FRITZIE

WOMEN AND THE AMERICAN WEST
Renee M. Laegreid, Series Editor

FRITZIE

The Invented Life and Violent Murder of a Flapper

AMY ABSHER

UNIVERSITY OF OKLAHOMA PRESS : NORMAN

Library of Congress Cataloging-in-Publication Data

Names: Absher, Amy, author.
Title: Fritzie : the invented life and violent murder of a flapper / Amy Absher.
Description: Norman : University of Oklahoma Press [2023] | Series: Women and
    the American West ; Volume 4 | Includes bibliographical references and index.
    | Summary: "One January day in 1923, a young boy came across the dead body
    of a twenty-year-old woman on a San Diego beach. When the police arrived on
    the scene, they found the woman's calling card, which read simply, 'I am Fritzie
    Mann.' Yet Fritzie's identity, as revealed in this compelling history, was anything
    but simple, and her death—eventually ruled a homicide—captured public atten-
    tion for months. In Fritzie, historian Amy Absher reveals how broader cultural
    forces, including gendered violence, sexual liberation, and evolving urban condi-
    tions in the American West, shaped the course of Mann's life and contributed
    to her tragic death. Frieda 'Fritzie' Mann had several identities during her brief
    life, and the mysterious circumstances of her death raise as many questions as
    they do answers. She was born in 1903 near the present border between Poland
    and Ukraine. She and her family were Jewish immigrants who traveled to San
    Diego to find security and prosperity. In the last year of her life, Mann became
    locally famous. She had reinvented herself as a flapper and 'Oriental' dancer. She
    claimed to have friends in Hollywood and a movie contract. On the night of her
    murder, she said she was going to a party to meet her Hollywood friends; instead,
    she traveled to an isolated roadside hotel where she met her death. An autopsy
    revealed that she was four and a half months pregnant. Absher guides the reader
    through the intricacies of this true crime story as it unfolded, from the initial
    flawed investigation to the sensationalized press coverage and the ultimate
    failure of the legal system to ensure justice on Mann's behalf. Like other 'new
    women' of her era, Fritzie Mann adopted roles that promised liberation from
    the control of men. In the end, her life and early death suggest the opposite: she
    became the victim of a culture that consumed women even as it purported to
    celebrate them"—Provided by publisher.
Identifiers: LCCN 2023006236 | ISBN 978-0-8061-9289-5 (paperback)
Subjects: LCSH: Mann, Fritzie, 1903–1923. | Murder victims—California—San
    Diego—Biography. | Women immigrants—California—San Diego—Biography.
    | Murder—California—San Diego. | Women—Crimes against—California—San
    Diego. | Trials (Murder)—California—San Diego. | Women—United States—
    Social conditions—20th century. | BISAC: HISTORY / United States / 20th
    Century | TRUE CRIME / Sexual Assault
Classification: LCC HV6534.S28 A274 2023 | DDC 364.152/309794985—dc23/
    eng/20230607
LC record available at https://lccn.loc.gov/2023006236

Fritzie: The Invented Life and Violent Murder of a Flapper is Volume 3 in the Women
and the American West Series.

For Carol G. Thomas, Abby Adams,
and Jon Bridgman

CONTENTS

ILLUSTRATIONS

ACKNOWLEDGMENTS

This book would not exist without the SAGES program at Case Western Reserve University. The idea came about as I was planning and teaching my undergraduate course "Murder in the Jazz Age" in the fall of 2012. In that course, each student received a sealed envelope containing a primary source from a Jazz Age murder or other crime. The students had to turn whatever they received in their envelopes into an original research paper. It was as if they were given one piece of a puzzle and had to figure out what the rest of the puzzle looked like. While collecting sources for this assignment, I came across a brief article in the *New York Times* about the murder of Fritzie Mann. Because it was California history, I couldn't assign the murder to one of my students; there were not enough resources available to them. So I assigned the murder to myself.

I am thankful to my students because through them, our discussions, and their enthusiasm for the class, I came to understand why these types of histories matter and need to be taught. Moreover, the teaching awards I received while a member of the SAGES faculty, particularly the Richard A. Bloom M.D. Award for Distinguished Teaching in the SAGES Program, helped me to fund research trips and to write during the summer breaks from teaching. My fellows—Brad Ricca, Michele Hanks, David Lucas, Lisa Nielson, Barbara Burgess-Van Aken, Annie Pecastaings, Bernard Jim, and Nácisz Fejes—and the SAGES staff—Sharmon Sollitto, Lance Parkin, Janet Alder, Peter Whiting, and Michael Householder—read early drafts and constantly told me to keep going. In thanking all those I knew while a SAGES Fellow, I am reminded of the halcyon days when we were a collective of educators, writers, and students pursuing the life of the mind.

Many SAGES students read early chapter drafts. I am beholden to all of them including Brenna Harrington, whose kind words helped me realize the value of the narrative structure; Ashley Sowers, who gave important notes on the abortionist chapter; Brittany Byrd, who was certain all this mattered; and Josh Sylvan, who offered insights into the medical aspects of the book.

My assistants Anthony Ghazoul, Robert Woods, Lucas Service, Gerome Spino, Diana Illingsworth, Steven Cramer, and Olivia Taliaferro all contributed significantly to the research efforts of this work. Sam Esterman assisted with the final steps to completing my first book, *The Black Musician and the White City*. Then he was with me through the important conceptualization and foundational research (including a lot of microfilm) for this book. I was honored to share a table with him.

I owe a great debt to librarians, archivists, artists, preservationists, and researchers who shared their expertise and showed me how to realize this project. They include the essential Theresa Mudrock, who pushed this project forward by finding a newsletter in early 2013 with an entry from the San Diego History Center discussing a scrapbook on the Mann case. At this point, there was no Wikipedia page, or publications, on Fritzie Mann. Quite simply, this is a book because Theresa told me it was a viable and vital topic. The interlibrary loan staff at Case Western Reserve University, Carl Mariani and Elanor Drushel, were herculean. To William Claspy I apologize. At the San Diego History Center, Lauren Rasmussen, Jane Kenealy, Natalie Force, and Ronald Teague were essential and supportive. Rick Crawford at the San Diego Public Library set me on the right track with an understanding of how the city's newspapers helped to create the historical narrative. The special collections staff at SDSU kindly permitted me to scan files for days, which I shared with them for their digital collection. Joyce Disraeli at the Jewish Historical Society connected me with local sources and people, including Leo Greenbaum's family, who were open and helpful as well. Ms. Disreali's kindness is something I remember fondly. At the Margaret Herrick Library, Genevieve Maxwell greatly assisted in clarifying historic events. From the University of Nevada, Reno, Libraries, Jen Wycoff, Usha Mehta, and Teresa Schultz located sources and figured out copyrights in the final days before my deadline. In Cleveland, the Dittrick Medical History Center's staff—Jim Edmonson, Jennifer Nieves, Laura Travis—gave me an intellectual home and access to their collections.

John Findlay, Richard Johnson, Sharmon Sollitto, Dennis Dworkin, and Rachel Kapelle all read chapter drafts and kept supporting and pushing me forward. My friends and mentors Carol Thomas, Abby Adams, and Jon Bridgman shaped my approach to the research in the early days of the project and suggested I consider *An American Tragedy* and *The Great Gatsby* as both scaffolding for the writing and fundamental sources for understanding the culture of murder in the Jazz Age. Also, Carol Thomas gave the project her sense of humor and her genius for understanding the importance of place to history. Her book *Finding People in Early Greece* was a guidepost for this work.

There were many strangers I met along the way. Clara Platter and LeAnn Fields helped me realize the larger argument and significance of the book. Roseanne Wells's and J. L. Stermer's classes on writing nonfiction proposals and marketing nonfiction books transformed this project. Sace Elder and Jane Little Botkin offered substantial and important comments on earlier versions of the book. Their efforts were fundamental to improving the work and are much appreciated.

I am fortunate to have had Alessandra Jacobi Tamulevich, Steven B. Baker, John Thomas, and everyone at the University of Oklahoma Press championing and molding my work.

Many thanks to Jen Hill, Emily Hobson, Meredith Oda, Christopher T. Morgan, Erin Stiles, Dennis Dworkin, and Greta de Jong for inviting me to teach in their departments. Also, in the last weeks of completing the manuscript for publication,

Courtney Hendrix was my teaching assistant. Her efforts in sharing the responsibilities of the classroom made it possible for me to meet the deadline. She was a miracle.

Then there were the friends and forevers: Theresa Mudrock, Rachel Kapelle, Sharmon Sollitto, Annie Pecastaings, Emmie Stevens, Roey Moran, Justyna Stypińska and Felex, Keiko Tsurumi, Dave Byrant, Stella Yee, Janel Fontana, John Mills, Jim Lea, Andrew Price Jr., Mariana Gatzeva, Mai Segawa, Arjun Khadilkar, Albert Chen, Brittany Byrd, Elizabeth Doolittle, Elanda Goduni, Josh Sylvan, Fiona Liu, Gerome Spino, Aaron PG, Kevin Smith, Diana Illingsworth, Belle Perez, Shreya Sekaran, Zach March, Do Hyeon Jang, Sunil Gollamudi, Alex Caveny, Matt Brown, Robert Brown, Yasha Duggal, Katie Cox, Kayla Pfaff, Garrett Dunlap, Emilio Colindres, Charlie Hu, Ren Ren, Han He, Zenobia Ofori-Dankwa, Anne Cardwell, Nicholas Heim, Vincenzo Volpe, Aishwarya Yenepalli, Anjuri Kakkar, Amaka Okocha, Sijie Peng, Elizabeth Perea, Ross O'Hagan, Dominic Kizek, Dixon, Emily Kane, Monica Ortega, Jojo Lambdin, Nadine Angel, Victoria Mathews, Noah Wagner, Victoria Almanzan, Sabrina Lillibridge, Alan Rocke, Mark De Guire, Iñaki Arrieta Baro, Roz Bucy, Tara Phuongnhi Tran, Anish Selvam, Prashant Bhagavatula, Qiyan, Chisa Oros, Angela Chase, Chelsea Brokmann, and Victor Guinto.

To my family, thank you for understanding.

INTRODUCTION

Fritzie Mann lived not one life but several. She was a twenty-year-old dancer who specialized in "Oriental" performances and worked private parties. She was also Jewish, a flapper, an immigrant from Galicia named Frieda, and four and a half months pregnant at the time of her murder.

Mann wanted to remain the product of her own imagination and deliberately bent her biography to her will. She made up stories about herself, her childhood, and her family. Then she hoped that the stories would illustrate who she would become. During her life, she steadfastly committed to controlling her own image with such shrewdness that knowing her wholly would be impossible. To understand what she meant when she said "I am Fritzie Mann" requires exploring the choices she made and how she lived, choices that illuminate the confrontation between the individual and the age.[1]

F. Scott Fitzgerald named the 1920s the Jazz Age.[2] The prominence of the Jazz Age in American national memory should not be understood as a postscript to the Victorian Age or seen as a novelty set between the horror of a world war and the solidification of the national identity during the crisis of the Great Depression. The decade was not an accident or frivolous escape from more

1

important things. The twenties were also about more than corporate growth, the automobile, and sexual liberation. By remembering the age as an afterthought, we preserve the illusion that as a nation we were once innocent.[3]

The life and the death of Fritzie Mann help to break that illusion by making the Jazz Age a West Coast history. For example, it was in the West that women first voted. Jazz musicians went to California before Chicago. The West does, then, have a claim to the history of the Jazz Age. Placing the focus on San Diego suggests how and why people sought to transform themselves, their communities, and their nation in the twenties. San Diego's history also articulates the experience of communities straining to embrace modernity with skyscrapers and highways while trying to maintain their white-only mythologies through class, nationalism, urban planning, and sunshine boosterism.

San Diego's history—more than New York's, Chicago's, or even Los Angeles's—suggests the experience of people living on the periphery of the national experience, because the shift to San Diego provides a view of history from the edges, which are sometimes frayed. This view is one of social and cultural history in which the rules of inclusion and exclusion take center stage. The Jazz Age story of Fritzie Mann and San Diego illustrates what it was like to exist on both sides of the identity border—between classes as well as between native born and immigrant—without belonging to either.

Because she was an immigrant, the roots of Fritzie Mann's story are in the destruction of Europe before and during World War I. The Mann family emigrated from Galicia, a province that lay between contemporary Poland and Ukraine.[4] Though fraught with violence and anarchy for centuries, in 1898 the violence in Galicia changed when the pogroms went from being occasional to a normative reality. Throughout the following decade, the looting and destruction of Jewish shops and taverns by Polish peasants in the villages of western Galicia, and the subsequent declaration of martial law, prompted many Jewish families to emigrate. Mann's family was among them. The 1920 census records show that the family immigrated to the United State in 1910 and had become naturalized citizens by 1916. All were able to read and write. The two eldest children were employed as office clerks.

After World War I, Poland geopolitically and administratively absorbed Galicia. The erasure of the territory on maps foreshadowed the eventual annihilation of the province's inhabitants in the Holocaust of World War II. The earlier immigration of Galician Jews to the United States meant that Galicia survived outside Europe. Galician Jews reshaped the United States by creating Yiddish theater in New York and the Hollywood movies from which evolved much of the core of American culture in the twentieth century.[5] Fritzie Mann was the child of this immigrant history.

Her family did not settle in New York City, as so many other Jewish immigrants did. Instead, they moved across the continent to the mountains of Colorado. After the death of Mann's father, and faced with her sister's continued failing health due to tuberculosis, they eventually resettled in San Diego.

By 1922, the last year of her life, Fritzie Mann was appearing throughout the city. Her dance performances were her own creation, but they were inspired by the popular films showing in the movie palace where she worked. She would meet up with her boyfriends at the US Grant Hotel downtown and go for car rides out to the beach or to Tijuana. She would make up stories about having friends in Hollywood and a movie contract. Mann chased freedom and fame. Her freedom ended with her pregnancy. Her murder brought the fame.

Can the death of a single woman help us in the early twenty-first century understand the salient contradictions of the Jazz Age? Perhaps it can, but not if we try to understand Mann's life through biography or separate her life (and death) from the media and judicial circus that unfolded in its aftermath. The story of Fritzie Mann is not just about a young woman attempting to claim her identity. In her life and in her death lies evidence of the cultural and social relationships that indict the historical conditions at the foundation of contemporary society. It is precisely because of the light she shed on these relationships that Mann's brief life is like a skeleton key to the mindset of her culture and an instructive framework for understanding what even people at the time, for better or worse, didn't understand about the early twentieth century.

Whether one thinks of the Jazz Age woman as a "flapper," the "New Woman," or the "modern girl," most people's image is of middle- or upper-class, native-born American youth. Part of Mann's significance is that she was not a member of this group, yet she epitomized the flapper. Her family lived in a German-speaking immigrant community in San Diego. She was not wealthy. Though she had a high school education, college and the "smart set" life were not possibilities for her, because she could not afford to compete for status as defined by class or consumer goods. Instead, like a true flapper, she focused on transforming her body into a canvas, a commodity, and eventually a persona that could compete.

Mann's choices suggest that the flapper was not a product of mass culture; rather, her greatness derived from her carefully cultivated aesthetics of self-invention. According to Zelda Fitzgerald, the flapper "flirted because it was fun to flirt . . . she covered her face with powder and paint because she didn't need it . . . she was conscious that the things she did were the things she had always wanted to do." Most of all she believed she had a "right to experiment with herself as a transient, poignant figure who will be dead tomorrow." Like other flappers, Fritzie Mann turned herself into her own work of art. She was young. She was lovely. She was calculating. She was intentionally shocking. She was simultaneously an object of admiration and an iconoclastic hyperbole of a person.[6]

Mann understood that she and the other girls of her generation had power. If they could dance, live, and love between tradition, on the one hand, and choice and hazard, on the other, they thought they could be not only free but also renowned. It is possible that she confused notoriety with fame. Nevertheless, it is also possible that she clearly saw the value in living on the periphery of society as well as the power of image to shape Jazz Age America. In the last year of her life, she sought a place in that culture. In her hands, sex was a performance. Revolution was a performance. So too were youth, virtue, and beauty.

A time of revolution is a dangerous time to live because it is easier to tear down a tradition than create a new one. Mann deliberately led an experimental life with a conscious awareness of the available choices. Like Gatsby in F. Scott Fitzgerald's novel, she believed in the green light. She wanted to be the boat against the current. However, she was living in an age that was not revolutionary enough. As it turned out, the new freedoms for women had not set them free. Consequently, when her life came into conflict with men who were hostile toward women whom they could not control through traditional means, she discovered the peril of the age.[7]

Mann's actions cannot by themselves account for the revolutions of the Jazz Age, because she was dead and the production of truth and power is the empire of the living. Nevertheless, over time and because of the times, reporters, doctors, lawyers, family, friends, and enemies collectively devised a myth that rewrote Mann's story. Her murder became a fusion of image and memory because imagining her helped them, the strangers and the friends, to create themselves and their understanding of the world in the twenties. She became the innocent and the wicked, the victim and the fiend, the object and the subject. The challenge—for the coroner, the reporters, the district attorney, and the modern reader—was and is to recognize the relationship between the flesh-and-blood Mann and the fictions they made of and from her. Mann's life and death reveal how and why the Jazz Age celebrated women while simultaneously destroying them.[8]

1

BEACH

Norh of San Diego ran the coastal highway. The road went through La Jolla, down through the low depressions, and up to a lightly forested Biological Grade. Across the mesa were the sandy beaches of the Torrey Pines Grade. The road moved in a westerly direction down the grade and made an abrupt turn to the right. Then it paralleled the ocean in a northerly direction all the way to Los Angeles.[1]

Torrey Pines was the gateway to San Diego, because it was at the most northern point of the city limits and was accessible by the state highway. Only in the previous year had developers finally, and successfully, built a resort on the rugged hills eroded by the ocean and by time. Wisely, they had built the resort from adobe, in a style inspired by the Hopi people, which made it blend into the hilltop. The local papers designated the lodge the most "attractive spot in all of Southern California." Rugs, pots, and artwork created by indigenous artists adorned the walls. Only native plants adorned the grounds. Rangers patrolled the surrounding park to assure the survival of the pine trees, a species that grew nowhere else except the Santa Rosa Islands. The lodge, the parks, the trees all suggested the wealth of the area. Designers and boosters desired to create a kind of managed

Torrey Pines looking northwest toward Del Mar, California, 1931. Del Mar Pier is seen partially at the far right. An automobile is parked on the shoulder of the beach near Highway 101. Though unlikely to depict the exact area where Mann's body was found, the photo gives a good indication of the terrain, road, and the proximity to the ocean. Photo by Walter Averrett. Courtesy of the San Diego History Center.

nature where the uniqueness of the site could be preserved and curated.[2]

As the road cut its way through Torrey Pines, on the west side there was a guardrail and fill that raised the road up ten or twelve feet above the level of the sand and wetlands. The fill, composed of crushed rock and earth, sloped away from the highway westward, extending out ten or twelve feet. Where the fill ended, the beach began. For the first twenty or thirty feet of the beach, the sand was absolutely dry— rarely knowing the touch of the ocean except during extraordinarily high tides accompanied by storms that carried the waves up onto the roadway.[3]

At the point where the road made its turn to the north, it passed over a bridge and then through a viaduct before turning to the northwest and running by a tiny garage. In this spot, a little ways beyond the road, there was a place where the ground was comparatively hard and automobiles could turn off and park. If one were to stand at that point, where the road curved off to the right, and looked in approximately a northeasterly direction, one would be facing the spot in which a child caught sight of the body of a young woman wearing only her slip and shoes. She lay parallel to the ocean, but not in it. Her hands were on her chest and her hair was "loose, laying in the sand, as though the water had washed it and carried it toward the ocean."[4]

It was January 15, 1923. The Chase family of San Fernando had stopped at the beach for a picnic. Despite the fact it was mid-winter, this was still San Diego, and the temperature seemed mild enough for the excursion. The family's nine-year-old son spotted the body. At first, it just seemed like an object, a mound, maybe a dead seal. He ran toward it, and only when he realized that it was a woman did he begin to scream for his father. Mr. John Chase came running. He was still holding his sandwich.

Mr. Chase would later recall that her eyes were open. They looked bloodshot. He thought that the waves had touched the body because the sand was wet. He would recollect little else with certainty regarding the state of the body. He did find help at the nearby garage and then guarded the body until the police were notified. He stood there and watched over the woman as small groups of people stopped their cars and walked down to the beach to have a look. He never did eat his sandwich.[5]

Next came Harley Sachs. He was working in his garage when he heard the news of a body on the beach. He thought it was a joke. So, before calling the police, he walked down to the beach to see for himself. He found the body and saw her hands folded across her chest. If her tongue had not been protruding, and had there not been white foam in her mouth, she would have looked relaxed. Sachs returned to his garage, but not to call the police. Instead, he fetched a piece of burlap. Returning to the beach, he covered the body. After his small act of kindness, he informed the police and walked back to his house.[6]

Having been in traffic court all morning, it must have been nice to be back on patrol, but motorcycle officers C. L. Matthews and Robert Bowman were quickly dispatched north of town.

They arrived at the Torrey Pines Garage and then proceeded to the beach. They left their motorcycles on the hard bit of ground just off the road. From there they could see no body. Not until they walked away from the road and down over the rocks did they see the figure.

Mathews raised the burlap. He would later recall that her eyes were closed. She had a wound on her forehead. A frothy fluid had run down her cheek and pooled under her head. Her silk undergarments were in place except for the left strap, which had fallen down off her shoulder, exposing her breast. She still had on her shoes and stockings. The officers remarked to each other that she had not been dead long; her skin seemed so natural, and the blood pooled in the corner of her right eye had not yet turned brown.[7]

They noted that her body lay parallel to the surf, and they looked around trying to figure out where she had come from. Had she jumped from the bridge off in the distance? Had she come from the road? A nearby hotel or motor lodge? The only tracks they saw in the sand were those of the Chase family and Sachs. The sand had been washed by the ocean and was now dry and hard. But it would not be for long. They could tell that that the tide was coming in. When they arrived, the water was twenty feet from the body. As the afternoon passed and they waited for the arrival of the coroner, they began to worry that they would have to move the body to save her from the ocean. As the hours passed, cars stopped on the road, and groups of people watched the two policemen as they watched the body. The policemen made sure the rubberneckers—an odd assortment of bellhops, tourists, and a sign painter—did not touch the dress they saw near the road. The dress looked like it had been laid out, just like the body did.[8]

At last, the officials from the coroner's office arrived. The coroner, Kelly, and the county sheriff, Bludworth, along with the driver of the "dead wagon" all lifted the body from the sand and placed her on the stretcher. No one took a photograph. No one would think to put a stake in the ground to mark the spot until the next day. Not until then did anyone think to draw a map of the scene. Bodies on the beach were not rare. No one thought to preserve the scene. The year was 1923, and forensic science was young. Because breaking the chain of evidence was not on anyone's mind, the two motorcycle officers finally left the beach to go back on patrol, as more officers appeared to begin the search for evidence on the beach.

Harley Sachs, who had been so thoughtful to bring the piece of burlap to cover the body, found it hard to sit still in his home. Eventually he felt the need to return to the beach. He walked along the sand, and it was not long before he began to find the bits and pieces of the woman's life. About 350 feet away from the body he found a small, brown, beaded dress. Nearby was a barrette. A little beyond the road, the guardrail, the fill, and along the beach was a blanket. He knew to touch nothing. Instead, he called for the sheriff. Sachs and a group of officers found a smallish suitcase, the kind called a "grip" in the vernacular. Sachs later recalled that the bag contained a small blue dress. The police would describe it as a kimono. There were also personal letters and newspaper clippings documenting the rising star of a local dancer. Just a little farther down the beach, there was a vanity case containing a calling card that read simply, "I am Fritzie Mann."[9]

2

BODY

A round five o'clock that same afternoon in January 1923, Dr. John Shea, autopsy surgeon, arrived at the basement of Smith, Goodbody & Dunn's, a mortuary at San Diego's Third and Ash. There, waiting for him, was the body from the beach. As he recalled later for the court, "When I saw her at the undertaking rooms on the table, when I first saw the body, there was a congested appearance of the face, as I remember it now." The doctor and the body were alone. He tied on his leather apron and unpacked his tools. He stood for a while just looking at her. First, he noticed how pale her body was, in comparison to her face. Then he noticed the bruises and abrasions. Shea examined "everything [even] the palms of her hands and the soles of her feet." He did not yet know her given name was Frieda.[1]

Nevertheless, it was Shea's job to provide the first answer to the question, Who was Fritzie Mann?

As was the procedure at the time, Shea was to conduct a preliminary examination. Over the next few days, Mann's body would undergo several examinations. The purpose of these was to determine the cause of death, the manner of death, and the contributing factors. Under normal circumstances, the coroners tried to assemble facts and statistics about the decedent objectively to satisfy the family. In a normal drowning, these questions arose: If she had drowned, did she know how to swim? Was it a hot day and had this contributed? Had the ocean been rough, or had she hit her head on a rock? Was the problem inebriation? Was the cause a heart attack or stroke? Sadly, these were not normal circumstances, and the questions that needed to be asked would bring few answers.[2]

Shea had attended Harvard Medical School. As a student, he had one course in postmortem examinations. His limited training was common at the time; forensic medicine was still in its infancy. Besides, the skills needed to do a postmortem were the kind of thing a person learned on the job. After graduating, he worked in general surgery and medicine in a Massachusetts hospital. Whenever possible he assisted the county coroner in autopsies. Volunteering to assist was the simplest way to gain insight into the principles of the field and the human body. In 1914, Shea moved to San Diego, where he became the county's autopsy surgeon and started a general medical practice. Over the next ten years, he estimated, he conducted somewhere between five and six hundred autopsies.

Despite all of his experience, the Mann case was a troubling one. Later, at the inquest and at two trials, Shea would be asked if his methods were thorough. He would have to explain his techniques and observations in language the average person could understand. What no one outside his profession seemed to comprehend was that he could never be completely thorough. At most, he could follow a routine procedure. He could even specialize the focus of the autopsy to certain parts of the body, but a complete understanding could never be achieved for the simple reason that each examination destroyed the material necessary for future investigations. It was dangerous to jump to conclusions about the body because, if he were to assume one part of the corpse was more important than the other, he would ignore another part of the body. Failure came from not thinking of the body as a whole. The great dilemma of the autopsy surgeon was that, to determine the cause of death, he first had to determine what the body was like when it was healthy, normal. Only then could he understand what was abnormal.[3]

Accordingly, Shea did not begin by looking for evidence of drowning. Instead, he began by detailing the outer appearance of the body. For Shea, as it was for his boss and colleague, coroner Schuyler Kelly and pathologist Dr. H. A. Thompson, the body was like a code that could be interpreted. Shea's job was to do the first examination. Then Thompson would examine the tissue and blood samples. Finally, Kelly would join the process to draw the conclusions of the team together. By reading the body's idiosyncrasies, all three men hoped to discern its history, its society, its nature, and its culture. As the medical examiners, their job was to transform the body from an object abandoned on a beach into a person. Shea would be the first one to give the body meaning through his discourse of coroner's objectivity.[4] Indeed, everything that followed his first examination, from the newspaper coverage to the trials, was just an extension of the autopsy.

Through this process of dissection, Mann's life began to emerge from the body. The transformation would never be complete. As the autopsy surgeon understood, and what so few others were willing to accept, it would be impossible to ever fully know Fritzie Mann.

Shea found Mann to be five feet four inches tall. She weighed about 120–130 pounds. Her body was pale, which was common for victims of drowning. Her face and head were red. Her skin had not corrugated, meaning that her skin had not loosened and taken on the appearance of a glove. This particular change in the skin "only comes on," Shea noted, "after a certain number of hours in the water—quite a long while," which was an indication that this was no run-of-the-mill drowning.

Her jaw showed signs of rigor mortis, as did her tongue. But there was no lividity, a pooling of the blood in the dependent parts of the body such as the organs. She had a black-and-blue discoloration on the outer angle of the right eyebrow the size of a quarter. Shea dissected it and found it to be superficial; the bruising, which was dark blue, suggested that it had happened shortly before she died. There were also abrasions on her forehead and the prominent parts of both cheeks. On her elbows, "there was just an abrasion as though the skin had been rubbed off." There was no foreign matter under her fingernails, which he dutifully scraped.[5]

With the body in as good a position as possible to conduct his work, Shea began to explore the interior. It was customary for the surgeon to stand on the side of the body corresponding to his cutting hand. Exhaling slightly as he pressed down on the knife, he made a clean cut from the base of the neck to the pubis. Her "blood was fluid" and "dark in color."[6]

At this point, he had several options. In his mind, Shea would have drawn on his experiences and the prominent textbooks of the era, because what he did next was of supreme importance. Of primary concern was whether to open the chest or the belly first. No solid custom existed at the time among surgeons. Instead, the procedure would conform to his desires. He began with the chest. Then came time for the sternum. Finally, he could view the diaphragm. At this point in the procedure, he resembled an auto mechanic more than a surgeon as he peered into the machinery enclosed within the two cavities of the chest and abdomen.[7]

By observing the thoracic organs, he could at once capture an understanding of the distribution of blood in the circulatory centers. Shea knew that all the body cavities underwent a certain set of changes following death. Therefore, he needed to pause a moment and not rush, because once he began he could not turn back the clock and start over. The body was a Pandora's box; there could be no retreat. Time, rot, and regret were all his enemies.[8]

In a way, the autopsy was like a war. As he observed, the tissues were turning a dusky purplish color as the postmortem changes progressed rapidly through the body, altering the nature of everything that was once living. The chief problem was how to move fast enough to stay ahead of the inevitable decay of the body while causing the least possible destruction of the relation of one organ to another. He had to choose which tissue to save and which to violate with the knife. Everything, even the blood and the odors, had to be noted. None of this type of evidence could be replaced or simulated. If Shea was to understand the fate of Fritzie Mann, he could not allow himself to see the mortar of the house as insignificant, nor was the fibrous skeleton of the viscera inconsequential.[9]

Having systematically looked over the organs presenting in the opening, Shea was now in a position to determine whether to follow custom or change it. Any choice he made he would have to defend in court, because the next step in the autopsy was to observe the lungs postdrowning. He delicately lifted back the edges of the lungs from the pericardium, noting size, drape, degree of distinction, vascularity, translucency, and special conditions. Any mistake, any pressure exerted, would destroy evidence. He held off. He did not remove the lungs. First, he had to determine the distribution of blood so as to establish the health of the organs and how they might have changed at the point of death. As soon as he had determined the distribution of the blood in all the important organs, Shea could begin to make such cuts as were necessary to remove or examine organs. Then he had to deal with the spilling of blood.[10]

A little blood had secreted from the arteries and veins of Mann's lungs, but only a small amount. Shea noted that her air passages were "smooth. . . . There was nothing that was out of the ordinary" in terms of color or texture. "The incision of the lungs and bronchi, for the purpose of finding any foreign substance there, revealed a frothy mucous," Shea recorded on his trusty index cards. "Frothy mucous exuded from the lungs" when he applied pressure. As he would explain later in court, "Frothy mucous means the mucous of the lungs mixed with air and water, churned up, they are both intimately connected; it always means there is air mixed with water." The fluid was white in color. Her blood was separate from the frothy fluid: "It wasn't mixed intimately . . . you could observe the whitish mucous" distinctly. He found no "free water," meaning there was no water separate from the fluid. He concluded that her death was due to drowning because he found in the fluid a mixture of mucus and air, as was common from drowning. Frothy mucus leaked from the mouth when pressure was placed on the lungs. Yet he found no sand or sea grass in the lungs, not even in the bronchi. Shea would need confirmation of these findings.

As always, Shea had options. He could make the "little window," a discrete set of incisions that produced a small portal through which he could examine the internal organs without disturbing them. However, there was also the "slop bucket" method, which was popular among surgeons for its speed. As its name suggested, all one needed was a bucket. Nonetheless, once he severed the stomach from the body, Shea would destroy the only possible means of rational observation of cause and effect. The gut was more than just tubing. It was impossible to understand the tissues and bacteria once it had been ripped out and washed. Indeed, in the handling of the digestive track, the surgeon distinguished himself from the mortician. Oh, Shea may have had to use the "undertaking" table in the basement of Goodbody & Dunn, but he did not need to view the stomach as a distended, bacteria-filled enemy that would decay the corpse and ruin the embalming procedure. No, he knew that the stomach was the sum of all things.[11]

Shea could wait. He would not disturb the stomach until a full study had been made of the exterior. He looked for evidence of inflammation or special changes. This care was necessary because Mann may have been drugged or poisoned, which could have facilitated the drowning. Shea still had to keep in mind the possibility that the drowning was only the outcome of a longer and more tedious death.

As he did all of this, the color continued to change and the drying or mortification grew more prevalent. These changes were at once the enemy and a friend. There was much value in noting them because their speed and character were indications of death. Here was his failing. He did not keep careful notes of these changes. He had no assistant. He had no audio recorder, such as a Dictaphone like businessmen used. Instead, he had to stop his time-sensitive work and make notes on index cards. He did not always stop to detail everything. He was sure he would remember these details later, because they were common enough to his work. Here was his regret—when months later the lawyers would find his explanation of time, rot, and customary changes unacceptable.[12]

Shea wrote down, "Stomach contained water and some undigested food." Specifically, her stomach contained no more than four ounces of water. Again, he found no "sea grass" or "indication of sand" in her throat, lungs, or stomach. There was the frothy fluid in her lungs. He concluded that this was "death due to drowning." He stopped. He would need to notify his boss, Dr. Kelly, that there was possible evidence of murder.

A few days later, on Friday afternoon, January 19, Shea, Kelly, and Thompson performed the second autopsy. At that time, the three colleagues removed the uterus and the fetus. She was four and a half months pregnant.

Though she had drowned, there was no evidence of the ocean killing Mann. Shea's findings suggested homicide, which forced Coroner Kelly to also contemplate the question, Who was Fritzie Mann? as well as what led to her murder. On the off chance that the body was not that of Mann, he called her family's residence. William Mann, Fritzie's brother, answered the phone and explained that Fritzie was not home but was expected to return in the evening. At that time, Kelly did not tell William that his sister was dead. Regrettably, William would learn this news from reading the *San Diego Union* the next morning.

The next day, Kelly had William Mann brought down to the mortuary to make the identification. He was positive it was his sister. Kelly then visited the Mann house, where he met Fritzie's mother, Amelia. He learned that Mann had been invited to a party in Del Mar. Movie people were expected to be attending the party. Mann, who had dreams of being a star, had told everyone she was leaving San Diego for Culver City, the little hamlet adjacent to the movie studios. She was excited at the prospect of mingling with the famous and wealthy at the party. Mrs. Mann had walked her daughter to the bus stop and waved good-bye. A few hours later, Mann called home to say that the party was no longer in Del Mar but had been moved to La Jolla. That was the last they had heard. Kelly inquired about the names of Mann's boyfriends. He knew at this point that she had been murdered and that she was pregnant. He also knew he would need to hold an inquest because Shea's findings were only the physical details of how Mann lived and how she died. Kelly, the district attorney, and the police needed the dirty little secrets that composed her life, which might connect Mann to her killer.[13]

Because Shea found that Mann had suffered a blow to the head before she died and did not show evidence of drowning in the ocean, the police were forced to return to the beach. Once there, detectives Richard Chadwick and George Sears did not meet with Mr. Chase, whose son had found the body, or Mr. Sachs, who had covered the body with burlap, or even the two motorcycle patrolmen, Matthews and Bowman, who had been the first law officers on the scene. Instead, they met with Mr. David Rannels, the owner of the Torrey Pines Garage. Sears and Chadwick were depending on Rannels to remember what the beach was like two days prior. "How high was the tide? . . . Where was the body?" they must have asked. They measured off distances by "stepping it off." They attempted to place stakes where each piece of evidence had rested. They went up the bridge that overlooked the beach and drew a map on a piece of cardboard. They did find an additional piece of evidence, "an olive drab blanket." The police had made mistakes in the previous days, and they were the kind of mistakes that could never be undone or fully explained.[14]

It might have been helpful if photographs had been entered into evidence. After all, the newspapers were full of photos of everything from politics to starlets. At the time, photographers argued that photography was an overlooked courtroom tool because lawyers lacked knowledge of photography and were unable to enlist the services of a photographer who really understood how to photograph so that the prints could be admitted as evidence. Adding to the difficulty of using photographs in court was the inconvenience of the technology. Photographers may have had the height of the available technology, but that height was flash-pan and powder, negative plates, color-sensitive plates, and panchromatic plates that provided a spectacular spectrum of grays but not color. To create the best possible photo, exposure time could be as much as fifteen minutes, which meant that the photographer had to swear nothing had changed in the crime scene during that time. Also, the same person had to make and finish the photograph and swear to this fact in court, because people already knew that that photos could be altered. There had been cases of theft, damage, arson, and murder in which photos were used as evidence, but it was not yet a widespread practice.[15] Consequently, the police at the beginning of the case, and later in the trial, could only offer their best guess as to the exact placement of the body and other articles of evidence.

Luckily for Chadwick and Sears, Coroner Kelly convened an inquest. Mann's flapper friends, her family, and the various police officials and witnesses were invited. Shea read his initial report to the coroner's court. At the news that Mann was to have a son in another four and a half months, her mother began to wail, and her brother yelled out, declaring his sister to have been a "good girl." Kelly was not trying to prove otherwise. Instead, he wanted to know how she spent her last days. What was her mood? With whom did she spend time? Above all, who was the father of the child?

For this last question, there was no sure answer. Some friends reported that she was dating a man who claimed to be a film director in Los Angeles. Others claimed Mann was seeing a local doctor at Camp Kearny.[16] In these two different possibilities lay the difficulty of investigating and then prosecuting suspects. First, questions about paternity exposed the limits of the science available to Kelly. There was not enough knowledge of DNA to use it as evidence in 1923 and thus no definitive way to tie a suspect—the physician or the supposed film director—to the paternity of the child. Second were the issues of class: Mann was dating a doctor with a "high position," as the district attorney's office described the physician's role at Camp Kearny, and his "pride" would not allow him to marry a pregnant, working-class, Jewish immigrant.[17] In going after either suspect, the police, the district attorney, and the medical examiner's office would be violating well-established hierarchies of power, class, and money. Third, the evidence they had gathered suggested that the answer to the question, Who was Fritzie Mann? was complicated. She was leading a life about which her family was unaware. In that life, she had traversed both the physical geography of southern California and its social geography. This life had brought her to her death.

For his part, Kelly kept a scrapbook of all his cases. No other case held him enthralled like the death of Fritzie Mann, because her death revealed the social and institutional relationships between citizens and the police. Most people in San Diego probably confronted the homicide with a mixture of curiosity and horror, but they were also exposed to the possibilities and limits of life in their city, especially for the working-class immigrants juxtaposed to the wealthy inhabitants of Coronado, the affluent city on an island in San Diego Bay. Kelly's job constantly brought him face to face with this reality and its accompanying wailing mothers in mourning. However, this one case so frustrated him that he wrote notes denouncing the injustices, which he rarely did, in the margins of his scrapbook.

On Kelly's suggestion, the police began looking for a hotel room or a home that could have been the murder scene. It didn't take long for them to find the Blue Sea Cottage, a clerk who recalled seeing Fritzie Mann, and a maid who had seen what looked like blood in the bathtub. To the press, Kelly explained that when Mrs. Mann had seen her daughter's body she began to scream and yell the name of the man she thought had killed her Fritzie. She had told Kelly how she had begged Fritzie to tell her more of her plans, but the daughter had only told her mother not to worry, that everything was going to turn out all right.

The day after the inquest, Kelly, Shea, and Thompson gathered beside the undertaking table in the basement of the Johnson and Saum Mortuary, where Mann's family had requested the body be moved, to begin the second autopsy. The family had questioned the findings of the inquest. Specifically, they did not believe that Fritzie was pregnant.[18] The autopsy team suspected murder, but they still had to rule out suicide and accidental death. Therefore, a second autopsy could prove useful.

In 1923 it was nearly impossible to determine the type of death caused by a blow without locating the weapon. The doctor would need to prove that the wound was inflicted purposefully so that the police and district attorney could prove the killer had something at stake.[19] The reality was that lawyers with little medical knowledge would ask them if the wound above Mann's left eye could have been inflicted in a suicide attempt. In this second autopsy, because their testimony would stand in for the victim's, they had to adopt the point of view of a courtroom of laymen and test for every cause of death imaginable. They felt the burden of having to speak for the dead.

As coroners, they knew a simple truth: drowning was a troublesome postmortem ruling. If a drunken man drowns, then nine times out of ten it is an accident. However, if a single, pregnant woman drowns in an out-of-the-way place, then it could be many things, but an accident was not one of them. Maybe it was suicide? They could have relied on statistics of suicide rates and just used the laws of probability as the basis of their judgment.[20] Well, they could have done a great many things. Even so, there would always be the matter of the wound on her forehead.[21]

Shea and Kelly knew that it was standard for abortionists to abandon bodies of patients who died from the procedure. In one extreme case, San Francisco police in 1920 executed a raid on the home of an abortionist. They found "girls and women recovering from the illegal operations" and unearthed several bodies from around the home of the doctor. The victims ranged in age from fourteen to their twenties. These crimes brought out Kelly's anger, which he regularly expressed to the press. It seemed that young women were coming to their deaths frequently because of legal barriers, medical ineptitude, and a black-market system run by fixers and abortionists.[27]

Having ruled out the botched abortion as the cause of Mann's death, the investigators moved on to the possibility of poisoning. Thompson did the investigation of the stomach and kidneys, which the morticians' embalming activities had made more difficult. He was unable to find any "volatile" poison present, which would have included, for example, chloroform, nitric oxide, chloral, cyanide, or other poisons of that type. The tests and autopsy did, however, reveal that she had been drinking.

By this time, it was a few days after the first autopsy. Thompson explained later in court that, "after the treatment that the body had had [from the morticians], it would have been, I would have been unable to find" any poisons in the organs. He had to rely on a visual examination of the tissues to eliminate poisoning from the possible causes of death.

Cyanide poisoning is unmistakable. If this was the cause of death, Shea would have seen the poison's impact on the body at the first autopsy, in the stomach, the back of the mouth, the pharynx, and the entrance of the larynx.[28] Also, the laboratory test for cyanide was simple and well known.

The existence of the test for cyanide did not stop murderers. In Los Angeles, in June 1921, police arrested a man for poisoning his wife with cyanide.[29] According to the San Diego Tribune, poisons were both common and easy to acquire. The paper believed cyanide to be the most common of poisons, along with arsenic and bichloride of mercury, because popular opinion held that it left no trace on the body, killed quickly, and had effects easily mistaken for a heart attack. Any killer could acquire the poison, which was commonly used in pesticides, furniture polish, and silver polish.[30]

The doctors also wondered if Mann had been anesthetized with, say, chloroform. If she had been chloroformed, this would explain the absence of foreign tissue under her fingernails. After all, killers found it useful in domestic killings such as the one in Modesto, California, in 1920 in which the killer first drugged a young woman and then strangled her.[31]

When used, chloroform causes the lungs to swell and rapidly fill with fluid. Given that Mann's lungs had fluid in them, chloroform was important to consider. Its presence could even be mistaken for the result of a drowning, if the autopsy surgeon failed to see if the mucous membranes, mouth, stomach, and intestines were inflamed, but Shea had checked.[32]

They could also rule out other poisons. Autopsy surgeons at the time knew their poisons. Nitric acid revealed itself with a remarkable yellow discoloration of the skin about the mouth. The riot of yellow continued into the mucous membrane, which appeared as though cooked. Hydrochloric acid made the fundus of the stomach appear thickened and the organs adjoining the stomach cooked. Sulfuric acid revealed a whitish-gray escharosis, a dry, dark scab-like burn, throughout the mouth; the stomach contents looked like coffee.[33] Thompson was confident from looking at the blood and tissues that Mann had not been poisoned with the most popular of poisons.

It was not just the body that showed no sign of poisoning. There had been a whiskey bottle in the cottage the police believed to be the scene of the crime, and Mann's blood work revealed that she had been drinking. However, it "came to naught," the newspapers moaned, when Dr. Thompson revealed that there was no poison in the bottle. The substance was not even whiskey. The police carefully checked the fingerprints on the bottle, but none related to anyone in the case. "This explodes the police theory that the bottle contained drugged whiskey, which was given to the girl before she was thrown into the sea," summarized the *San Diego Tribune*.[34] Concluding that they would have noticed any evidence of poisoning during their two examinations of the body, tissue, and blood, Mann's team of doctors let her rest.

Regarding the cause of death, Thompson was clear. It was drowning. The question that remained was where she died. Shea did not have access to a microscope and could not offer a comparison of tap water versus ocean water. He would have to rely on the contents and appearance of the lungs. The small amount of water, the froth, and the way the lungs did not deflate as water-soaked lungs would when removed from the body made him concluded that Mann's body was removed from the scene of the crime, which was most likely at the Blue Sea Cottage, and dumped at the beach.

The doctors knew that Mann died by drowning. The blow to the head suggested murder. Since she was pregnant, they suspected a crime of passion. Yet for such a crime the body was remarkably bloodless. There was only the one marked sign of violence, no indication of strangling, no evidence that she had been forcibly held under the water, and no skin under her fingernails. This case was so unlike a murder of the previous year involving a woman who shot her lover because, as it turned out, he was married with two children. The lover survived.[35] Or the case of moonshiner who had bludgeoned a rancher to death: The moonshiner claimed self-defense because the rancher had first hit him with an empty bottle, then come at him with a butcher's knife, and finally an iron rod—all supposedly justifying the moonshiner to beat the rancher to death. Then, while the rancher's wife was still covered in her husband's blood, the moonshiner asked her to run away with him.[36] This is what crimes of passion looked like in San Diego. The moonshiner and the bigamist cases were the two crimes that shared the pages of Kelly's scrapbook with Mann's case. In comparison to her case, they were overtly and unforgettably violent.

The lack of apparent violence did not mean that no crime had occurred. All it meant was that Mann knew her killer or that her killer was highly skilled and knew what to avoid. In the twenties, the most telling crimes were not the political fighting, the race riots, or Prohibition violence. Rather, everyday domestic violence permeated the city as it transitioned away from prewar values. Fritzie Mann's murder revealed the anxiety of the community regarding the Jazz Age's social leveling and fragmentation.[37] In death, as in life, Mann was a threat to the social order because her body, and that of the fetus, challenged any understanding of San Diego as a paradise by the sea.[38] Mann, with her ability to transgress all social norms and barriers in both life and death, offers a view of the United States at its most resplendent, rebellious, and vicious.

There was something more to note, Dr. Thompson explained to the court: the fluid in Mann's lungs suggested that she had resisted: "The point is this: that if you are not taking deep [breaths], there is more voluntary effort there than there is with the involuntary effort that you get after respiration with a person unconscious." The lawyers, the public, and the police were asking if she had willingly gone into the water as an act of suicide or was unconscious from hitting her head on a rock and died by accident. Thompson was pointing out that, when a conscious person goes into the water, they try and hold their breath as long as possible; they might not have lungs filled with water at the time of the autopsy because they had held their breath. Finally, when they cannot hold their breath any longer, they battle to take in air because their body is taking in only water. People do not "give up the fight," he argued, "until they are practically anesthetized, and the reason they are anesthetized is because of the mixing of the air and water and mucous in the lungs." Thompson continued, "In cases of drowning you usually get frothy air—that is, air mixed with fluid," which was precisely the state of Mann's lungs. It was important from Thompson's perspective to understand that "the whole picture varies according to the struggle of the individual." If she had been unconscious the entire time she was "churning," as he called it, "there would not be anything" like what they had found. He offered more. The level of carbon dioxide in her blood ultimately led to a "paralysis on the respiration," which killed her. The amount of froth and carbon dioxide suggested that there had been a "struggle." She had not just drowned. According to Thompson, no matter how briefly, she had resisted.

3

NEWS

While the police and the doctors worked to construct a case, the press was conducting its own autopsy. At first, there was a mistake. The *San Diego Tribune* announced that the body of a man was found at Torrey Pines.[1] Quickly, what began as a hundred-word account of a drowning became headline news. "Body of Pretty Young Woman Cast Up by the Waves," rang out the headline in the *San Diego Sun* on January 16. "If it was not murder," proclaimed the *Sun* as it speculated on suicide, "then something drove her to her death, something so vital to her continued existence that she preferred the balm of the grave to the bitterness of life, for life must have seemed bitter to her when she faced the ocean and strode in to end it all." "For her," the *Sun* reporter opined, "the mystery of life, with its cross purposes, its frequent injustices, had been solved in death." "Fritzie," regrettably from the perspective of the reporter, "locked her secret within the depths of her broken heart." Or maybe she had looked sweetly into the face of her killer "when the final blow fell."[2]

The press was claiming moral authority in the case and the right to guide the public perception, which they asserted preempted that of the police. What the press understood far better than anyone else in the city was that their readers were both

This front-page photo from the *Los Angeles Examiner*, January 17, 1923, shows Fritzie Mann in a costume with a white-plumed headdress and a bodice covered in pearls and jewels. The placement of the Mann headline immediately below the war headline indicates the sensationalism and importance her death received in the press.

citizens and consumers looking for sensation and entertainment. The trick to selling newspapers on the backs of a murder was to make the readers feel as though they were being mobilized in a conflict over values. The social violence was not an invention of the press, but they did commodify it.[3]

Suddenly, readers of the local papers where engrossed in the "quest" to find "The slayer of pretty Fritzie Mann." Three weeks earlier, the paper explained, Mann was "the toast" of the "Palais Royal, a bright light café and cabaret on Spring Street," in Los Angeles. "She was a favorite there—as she was in San Diego." The lucky girl had a "host of admirers who feted her and entertained her." Fritzie was "popular," the stories declared, as though the loss of a popular girl made everything that much more tragic.[4]

The reporters confirmed that every detail, no matter how small or how incorporeal, was important. For example, the night before her death she told a friend, "Some of my moving picture friends are coming down for a house party Sunday night. We are going to have some fun." She began to pack the "night dress and kimono" and went off to "meet them—or at least HIM." "It was the trip," the papers lamented, "from which she failed to return." "Who were the moving picture friends?" reporters asked. "These are unanswered questions, but they are questions that may have to be answered before the curtain falls on the last act of Fritzie's sad drama."[5] The curious thing was not so much that the newspapers dramatized her death, but that they seemed unaware that Fritzie's life was already a fiction created by the girl herself. In other words, she was a Gatsby.

In meeting Fritzie Mann, the reporters were meeting their equal; the only true thing about her was that she was dead. Nevertheless, the press accepted the fiction. Truth was not what the newspapers sought or published. In early 1923, they wanted a story.

Nothing was more entertaining than crime. Newspaper editors had known this for decades. The *New York Herald*, founded in 1833, began to sell massive numbers of papers in 1836 only when it carried extensive coverage of the murder of Helen Jewett, a nineteen-year-old prostitute. Her landlady-madam found her battered body in a smoldering bed. Jewett's lover became the prime suspect. With this case, the newspaper had found a reporting model that would sell endlessly. The scandalous profile of the victim, presented by firsthand descriptions of eyewitnesses, balanced the interviews with bereft friends and family. There were the details of the crime, the police interviews with the suspect, the trial, and finally the corrupt machinations of the justice system. Then there were the challenges to the social order because the suspect came from the upper class and the teenage victim worked as a prostitute. The Jewett case demonstrated how the press might shape the news into its most whorish form. Basically, with this story, papers like the *Herald* could transform "news" into a word that did not mean information; instead, its meaning derived from the idea of latest, fresh, or innovative.[6]

William Randolph Hearst, with his *New York Journal*, decided in 1895 to shift the format of the paper from information to stories, thus contributing the exposé to the emerging tabloid form.

Illustrations soon filled every publication, which made images the driving force in journalism. For the reader the inclusion of illustrations meant that appearances could replace factual information. For the culture, it meant a rejection of Victorian sentimentality. The newspapers were swapping long-held values with a trivialized, fabricated, and meaningless world that the papers sold as news.[7] For these reasons, the newspapers are essential to understanding how Fritzie Mann transformed from a person into a paper doll cutout of the half-nude victim of a changing society.

As the decade opened, it was hard to miss the fact that "most criminal cases are tried in the newspaper headline, but it is from this form of exaggeration and condescension that the great public gleans its impressions," as the *Saturday Evening Post* explained in an attempt to illustrate how far civilization had slipped. The tabloids had won. Editors and reporters now offered a "sustained press campaign that could headline an innocent man into the death house; certainly it works often enough the other way, for most of the malefactors who go free can thank the gush purveyors of the press." The *Post* predicted that no measure of reform would occur until editors accepted that their "function is to give the news, and that verdicts are the business of juries."[8] It was not just a yellow press; it was "the saffron press."[9]

In this news format, murders made great copy because sex or money, or both, were the cause of most of them. There were photos, love letters, and confessions to publish. Suspects and victims could be turned into characters and celebrities. Moreover, a murder investigation lasted weeks, the trial could last months, and the deathwatch before the execution could give dozens of stories. Afterward the paper could do exposés on the morality of capital punishment, the ineptitude of the police, the quarrels of the jury members, and the corruption of the judicial system. Even mediocre editors could spin a murder for months; murders were the perfect story precisely because the murder was only the beginning and ultimately no one knew how it was going to end. A murder presented an opportunity for any editor who understood that the group of readers seeking to be entertained far outnumbered those who wanted to be informed.[10]

Placing crime on the front page made crime popular and criminals celebrities. Coverage of criminals also fed the anti-Prohibition movement, which found the newspapers useful for suggesting that there had been a rise in crime with the onset of Prohibition. Every newspaper front page seemed to imply that life was not healthier, thrift was not virtuous, village loafing had not ceased, and schools were not better off.[11] On the contrary, the world seemed more complex and certainly more violent.

Though all the tabloid antics existed well beforehand, the Jazz Age raised the practice of sensationalizing tragedy to new levels. Arguably, the fascination with scandal began in earnest the summer of 1920 when police found the body of Joseph Elwell, a well-known gambler attractive to both sexes, according to the newspapers, in a room that locked from the inside. The New York police gathered all the evidence and interviewed dozens of suspects. Yet they were unable to solve his homicide.[12]

Then in San Francisco, in September 1921, police arrested famed comedian and number-one box-office draw Roscoe "Fatty" Arbuckle for the murder of a young woman at a wild three-day party that featured bootleg liquor. The scandal was so severe that the Hollywood studios pulled his films and refused to release any new ones. Arbuckle stood trial three times. Once a jury had finally acquitted him, Arbuckle attempted to regain his career, but it was too late. City councils and morality groups pressed for bans of his films throughout the country. The jury had gone his way; the court of public opinion had not.[13]

The most mysterious of the Hollywood scandals was the death of William Desmond Taylor in February 1922. His neighbors reported to the police that they had seen a man near his apartment late at night. Shortly thereafter, a shot rang out. Taylor, a prominent film director, had entertained famed actress Mabel Normand earlier in the evening. She told the police that Taylor had walked with her to her car and then returned to his apartment. Shortly after she departed, Taylor's only servant left for the evening. When the servant returned in the morning, he found Taylor lying dead on the floor of his living room, shot through the back. The servant did not call the police right away. Instead, he called the Famous Players–Lasky movie studio. Publicists and lawyers from the studio descended upon the apartment and burned vital evidence in the case, such as Taylor's letters. Someone moved the body. Actresses began to show up to claim their belongings. Investigators found the body in a locked house. The people from the studio had tampered with the position of the body and destroyed evidence. He was bedding every major actress in town. Despite dozens of suspects, his murder was unsolved. In short, Taylor's death was perfect for the newspapers.[14]

Ultimately, Arbuckle and William Desmond Taylor were upstaged. In late August 1922, the Reverend Edward Wheeler Hall and Mrs. Eleanor Mills, the choir leader in the reverend's church, were found shot to death on an abandoned farm near New Brunswick, New Jersey. Murderer, or murderers, had arranged the bodies. Several bullets had been fired into the face of Mrs. Mills, and her head had been severed nearly from her neck. The couple's love letters were flung about the bodies and shoved into Reverend Hall's pockets. Against his shoe lay his calling card. There were signs of a struggle. The reverend had bruised knuckles. There were also signs that they were killed by someone they knew, because a handkerchief covered Mrs. Mills's face.[15]

The constant presence of the Hall-Mills murder case in newspapers from the fall of 1922 speaks to the lessons these cases taught the media concerning the importance of violence and sexual impropriety to selling papers. Nonetheless, the papers were not driving all of the interest. In fact, the public's interest seemed to shock the press at times. In reporting on the rise of murder tourism, a journalist expressed disbelief in the fact that, "for a nice Sunday motoring into the country or to some quaint village or little appreciated town, there really is no inducement so compelling as a fine bloody murder." "If there is no murder scene," the reporter sarcastically noted, "within easy motoring distance, perhaps the pilgrim-motorist may be able to reach some picturesque spot where there almost was a murder. . . . Failing that, the vicinity of an assault and battery" might suffice. The reporter likened the times to a hundred years earlier when "it was a widespread genial custom to hitch up and drive miles to the country jail, there to attend that social event known as a 'hanging.'" Of course, people were still attending lynchings in this way, but the reporter seemed oblivious to this fact about his culture. So many people found entertainment in murder that he suggested signs be posted "on that spot the crime was committed. Entire spot has been carried away by souvenir hunters."[16]

According to the newspapers, the sordid, sad tales of Taylor, Arbuckle, and Hall-Mills were also a story of America. The murders showed religious leaders like Mills to be adulterous hypocrites, reporters were able expose inept police and corrupt officials, and Hollywood was not a dream factory after all.[17] Crime reporting transposed life (and death) into narratives defined on all sides by envy. The narratives defined society by wealth, status, and power. These were stories driven by ineptitude, promoted by viciousness, and encouraged by perversion. America, as written by the tabloids and newspapers, was an invidious country of suspicions and rumors rather than high morals and values.[18]

If the newspaper coverage of scandalous murders in the early twentieth century turned murder into entertainment, it also forced nearly everything in the news to turn into entertainment in order to attract public attention.[19] The result, as Burton Roscoe, the Chicago Tribune's cultural reporter, observed at the time, was that life was "not dramatic." Rather, "it was melodramatic." It had "elements of low comedy," which the reporters all recognized. The pathetic spectacle of the murder mystery, lit only by the dim reality of lost ideals, upheld the myth that everything was ephemeral.[20]

To make the public care about Mann, the newspapers first had to make them aware of her youth, beauty, and loss. Editors published Fritzie Mann's publicity photos, which resembled the bathing beauty shots the papers usually ran. They dedicated entire pages to recalling the details of her life. She had been in San Diego for a little over a year. The family had immigrated first from Europe to Colorado, and then to California. Her sister, who had tuberculosis, lived in a sanitarium. Because they had a "fatherless" household, the papers identified her brother as the man of the house. Her life, as laid out in this way, would seem unremarkable had it not ended in murder. Suddenly, the girl who had worked in a music store in Denver and had danced in local exhibitions in San Diego was a rising star who had "reportedly signed a contract with [Lasky's] Famous Players."[21] Here was the "Body of Pretty Young Woman Cast Up by the Waves." She was tragic in the article titled "The Dancing Feet of Fritzie Are Stilled." She was the "almost nude body . . . found in the surf." The newspapers transformed her into an alluring "girl" "clad only in silk undergarments" in a "delicate condition" who may have been "secretly married to a Hollywood moving picture actor."[22]

Initially, they did not focus on the scandal of her "delicate condition"; instead, they became caught up in the notion of naiveté. Her youth and her beauty, they speculated, made her susceptible to disreputable men who wanted to prey on the innocent. "It may have been that she was lured by false promises that made her trusting heart happy," speculated the *Sun*. "Perhaps she did not know when she made her way to the seashore that the ocean was to be her tomb," which suggested that the reporters needed to believe she killed herself. Nevertheless, another "player in the drama" may have "sought the most desperate way out." Again, the lack of facts forced the reporter to imagine: "Perhaps Fritzie's smile was turned upon that other face when the blow fell." "Her belongings, speaking outright of the girl's love of life and the pursuit of happiness, were found on the beach. Her frigid body, with eyes staring at the stars, was found half buried in the sand." The reporters sounded as if they could only repeat the sad details of the beach because they too mourned her loss. "Notes and cards in her suitcase gave the clue to her identity," and still the investigators knew nothing. Reaching from the beach into the city, "grief went into the home of her family on the revelation [of] her death." The *Sun* concluded, "It was a terrific blow to them all, almost more than Fritzie's mother could stand. Thousands who knew the little dancer were shocked."[23] What the *Sun* revealed was a shared voyeurism between the reader and the reporter.

By January 17, three days after the recovery of the body, the *San Diego Union* ran full-page articles featuring Mann's publicity photos. The photos converted her from the corpse to the sexualized youth. At this point, the *Union* reported that the police were pursuing the "theory of murder." She must have been an attractive corpse, because they continued to detail how, "when found, the body was half clad in silk undergarments. The woman also wore silk stockings and black satin pumps with French heels."[24] By the nineteenth, the *New York Times* had picked up the story and related the Hollywood connection and the victim's identity as a dancer "whose partly clad body was found on the beach." The *San Diego Union* detailed the screams of Amelia Mann at the inquest proclaiming that her daughter had been murdered: "Oh my little girl, my darling. I know it's a dirty murder."[25]

The *Los Angeles Examiner* began to feature stories about Mann, to publish her letters, and to detail the case every Wednesday, the day of the week dedicated to "women's news." Like the crime and sexual escapade magazines popular at the time, the newspaper focused its Wednesday coverage on what could euphemistically be called missteps of chorus girls (such as in "I Married a Ziegfeld Follies Dancer"), actresses, housewives, and debutants. The *Examiner*'s style of journalism was proved a moneymaker by *True-Story* magazine, launched in 1919. By 1923 it was selling 300,000 copies. By 1924 it averaged 848,000, and by 1926 sales approached two million. Regular newspapers had to compete with the murder magazines.[26]

In death, Fritzie Mann attained what was impossible in life. She was famous. Yet on the national scene there were other crimes to report, such as the overdose and death of film star Wallace Reid. In addition, Roscoe Arbuckle was trying to revive his career at that point and making daily news. The Hall-Mills trial was just starting. In San Diego, though, the story continued as "Fritzie's death has overshadowed all local news events in the newspapers of the Pacific coast." Her face "gazed out from front pages morning and night." The case had become the topic of conversation for the entire city.[27]

Given the focus on Mann's half-nude victimhood, what if things had been reversed and Mann had been the killer instead of the victim? Would there have been a difference in the coverage of the crime? Would there have still been the bathing beauty photos and sentimental stories about the tragedy of youth? Luckily, to answer these questions one need look no further than Los Angeles in the summer of 1922. Clara Phillips, twenty years old, killed her husband's lover with a fifteen-cent hammer purchased for the crime from a hardware store. Clara had approached her husband's lover, Alberta Meadows, a twenty-year-old widow who worked as a bank bookkeeper, as Meadows left work. Phillips asked for a ride and then directed Meadows to "lonely" Montecito Road. There the women argued, in and then outside the vehicle. Phillips began to bash Meadows's face and head. She later told her husband that she had "struck at Mrs. Meadows' head again and again with the hammer." "When all life was gone," the sheriff later related to the press, "and the head crushed in several places," Phillips left the body "where it had fallen." She then took the dead woman's car and drove toward home. Her clothes were "blood-soaked" and her hair "disheveled." She felt as though she were "on the verge of collapse." "She rushed into her husband's presence, crying: Don't leave. Don't Leave. I've killed the one you love best. You'll never see her again. Oh, I can't live without you." Her husband helped her escape. Without his confession, the next day, the police would have been unable to identify Meadows's body, which suggests the level of rage Phillips felt as she destroyed her competition's face.[28]

Three aspects of the case distinguished Clara Phillips's crime from the other famous murders covered at the time. First, she took a friend, Peggy Caffee, with her to the murder. Phillips required proof that she was the killer. She needed an audience more than she needed to maintain the image of innocence.[29]

A second distinction between Mann and Phillips was the language used by the press. When the police captured Phillips and were transporting her back to Los Angeles, they "secretly" took Caffee to meet the train and identify Phillips as the killer. The press reported that Caffee "quavered" as she "faced the prisoner." The use of this language by the press suggests that the newspapers were making clear that Phillips was not a victim.[30]

As Phillips stepped from the train at the Southern Pacific station in Los Angeles, cameramen were waiting to meet her. "For a moment the shutters clicked and her teeth flashed in a succession of smiles," noted the Associated Press. When she began to step into the sheriff's vehicle, a photographer asked her to pose. Phillips eagerly complied by smiling and "mounting the running board, head and shoulders above the large crowd of spectators which thronged the street." As she smiled, a strange kind of celebrity was born. When it was time to transport Phillips to jail, the officers had to force a lane through the crowd of spectators gathered to see her. Again, she posed for photos, only this time she stuck out her tongue instead of smiling.[31]

Here arises the media-created persona of Clara Phillips, "Hammer Slayer," as the newspapers quickly named her. She had been a bathing beauty in Hollywood pictures. "The attractive smile that marks her pulchritudinous photographs," the *San Diego Tribune* explained, "of the motion picture bathing beauty days here . . . greeted spectators when she was brought here yesterday." She had smiled for her mug shot. She smiled at everyone and everything. To the press, anxious to interview her, she said, "Good Morning, did you wish to see me?" Her attorneys said insanity would be her defense, but they were not sure if they would argue permanent or temporary derangement.[32]

A third aspect that made Phillips a sensation and distinguished her from all other female murders and female victims was that on December 3, 1922, Clara Phillips escaped from the police. In a string of run-on sentences, the respectable *New York Times* announced that Phillips had "wriggled through a small opening made in the window of her cell, and [gone] from there to the ground by a perilous route which included, it is believed, rope ladders and a sheer descent down a drainpipe." Footprints indicated that she was barefoot. Evidence that the bars to her cell, which was on the third floor of the county jail, had been sawed suggested that she had accomplices among the police.[33] After her escape, Department of Justice agents determined that her stolen plane had landed in Mexico, where the trail went cold.[34] In only a few short months, the newspaper coverage of Phillips had gone from "housewife" to "slayer."[35] She was a beauty queen with ties to Hollywood. She was vicious, possibly crazy, and willing to be photographed. Now she had also outsmarted the police and federal agents. Phillips was scandal personified.

In striking contrast, Mann was mysterious. Unlike Meadows, the bank clerk victim of Clara Phillips, she was an "Oriental dancer" and "the butterfly girl" who performed for the wealthiest people in the city. Mann's scandal revealed the dirty underpinnings of a society, because the newspapers could focus on speculation and rumor rather than facts. Quite the opposite, Phillips individualized the act of murder; she made it about herself rather than her victim or society.

For the Mann story to work in the newspapers, the reader's perspective had to become the center of the coverage. The reporters wrote about Mann as if they were observing society, the police, and the suspects. The onlooker reporter's and reader's perspective all became essential because their perspectives could transform an event like a murder into something that was subjective. Reporters were not manufacturing the seriousness of the crime by taking on the role of the bystander; they were shaping a narrative that resembled the truth about the changes under way in their culture.[36]

The first step to discovering the Mann story was the coroner's court and the inquest. District attorney Chester C. Kempley personally conducted the questioning of witnesses during the inquest. The *Union* was there to report: "The district attorney has taken an active interest in the case from the start and has assigned men to co-operate with the police in the investigation." Moreover, "while authorities were busy on the trail of those who abandoned Miss Mann's body on the lonely beach north of Torrey Pines," the *Union* repeated the now familiar tropes, "another scene in the drama was enacted in a room at the local morgue yesterday afternoon." It did matter who killed her, but a more important question arose, at least from the perceptive of the press: Who was Fritzie Mann?[37]

William Mann, her brother, distrusted the inquest findings. After listening to the evidence, he stood and gave a statement that defended his sister and condemned the investigation. The first thing on his mind was that he felt the coroner's office had showed little regard for the family. Coroner Kelly, in his first statement to the press, explained, "When I received the call I went at once to the place where the body had been found. Nearby was the vanity case containing such things as a girl might be expected to carry and with a card containing the words, 'I am Fritzie Mann.'" In these opening lines, Kelly contributed to the growing sense that Mann was a girl, not a woman. In being a girl, she was a victim. She was small, vulnerable, and fragile. "The girl's dress and a small satchel containing a kimono were picked up by John Bludworth, deputy sheriff, some distance south of the body near the highway as if someone and thrown them from a passing machine," he said, using the popular word for an automobile at that time. "I called the Mann's house Monday night and asked if Miss Mann were there. A man answered and said she was not home, but probably would be back late in the evening. I then asked when I could see her and he thought possibly in the morning. I did not know at the time that the body was that of Miss Mann, but thought she would be able to assist in the identification."[38]

By calling the house, he had inadvertently added to what would become an insurmountable family tragedy. He left out the fact that the family learned of her death from the newspapers. Then he recalled, "I visited Mrs. Mann and she told me of Miss Mann's intimates," meaning the boyfriends. "One in particular was mentioned by Mrs. Mann as being a particular friend of the girl's. Mrs. Mann only saw him once, she said. When Mrs. Mann visited the morgue and saw her dead daughter's body she became hysterical and cried out the name of the man she believed responsible. Mrs. Mann had known of her daughter's condition for several months." In this Kelly overstepped. Mrs. Mann suspected that something was wrong. Because of Kelly's investigation, she did not know all the details of her daughter's death until the inquest. He continued, explaining Mrs. Mann's insights: "[She] pleaded with her child to tell her troubles. But the girl would only say that everything would turn out all right and not to worry." These details left William angry.

William Mann recalled the phone call from Coroner Kelly differently. He told of being called and asked if Fritzie Mann were home. He responded in the negative and asked who was calling. The voice on the other end replied, "This is Kelly." The phone call seemed an obscure moment until the next morning gave it meaning. William picked up the morning paper, the *San Diego Union*, and read the description of the "half-clad girl" found on the beach. He knew then that his sister was not coming home. "I saw the description and while it was not absolutely correct it was close enough to make me curious." He went directly to the morgue and identified the body. William believed the man who had called to be the coroner and, had the coroner given his title, William declared, he would have "come down at once and unraveling of the case would have been set at least 12 hours ahead."[39]

The newspapers also dutifully reported the police complaint that the coroner's office was too slow to turn over evidence. They maintained that the coroner had failed to release the card inscribed "I am Fritzie Mann" until the morning after. They claimed that all they knew for the first twenty-four hours was that "the body of a half-clad girl had been found in the sand near Torrey Pines."

The proceedings were too much for Fritzie's brother. He implied that the coroner and the investigators seemed to be trying to besmirch his sister's memory when they should have been looking for the killer. He declared the killer to be Rogers Clark, movie director. "Clark frequently visited my sister," William explained, "but as far as I remember, never came into the house." Clark was the kind of man who would wait outside and honk his horn until the girl came running out to join him. Automobiles helped embolden a driver's sense of entitlement and thereby created new dating rules, which never would have happened in the prewar years, when men had to meet the family and dates had chaperones. William continued, "My mother distrusted him so much that she arranged a meeting on a pretext, just to get a look at Clark. It was one time when Clark wanted to take my sister to Tijuana." His mother distrusted Clark enough that she wrote down a description of him and refused to allow Fritzie to go on the date alone. "My mother didn't like it but she arranged to go along as far as the Paradise valley sanitarium, where my other sister was at the time. This was early in November." "Fritzie was a good girl, I know," William insisted, when one of the coroner's jurors asked who could be the father of the baby. She was a popular girl with many friends, "but none I know of who would prevail upon her to give herself to them. I am almost willing to swear that she was taken advantage of in some manner, probably when not in her right mind. When we first became aware of her condition she said she did not know exactly what was the matter." William Mann concluded from all the available evidence that his sister was "unconscious when the thing happened."

At this news, Mrs. Mann collapsed. According to the same *Union* article, she mentioned Clark's name frequently during her "hysterical outburst, and at times relapsed into her native tongue." Those in attendance also began to cry as they watched the court officials try to console the mother. She managed to regain her composure through "obvious effort." Men escorted her to the back of the room, "from which point she listened to the rest of the testimony at the inquest." However, there was nothing a mother would want to hear. Mrs. Mann was learning that she knew Frieda but had not fully known Fritzie.

As his mother grieved from the backbench, William "threw another bombshell." According to him, Rogers Clark once declared he would give $1,000 "to get acquainted with Fritzie." Fritzie was selling tickets to a performance at the Barn, a local nightclub. She was approaching the guests in the lobby of the Grant Hotel, which everyone knew meant the speakeasy in the Grant Hotel. Clark's reaction to first setting eyes on Mann speaks to how breathtaking she was and how hard it was not to notice her. "I am not positive," William explained, "as to the exact date. Clark saw her in the hotel, and I am informed," by mutual friends, that he "remarked that he would give $1000 to know my sister." Though he delicately veiled the story in euphemisms to protect his sister, his accusations indicated that Clark was a cad.

Jubilantly, the newspapers announced on the twenty-third that the police were ready to make arrests, a week since the recovery of her body. With arrests, the drama that sold papers could finally move away from describing the nude body on the beach, which had become increasingly undressed with each passing story, to subjecting individual suspects of the case to trial by headline. There were two potential suspects: Rogers Clark of Los Angeles, a purported producer-director-actor in the motion picture industry, and Louis Jacobs, a physician in San Diego. Both were suspicious.

Chief Patrick believed, as he openly told the press, that some of the witnesses were covering up certain phases of the case, "which if exposed would unveil a series of scandals" in southern California. The investigation again turned to Los Angeles. Detectives Sears and Chadwick left San Diego for Los Angeles to retrieve a parcel of letters said to have been stolen from among the young dancer's possessions after her death. They also intended to interview some of the girl's friends in Hollywood.[40]

It took several days to track down Rogers Clark. The rumor that he had secretly married Mann appeared in the papers. The truth was that he was a car dealer in San Pedro, which the newspapers reported only once. He had not married Mann. In fact, though he claimed to be divorced, he was still married. He was not a film director. He was just a guy using a pickup line in bars.

Nevertheless, the press's story presented the fantasy instead of the truth. The newspapers spun other rumors about police questioning a "well-known motion-picture star and a photoplay producer" concerning the incidents in the final days of Mann's life. Supposedly, the names of two motion picture persons were found in Fritzie's vanity case. Detectives also interviewed twelve others persons, but they uncovered no leads.[41]

Clark had originally lied to police about his whereabouts and then fled, only to be arrested in Los Angeles while driving a car with visible blood spots in evidence on the dashboard, where the cases of some of the instruments were also cracked and shattered. The rear seat, they reported, had bloodstains and showed evidence of attempts to wash off the marks.[42]

Chief Patrick, sensing the seriousness of the case, traveled to Los Angeles to question Clark. The *Union* reported, "The chief's quiz of the murder suspect began shortly afterward."[43] The police also had to retrieve Mann's belongings from her friend's house in Long Beach, outside of Los Angeles, where she had spent several weeks. She told her family and friends she had a film contract. The reality of the situation, which the newspapers had yet to uncover, was that she had no such contract. She was not a rising star. She had moved to Los Angeles to conceal the pregnancy and to escape the pressure placed on her, by Louis Jacobs, to have an illegal abortion.

Louis Jacobs, upon hearing of the death of Mann, came to the police station voluntarily and told the police of his relationship to Mann. He had sometimes taken her driving, but they were just friends, he insisted. The police had in evidence more than a dozen letters and telegrams between Jacobs and Mann discussing her "condition." He told them that his motivation was natural human interest in a friend in trouble.[44] "Damned Fool altruism," he called it. He had only shown an interest in the girl, he explained, because she was Jewish, as was he, and she had said her husband treated her "cruely." When the police showed him the letters, Jacobs denied knowing who was responsible for Mann's "condition" and claimed that she had never said the name of her husband. "How does it happen," asked Chief Patrick, "that you took such a part in her affairs, and still did not know the identity of the man who was responsible?" "I don't make it a business of prying into other people's affairs," Jacobs announced.[45] The chief asked Jacobs about the bruises on Mann's body. "I may have stepped on her feet while we were dancing."[46] Eventually, and temporarily, Chief Patrick had to publicly announce, "We are unable to obtain evidence to connect Dr. Jacobs with the alleged murder of Miss Mann." Everything they had was circumstantial evidence, and Judge Spencer Milton Marsh ruled Jacobs be released.[47]

Clark was able to offer an alibi that included spending the evening with Gladys Flowers, stepdaughter of a prominent civic leader, until after midnight, which she and her neighbors corroborated, and then visiting the Golden Lion, a crowded restaurant with ample witnesses, to meet up with friends.[48] The blood in his vehicle came from helping a injured motorist to the hospital, which the Los Angeles police verified.[49] Clark was also over six feet tall and in no way matched the physical description of Mann's companion that night. Jacobs, who was of average build, also offered an alibi; however, he lied when the police presented him with Mann's letters. Jacobs became the central suspect.

With the announcement of suspects and the holding of the coroner's inquest, the San Diego Union, the conservative city paper owned by railroad and real estate magnate John D. Spreckels, began to devote long-form articles detailing every aspect of the case. Spreckels prided himself on being a creative newspaper publisher who had long pushed illustrations and photos as instrumental to the news. Serial novels, comics, puzzles, and political cartoons all pushed readership as Spreckels sought to outsell his competitor, the Scripps-owned San Diego Sun. Spreckels could not buy out the Sun because, like himself, its owner was a millionaire. He had no choice but to outpublish Scripps. Mann's murder offered yet another opportunity for the Union to do so.[50]

The Union reported early on, "Arrest of Clark in Los Angeles was requested by Chief Patrick yesterday morning when evidence seemed to point strongly toward the motion picture man." Then it had the story: "The detention of Dr. Jacobs, who came to the station yesterday morning by appointment with the chief, was almost a foregone conclusion after letters sent by the doctor to Miss Mann while the dancer was in Los Angeles had been read. Information gathered by the police and operatives from the district attorney's office enabled the authorities to reconstruct

the happenings Sunday night and to weave a strong net of circumstantial evidence."[51] Therein lay the problem.

More evidence came in, and the newspapers reported it. A
blanket from the Blue Sea Cottage was found on the beach and
been identified by the hotel manager. The manager had identified
Mann from a photo and indicated that she had signed in with her
unidentified companion as "W. Johnstone and wife."

Grasping at any available new information in order to keep the
story going and the papers selling, the *Union* went on to explain
the police theory that the blanket had been wrapped around "the
young dancer, unconscious or already dead," as the killer transported her to "her last resting place in the Pacific." "On the way
back to La Jolla or San Diego," the police speculated, "the driver of
the machine, according to this theory threw out the blanket, the
girl's dress and the small satchel containing the kimono." With the
recovery of her belongings, all indications pointed "to a desire on
the part of the murderer or murderers to give the impression that
Miss Mann had committed suicide." Through the theories and the
speculations, the papers created the image of a violent murder.

Once the police began to go through her things and found the
letters, the papers could start to present the murderer as a preda-
tor and maintain the image of Mann as the nude girl. The *Union*
reported, "Dr. Jacobs, Camp Kearny public health service officer,
came into the case a whole lot more prominently than he had figured heretofore." He had sent more than half a dozen telegrams,
some signed "Louis L. Jacobs," others "Louis," and a few merely
"L.L.J." These documents threw a "flood of light on Miss Mann's
condition," meaning her pregnancy, "and did not agree with some
of the doctor's statements made to the chief Wednesday when he
voluntarily appeared at the station," police sources revealed.

Troublingly, the letters contained the details of Jacobs's
efforts to obtain a nurse and an abortionist for Mann, "although
just what the professional help was to do was not stated." Other
letters further destroyed Jacobs's story that he had known her
only a short time. One letter, from July 1922, "showed that the
acquaintance extended that far back at least." "It was the letters written by Dr. Jacobs that engaged the more serious attention of the police." The police summoned Jacobs to the station.
"The doctor, who wears the bars of a captain in the United States

public health service, appeared at the station at 11 o'clock yesterday morning. He drove down in his Hudson sedan. He awaited his appointment with the chief. Soon his opportunity came and he was closeted with the head of the police department." If Jacobs had killed her, her murder happened after months, according to the letters, of committing the social crime of trying to force Mann to have the abortion. By including the details about his job and his automobile, the newspapers clarified for the reader that he had the financial ability to marry Mann as well as the medical knowledge to understand the dangers of an illegal abortion.

With two suspects, her mother's declaration of "dirty murder," and the evidence of Mann's fragile "condition," the papers advanced a theory. The police were convinced it was not suicide. So who had killed her? The *San Diego Sun*, owned by E. W. Scripps, the creator of United Press Association, argued that "the man was an ardent admirer of Miss Mann."[52] Scripps used the *Sun* to relentlessly attack the *Union*, the *Union's* owner John Spreckels, and the Republican politics of both by championing the downtrodden of the city.[53] The *Sun* cited Chief Patrick as its source and began the narrative of the fall of Fritzie Mann. The house party had not "materialized." Nonetheless, an "admirer" of Mann's had driven "down from Los Angeles alone" in his "enclosed roadster." Miss Mann left with him. They went to the Blue Sea Cottage and took a room for the night. For some reason they did not stay long. With a "quart of cheap whiskey" in the car, they sped along the oceanside highway north. "Miss Mann became violently ill, from the effects of the liquor combined with her delicate condition." At some point in all of this, though the *Sun* was not specific, they had returned to the cottage. She most likely fainted; the newspapermen imagined she had "perhaps struck her head as she fell." Then the *Sun* showed mercy on the accused. "The man," they fictionalized, "tried desperately to revive her, failed, and believed her dead. . . . Seizing an army blanket from the stores of the cottage he carried her to the machine, went back for her clothing but left her hair net and an ornament, later identified by the girl's mother as her own." He sped along the highway, wishing to put on as much speed as he could as he drove north from La Jolla toward Los Angeles. At the first beach, he "carried the unconscious form of the girl into the waves, wrapped in the blanket, and dropped her." Then, in a clear indication that the reporters believed Clark to be the killer, they added, "Getting into the car he put on speed, tossing the garments out as he dashed toward Los Angeles." To be fair, they then had to explain that Clark had provided an alibi.[54]

Meanwhile, the *San Diego Tribune* was busy. Of the city's newspapers, the *Tribune* had always been the most tabloid and incendiary. Spreckels also owned the *Tribune*. Having the higher-end respectable *Union* and the lower-end "working man's" *Tribune* allowed him to dominate the city's media and Republican politics from "the top to the bottom."[55] From the *Tribune* came the rumors and the scandal. A truck driver happened to be passing the murder scene. The acetylene lamps on his truck cast a wide light, illuminating even the sides of the road. There he and his wife saw a man and a women "quarrelling violently" inside a car. "It appeared to be a closed car with the front glass dropped," the witness said. "While I did not see them actually struggling together, it was perfectly apparent that a quarrel was in progress. The car was of dark finish and was at the left side of the road, facing north, as though it had been driven from San Diego."[56]

The confusing rumors continued to pour into the papers. Harley Sachs, the man who had covered Fritzie Mann's body with a piece of burlap, had been on his way to church that Sunday night. His wife accompanied him, and they both said they saw an automobile standing at the side of the road headed toward La Jolla. The car was empty, and the lights were out. Sachs's wife recalled that they had wondered what had become of the car's occupants. Another man told the police that he too had seen a vehicle. Only this automobile had two men standing beside it engaged in a fistfight. He thought there were other occupants in the car. The police dismissed the pugilists' car as having nothing to do with the case, just as they were quick to dismiss the sightings of Fritzie that came from people all over San Diego.[57] The *Tribune* also advanced the theory that Mann's body had been thrown from a bridge and drifted in the tides until it struck land, which completely ignored all of the coroner's findings.[58]

The conservative *San Diego Union* exercised more caution in reporting the rumors than its competitors did. The paper was less cautious in announcing all of the unanswered questions that still existed five days after the murder. To begin, they asked, "At what time did [Fritzie] meet her death? At what time was her body thrown into the sea?" These two questions were an indictment against forensic evidence and the coroner's office. "Was she conscious when she reached there? What caused the bruise over her right eye? How long had her body been lying on the beach before it was discovered?" In asking these questions, the paper both tugged at the grief of the readers and made it sound as though the authorities had no evidence to answer the questions. How long she lay there was something the public might have felt they knew, because the public had discovered her. "How was she taken to the beach north of Torrey Pines? Who took her there?" These questions challenged the police, who had leads and suspects but could not seem to hold anyone in jail. The *Union* asserted that the police had to answer these questions before they could penetrate the "thick veil of mystery that now enshrouds the investigation" and bring the "alleged slayer" into "the light." The editors and reporters continued to condemn the police for their "failure to acquire direct evidence"; the police investigators still believed the suicide theory had merit, despite saying "firmly" that the "pretty dancer met her death by foul play."[59]

Their production of crime news suggests that detectives and reporters collaborated in determining what became a crime story. For a time, they were coauthors deciding where the story began and ended, who the protagonists were, and what roles they played. Their collaboration was a tenuous one because the press needed to create a sellable product while maintaining its image of neutrality. The San Diego papers were playing at presenting themselves as objective so as to create a false sense of distance, with the end result of their reporting seeming above the fray. The newspaper stories—like stories told in courtrooms, police stations, and everyday rumors exchanged across back fences—raised important questions about violence. Only the newspapers, according to the newspapers, had the power to suggest that the murder of Fritzie Mann represented all that was wrong with an entire population. Newspapers, particularly the *Union* and the *Sun*, saw their role in reporting the murder as an opportunity to expose issues of class, gender, nationality, and sexuality. If mistakes were made, they were the result of the police investigation, not the press, or so the press told the readers. Because the news-papers created the first public narrative of the death of Fritzie Mann, they became the first authority to which the other partici-pants had to answer. True, the presumed killer would be judged in court, but the police would be on trial in the papers for having failed to reveal the truth faster.[60]

Though the police may have delayed in investigating, the press did not. Because of its speed and efficiency, the press cre-ated and controlled the narrative rather than the police. From Coroner Kelly's point of view, the press must have been an essen-tial part of his autopsies and inquests. This seems evident from the scrapbook he kept of articles published about all of his cases. Had they been saved for vanity, one would imagine he would have preserved only the articles featuring his interviews, or that he would have given constant interviews, or that he would have favored the articles from the *San Diego Union*, the respectable paper. Instead, he collected from all the papers, even the *Tribune*. The publicity and fevered pitch of the coverage made success on the part of all involved necessary. Coroner Kelly knew it.

The police also saw the press as essential. They were seeking to inform the press in the hope of keeping their hands on the story and protecting the reputation of the force. The police wanted to make clear to the press that those questioned in relation to the murder were holding back, that her friends knew who the "pale and trembling young man," of average height and weight, seen with Mann at the Blue Sea Cottage, was.[61] They feared he had fled to Mexico, and a county detective left for Ensenada to check on leads. Meanwhile, the motorcycle squad continued to hunt up and down the coast in search of Mann's hat and coat.[62] Shortly thereafter the police identified the Blue Sea Cottage, a small hotel on the La Jolla coast with private bungalows, as the scene of the crime. The owner had described Mann as being chipper when she checked in with an unidentified escort who signed the register as Mr. and Mrs. Johnstone. Nevertheless, in late January 1923 the district attorney presented the evidence to a grand jury, held up the blanket, questioned everyone involved, and brought in an indictment of Jacobs for the murder of the young dancer, scantily clad in silk underwear, found on the Tor-rey Pines beach.[63]

A week after her death, it was time to bury Mann's body—but not the story. "Fritzie Mann carried the secret of her tragic death to her grave this afternoon," announced the *Los Angeles Times*. The paper claimed that in death she had made her way into the hearts of everyone in San Diego. The release of Captain Jacobs on a habeas corpus writ, two hours before Mann's funeral, "has left the death of the little oriental dancer enshrouded in an apparently impenetrable veil of mystery," the Los Angeles reporter mourned. Only her brother, her mother, and two friends attended the funeral. It had been a week. The police had arrested and released two suspects, having made no progress, the papers reported. Jacobs had given up no additional evidence. No solution had been found to explain how the "seminude body of Fritzie" came to be on the beach at Torrey Pines.[64]

This was 1923. The city was at the start of a decade-long, titanic level of social upheaval and violence previously unimagined in its details and pervasiveness. For those who watched over the body, who reduced it to its core meanings, and who pieced together Mann's final days for the newspaper reading public, ultimately the only way to understand Mann was as a tragedy.

Given the misfortune of her life and the failure of the police investigation, the *San Diego Sun* decided that Mann's obituary was really an obituary for her generation. It was January 1923, and this generation was already, as F. Scott Fitzgerald called them, the "beautiful damned." Mann was "one of hundreds of young girls who live for the gay nights, the slender, chic, silk stockinged girl [who] had dropped out of sight. The heartless waves of the Pacific beating over her silk-clad, almost naked body, had played her last jazz tune. . . . But last night," as the cocktails were passed around, "one familiar face was missing." While "this little girl lay in a casket in an undertaking parlor . . . the jazz was at its top speed." As the "grim faced" police "were scouring the city" looking for the killer, "the hilarity which she so enjoyed, and the merriment which she so often contributed to[,] was at its height." A "hundred other girls were ready to take her place" as the jazz band played on.[65]

4

FANTASY

In a eulogy for Fritzie Mann, the *San Diego Union* wrote that the city had a "night life of gleaming shoulders, glistening limbs, hip gin, racing automobiles, glued cheeks and jazz—always that eternal unending, hypnotizing jazz." The young people of the Jazz Age city sought out the places with the "shrill laughter" and the "pet names," where a "slender drummer, in a shiny suit, low collar and small bow tie" played a "long roll on the snare drum." Every night it started the same way in the bars and small clubs north of the city line. The parties inevitably moved over the border into Mexico. At first, there were only a dozen couples on the floors "swaying to the jazz tune." Suddenly, magically, another dozen appeared and then a third. "And now the floor is packed, a mass of humanity dipping and sliding and twisting under the gala decorations of the jazz palace." Fritzie Mann had been a "girl of twenty, a slim, athletic, attractive girl, who first was a spectator, then a participant, and finally a popular star in the gay night life."[1]

During the day, the city was a very different place. Fritzie could have gone for a walk through the hills of the Market District overlooking San Diego Bay. Perched atop one of those hills, she would have seen a truly beautiful city. There were warships entering and leaving the harbor. Navy aircraft regularly flew over

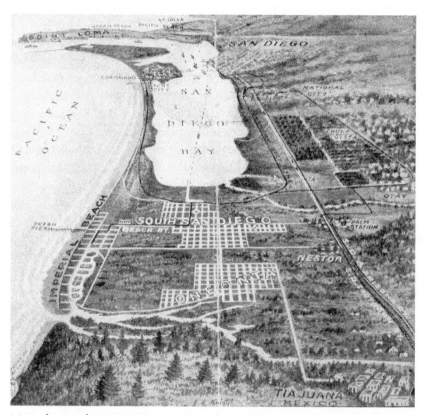

Map of coastal San Diego County in about 1910. From the Mexican border it looks north toward San Diego Bay and the city of San Diego. Coronado is the thin strip of land to the left of the bay. La Jolla appears at the top of the map, beyond Point Loma. Torrey Pines and then Del Mar—not shown on the map—are farther north of La Jolla. Cartography by RA Harris Realty Co. Courtesy of the San Diego History Center.

the Spanish-inspired homes accessible by paved roads and tree-lined streets. Back from the water, the residences reached to the southeast along the waterline to National City, and north and east into the mountainous country. In the center was the perennially green Balboa Park with its gleaming pools.

In the background were the mountains and the cultivated fields of the country, the orchards, and the paved roads, which enabled the farmers to bring their produce to markets inside the city and beyond. Leading off from the coastline to Los Angeles was the highway to Camp Kearny, a former naval base that once

housed the 40th Division, known as the "Sunshine Division."
At one time, the camp accommodated 40,000 men, but in 1922
it became a public health hospital where Dr. Louis Jacobs, thirty
years old, specialized in cardiology and pulmonology.

San Diego was simply a paradise of everlasting mornings,
according to its boosters, where the flowers bloomed all year, and
the roads were paved with concrete. After all, according to the
Union, there were "ideal climatic conditions" for a person to "get
the most out of life in San Diego," the "land of perpetual sunshine" where "life was worth living."[2] Like the city, Mann was
also looking for ways to remake, market, and present herself as
the modern gleaming ideal.

In the mornings, every day of the last year of her life, the
primer for the working-class modern girl arrived at Mann's home.
It was the *San Diego Union*. The newspaper displayed the achieve-
ments of middle- and upper-class women, such as bridge playing
and flower arranging, still defined by prewar standards. The paper
also propagated a fantasyland in its daily serial, a fictional story
presented in parts: "Starlight" chronicled the life of Virginia Fairfax, a girl unhappy with the "puritanical rule of her grandfather
[who] runs away to Hollywood" to become an actress.[3] Mann's
work toward becoming a star matches Virginia Fairfax's fictional
arc, which means the newspaper offered a fictional diary that
paralleled the aspirations of, or perhaps inspired, the life a young
woman months away from death. The fictional Virginia pushed
at the boundaries to find success as an actress, but in the end she
moralized and upheld the prewar values. Mann's end, in contrast,
reflected the reality of the boundaries of the Jazz Age city.

Things fell into place quickly for the fictional Virginia Fairfax. She met movie people, went to parties where she witnessed
the tragic behavior of her female friends, and eventually caught
the eye of Theodore Stratton, star.[4] The week Fritzie was dancing in the prologue, a live performance presented before a motion
picture, at San Diego's Colonial movie theater, the newspaper's
imaginary heroine Virginia was in Stratton's car. In this episode,
she sat looking at him but could not see past his fame. She tried to
conceal her naiveté and apprehension. As his car slowed in front
of her apartment, Virginia felt herself blush. Everyone looked
and recognized his car. Because Virginia Fairfax represents the

Victorian values of reputation and hard work, she scolded herself: "I really sensed the mistake I had made in allowing him to bring me home or pay me any individual attention." She knew that nowhere else in the world did "the tongue of scandal wag as it does in movie land. No one is ever given the credit of succeeding by sheer hard work," she realized. "If you speak of some big actor, he has always gotten his position because some woman was in love with him at his beginning, and, being a power on the screen, she made him." It was even worse for girls, "no matter how impeccable her conduct"; a girl linked to scandal "never escapes the lifting of the eyebrow and the compression of the lips which intimates something dark and shadowy in her past if she reaches the top." Virginia reflected that any young woman pursuing a career in pictures, which meant she was speaking directly to girls like Fritzie, "must be inured to this; she must regard her own conscience as her standard and let the world judge as it will."

Virginia knew her neighbors were all watching her; she lingered in the automobile "longer than was necessary." She extended her hand to Stratton, and he held it "a wee bit longer" than she had wished. Even though she feared he would say yes, she invited him to see her apartment. Stratton demurred. He understood far too well the stain scandal made on the life of a young woman. He explained: "The motives of men who are much in the public eye are always misunderstood. I have to be careful not only of your reputation, but of my own. If I should visit your apartment every eye that is watching us right now would grow rounder and larger for the moment—then it would narrow with sinister suspicions. That is the sad thing about our profession. Our motives are always suspected."

To this declaration of propriety, Virginia's heart leapt. He seemed generous, wonderful, and she felt fortunate to know him. She extended her hand again. "Careful, careful, my dear child," he said, barely touching her fingers. "Remember: you are always on exhibition." Then he raised his hat in the manner that distinguished him on the silver screen.[5] Here Virginia was the reticent Victorian maiden and Stratton was the self-made man who had not been seduced by the hedonistic morals of the Jazz Age.[6]

Reality contrasted greatly with the newspaper's Virginia. Fifty million Americans who went to the movies in one of the

15,000 theaters in the nation each week saw "hot love making." Most of the films ended with a moral lesson, but few in the teenage audience seemed to notice this because they frequently left the movie early. They went to their automobiles, where they could touch each other unseen.[7]

The films that drew in the youth audience were those that offered adventurous characters pushing at the edges of socially acceptable sexuality. In the summer of 1921, there is no doubt that Mann would have watched *The Four Horsemen of the Apocalypse,* because everyone saw it. The film starred the "Latin lover" Rudolph Valentino. Famously, Valentino danced the tango in *The Four Horsemen,* which represented his exotic sexuality because the tango required the woman to push him toward ecstasy. From 1921 to 1922, Valentino's performances and films redefined masculinity by creating a fantasy world in which the desirable man had to be socially accountable, possess sexual and emotional openness, and above all be nonviolent. He was the sex symbol for women like Mann and the fictional Virginia, who desired the chase but wanted to make the decisions about sex.[8]

The Four Horseman would become the most profitable picture of the year for Metro Studio.[9] In December 1921, advertisements in the *San Diego Union* announced that *The Sheik,* also starring Valentino, had been playing to a packed house for five weeks in the Rialto Theater.[10] In addition to the rise of Valentino as the smoldering Latin lover, beginning in 1922 Mann could have also seen *Polly at the Follies,* which featured all of the Ziegfeld Girls and Constance Talmadge performing a dance dressed in Egyptian-inspired costumes, and *The Ido Dancer.*[11] In these films, the man chases the woman, but the woman decides when they have sex. Through her own sexual expressions, such as through dancing, she turns the man into the pliable partner who bends to her will.

For a young dancer dreaming of stardom, these films offered powerful lessons. At the time, probably no performer was more instructive in the art of the erotic than Alla Nazimova in such films as *Revelation, The Doll House, Camille, Out of the Fog, Stronger Than Death, and The Hermit Doctor of Gaya.* In these films, Nazimova performed dances as an Indian priestess, as a gypsy, as a harem girl, or in nude silhouette against a scrim curtain while a Black jazz band accompanied. Sometimes she performed

Alla Nazimova in costume as Salome, February 1923.
The costume features a large white-plumed headdress
and cascading pearls down the bodice. Posters, advertisements in newspapers, and photospreads in fashion and fan
magazines throughout 1922 highlighted images of Nazimova similar to this one. Nazimova also depicted herself
as a geisha, a gypsy, and most famously a Spanish dancer
alongside Valentino. Mann's self-promotion and publicity
photos showcased similar modes of self-creation. Photo by
Arthur Rice. Courtesy Getty Images.

in a jungle setting and danced with the seven veils. She told the
press she was Russian or that she had gypsy blood. This gave her
mystery. Every newspaper portrait of her depicts her in costume
for one of her roles.[12]

Given Mann's use of pearls and feathers in her promotional
photographs, it is not hard to imagine that she, like her peers,

became enamored with Nazimova—a film star with her own production studio. She was not just beautiful or exotic; Nazimova was an indication that beauty and desirability were no longer the sole possession of the Gibson Girl, the pure girls of the turn-of-the-century advertisements, or even the girl next door. Nazimova both on and off screen was a feminist, an intellectual, and independent. She sought passionately sexual and companionate relationships with both women and men. She played sports, she hiked, and she believed that the outdoors were essential to life. She was also unabashedly short, Jewish, and foreign. In late 1922, when the newspapers were flooded with photos of Nazimova as *Salome*, there was a possibility that the New Woman could speak with a foreign accent.[13]

In real life, immigrants surrounded Mann. Like Mann, San Diego was fully American because its citizens refused to be bound by the past. Like the rest of the country, San Diego experienced a boom in business and population growth. Between 1910 and 1920, San Diego's population had almost doubled—reaching 75,000. By 1921, when the Mann family arrived, the population was 97,776. In fact, in the years 1920 and 1921 there was $3,520,082 worth of building construction in the city, an increase of $1 million over 1919. The official reason for the constant and impressive growth was that "tourists stay."[14]

The complex reason for the growth was the influx of German immigrants, the California Pacific International Exposition, and the military. The influx of immigrants and the military meant that Fritzie Mann was living in a young city. In 1917, North Island became a joint Army-Navy aviation station, for training pilots. When the Navy returned Balboa Park to the city, it gained the right to establish a naval hospital in the Park, where Mann's boyfriend Louis Jacobs worked. Point Loma, where Mann frequently performed, became the home of the naval training station and marine base. Thirty-Second Street also featured a naval station. By 1925, no one could have denied that San Diego was a military town.[15] Wartime money built modern San Diego. The harbor, the airfields, the military bases all expanded, as did the need for San Diego to be the leading American city in Panama Canal traffic. While Europe suffered the carnage of the war, San Diego and Mann benefited.

As 1922 began, Fritzie Mann was dancing at the Colonial, the new motion picture house that boasted of being "modern" because of its new heating and ventilation systems. An audience member never had to fear being "too cold or too hot." Though she was performing her "Dance of Destiny" as part of the prologue before the picture and had to share the bill with other performers who sang and did pantomime, it was a significant opportunity because the Colonial's manager had purchased the sets for the prologue directly from Metro Studios, Valentino's studio. Fritzie was dancing on sets once used in Hollywood pictures.[16] She was so close to achieving her dream and yet still so far away. What was she to do?

If Virginia's fictional story in the newspaper had anything to teach a young woman dreaming of stardom, then one of the first steps toward stardom was the importance of being noticed. To this end, Fritzie Mann and her friend Dorothy Armstrong sought a photography studio that could take promotional shots of them. It was the first step toward distinguishing between her life as Frieda and her life as Fritzie. In her photographs, which displayed her full body, Mann attempted to convey the luxuriousness of the costume. More than that, at least for the people who saw them in the paper after her death, the photos captured her soul in silver and albumen. The images feature an expressionless face, a dramatic cupped hand across the chest, and an expanse of exposed skin. In them, Mann seems like a young girl who wants to be desirable, beautiful, mysterious, amusing, dangerous, and talented all at once. The photos capture the looks, attitudes, and gestures learned from contemplating stills of actresses and glamour shots, such as those featured in the *Harper's Bazaar* or the *Los Angeles Times*. It is as if Mann had practiced these poses in the mirror at every opportunity until she could afford to pay for the professional sitting.[17]

Studying the magazines and newspapers, an eager student like Mann would learn that the elements of style change a woman's figure and hide her identity. A young woman with a frivolous mind might "extend a gracious little black-velvet gloved hand, or she may keep both her hands concealed from you so that you have no idea of the sort of person she is, where her hands have the subtle modeling of the Mona Lisa or whether they are direct,

The photos of Mann featured in the newspapers at the time of her death appear to be from the same photo shoot at the Hartsook Studios as this picture, for which she posed in 1922. She is in the same costume and headdress. Her photos depict her the way she saw herself and hoped others would see her—as an artist, as a beauty, and as Fritzie. Courtesy Getty Images.

straightforward boyish hands that are tell-all of her character," professed *Harper's*.[18] In *Cosmopolitan*, which at the time focused more on words than on fashion, the blurbs beneath the pictures of the new Broadway stars, the lucky "girls" who had recently signed contracts with Paramount, described their hair as being like a Botticelli.

There were rules for posing for the photographs. In *Cosmopolitan*, the photos were glamorous headshots that promoted the sweet girls, like Shirley Vernon, the star of Broadway's "Sally." Smudged filters ruled this type of photography. To appear innocent while being alluring, the young woman looked over one shoulder toward the camera but not at the camera. The vivacious girl, such as Florence O'Denishawn of the Ziegfeld Follies, also looked away from the camera while smiling ever so slightly. The daring girls, like Marguerite Marsh, appearing with Lionel Barrymore in

Boomerang Bill, looked into the camera. However, the established stars, meaning older, like Lillian Russell, did not appear in tight closeup. Their photographs were full-body, showing the costume and the presence of the woman. Fritzie Mann's choice in poses suggests which type she thought she was.[19]

Luckily, Mann lived at the moment photography was undergoing a shift away from merely cataloguing reality. As the twentieth century dawned, the photographer began to interpret, legitimize, and survey. It was a "Graphics revolution" that had begun in the late nineteenth century as illustrations and advertisements. In the twentieth century, photography changed the nature of information and of the self as represented in photography.[20] Mann used photography as publicity and as a tool to realize her preferred self.[21]

Like many others, Mann sought the photography studio to the stars: Hartsook. Founded by Fred Hartsook in 1910, the studios were a chain of photography firms founded on the principle that the regular public would pay extra to be photographed in the same settings as celebrities, just as they would pay to see dancers perform on old Hollywood sets at the Colonial Theater. The general public knew Hartsook's name because his studios distributed photographs with a provisional waiver of copyright, permitting any paper or magazine to print an image provided Hartsook Studios received credit.[22] The photos would have also appeared in the lobbies of the movie theaters where Mann was performing and in the *San Diego Union*.

Though the Hartsook studios lasted only until 1927, they did produce the best photographs of Lillian Gish, D. W. Griffith's favorite actress, and Alice Terry, who in 1921 rocketed to fame opposite Valentino in *The Four Horsemen of the Apocalypse*.[23] Mann's choice in photography studios suggests that she saw the Hartsook mark on the photos in the paper and knew their link to Hollywood. She also knew the importance of the photograph to her career.

Despite having the best photographers available, Hartsook employed skilled but less talented photographers, who were willing to work for minimal pay, to do family portraits. The photos that exist indicate that Mann met Hartsook's basic employees. Had an upscale artist in Hollywood photographed her—the kind that the movie stars and Los Angeles debutants had access to—the shadows in the photograph would have been gradual rather than starkly contrastive. Her skin would have appeared luminous so as to suggest warmth rather than drama.[24]

The photographers were essential, according to actress Norma Talmadge, because the movie camera was "fickle," meaning the still camera was discerning and showed the star quality better than the moving picture camera. Stills, she maintained, showed whether or not the aspiring starlets, who came in the hundreds every day to Hollywood casting offices, "registered." Many at the time believed that the still camera could see something the naked eye could not. Mann had "it." Without a doubt there was an ineffable star quality. Though "it" could not be explained, if the subject had it the camera would know.[25]

In pursuing the perfect photograph, was Mann attempting to alter one or another part of her identity—be it her gender, her "race," her culture—so as to create an acceptable American without the Jewish qualities that marked her as different and unacceptable? Certainly prior to and after the world war other Jewish girls were attempting to transcend their origins. The practice was common enough that the Yiddish magazine *Jewish Daily Forward* published weekly beauty shots of young women with bobbed hair, wearing pearl necklaces and makeup. In 1918, the *Evening World* declared that these girls were trying to assimilate by adopting non-Jewish dress and habits. There was even a term for this generation: "ghetto girls." The definition was similar to that of "flapper." The ghetto girls had a desire for consumer goods, fashion, and leisure. They wanted freedom from the family and control over their own money. They provoked anxiety among conservatives, as did the flapper.[26] Mann's actions do seem to reflect this "ghetto girl" urge. Her choices align with those of other Jewish youth and the wider changes in youth behavior, which demonstrates that "modern youth" was a nation-wide phenomenon.[27]

Her photographs also suggest that Mann dreamed of power and fame. She thought she might access her dreamed-of life through creative reinvention of herself. Some might call it lying. Yet, rather than seeing it as deception, let us instead see what kind of realities she selected. By examining her tangential relationship with the truth, the persona she constructed, and the constraints under which she embellished stories about herself, it is possible to glimpse her internal self.[28]

Placed in the context of her family, Mann's choices of persona are significant. Her mother, Amelia, found a place in the city's German-speaking neighborhoods, and her brother, William, found work as an accountant. Then there were the two sisters: Helen and Frieda—two radically opposed figures representing the same culture and city. Helen was, as her mother put it, the "sick daughter." She found her place in the modern hospital and represented the family's immigrant side. It was not uncommon for people at the time to associate illness with the foreigner. Indeed, at the time, culture, politics, economics, and social emphasis were more important in configuring an understanding of disease than was any diagnosis or prognosis.[29]

Frieda, on the other hand, sought out a different city and thus a different life. While her sister experienced the material of the physical poverty of disease, Frieda worked to create an imaginative wealth by becoming Fritzie Mann.[30] Leisure palaces and speakeasies made up Fritzie's city. She could be found waiting in the lobby of the Grant Hotel for a boyfriend to pick her up and take her to the Golden Lion Tavern for dinner or to Tijuana for a day trip.[31] Mann's San Diego was a Jazz Age city suspended somewhere between the "night life that extends from Tijuana on the south to those mysterious places along the highway on the north—where no questions are asked and no registers kept."[32]

Despite all the sunlit uplands of San Diego, there was darkness. California Jews did have to contend with widespread, openly celebrated anti-Semitism. To be sure, California had a Ku Klux Klan. However, the daily problem for Jews in California were the social clubs restricting membership, college fraternities banning Jewish students, and schools and universities setting quotas. California Jews also fought court battles to ensure the separation of church and state. Those that had acquired wealth, such as the Levi-Strauss family, invested in community stewardship in the form of building community centers and schools and fostering the arts to raise the profile of the Jewish community and to enrich their cities.[33]

Fritzie Mann was, however, of a different generation than the Jewish community leaders. Underlying the cultural shift of the Jazz Age that made her own transformation from Frieda to Fritzie was the war. Mann's freedom, like San Diego's, rose from the ashes of the Old World. Looking at San Diego at the start of the twenties is to look at a city transformed by World War I. While Europe crumbled, San Diego, with its military bases and harbor, flourished. Everything positive that came from that war came to San Diego, including the military and technological advancements of a new age. The city also embraced jazz and women's liberation. In short, the "air of the modern world gave such opportunity for full, deep breaths of freedom,"[34] which were unknown to Fritzie's mother's generation. Nevertheless, Prohibition, quotas, and the Klan represented the urge to control a society moving swiftly toward social change.

"It was not only the war," Zelda Fitzgerald, the prototypical Jazz Age woman, insisted. "The war was merely a heightening and hurrying forward of the inevitable reaction against the false" Victorian "premises" their mothers preached.[35] In a sense, the world did not change in a blink of eye because there was not enough time to blink. In just a few years, automobiles filled the streets, nearly every home had electricity and access to a telephone, Einstein promulgated his special theory of relativity, Marie Curie isolated radium, Ford's assembly line became the norm, Gideon Sundback invented the zipper, Georges Claude displayed the first neon lamp, Stephen Poplawski invented the blender, Thomas Edison demonstrated the first talking motion picture, and Leo Baekeland invented the polymer Bakelite.[36] They, the pre–World War I generation, had seen the remaking of society into what seemed like a modern age where anything was possible, such as a war bringing about greater peace.[37] Then came the war. Leaders said the war would save civilization. It would destroy all the remaining evils of the old world. In the end, the war destroyed everything except war.[38] As Zelda Fitzgerald concluded, "A whole generation accustomed itself to a basic feeling that there are two ways to be: dead and alive, preferably alive and probably dead."[39]

Fitzgerald and her husband, the author of *The Great Gatsby*, responded to the postwar world by moving to Europe, to drink. Hemingway, who in *A Farewell to Arms* wrote, "I was always embarrassed by the words sacred, glorious, and sacrifice," moved to Europe as well. Exile appealed to artists. They were "the war generation," "the lost generation," and in Europe they were choosing to stay at the funeral too long. The exiles left America of the twenties to the older generation of intellectuals, like essayist and editor H. L. Mencken of *American Mercury*, who publicized the "smart set" version of the Jazz Age,[40] and to the youth, such as Fritzie Mann, who rose up and became, briefly, fearless.

In early 1922, Fritzie Mann, as a performance rather than just a name, began to emerge into reality from the mind of Frieda. In February of her last year of life she was dancing "Spanish dances," like Valentino, at the Point Loma Golf Club. Her accomplishments appeared in the advertisements and in small paragraphs at the bottom of the page of the newspaper. Meanwhile, filling the remainder of the same page of the *San Diego Union* was a photo of Mlle. Bessee, a "character dancer" the paper called a "Premiere Danseuse." In the photo, she poses in full costume and looks nothing short of magnificent. Her costumes are "oriental" and move between "very Frenchy" creations of "black frills and jade plumes, which strikes a distinct and novel note in costuming," and costumes of "pure white chiffon, the beauty of which is enhanced by great quantities of diamonds and pearls, giving it an exquisite shimmery effect."[41] Mann, who clipped and saved all of her newspaper mentions, which were found in her suitcase at the time of her body's discovery, would have seen Mlle. Bessee's noteworthy and instructive photo. Bessee performed imitations of dances from motion pictures. She was "Oriental," like Nazimova, and unlimited in the types of exotic performances she offered audiences. Bessee embodied everything foreign and forbidden. Soon, Mann would have a new performance style.

For Washington's birthday, the city erupted in parties. At the Bostonia there was a "syncopated" band. At DuPron's a seven-piece band that included two grand pianos serenaded a "Masque Ball." Even Tijuana shared in the party. The Tijuana Bar and Café held a Mardi Gras ball as part of its grand reopening. At the Point Loma Golf Club, as the newspapers advertised, "Miss Fritzie Mann will again delight the guests with her nimble feet and shapely form. Miss Mann is one of those dancers—she always had something new and generally something startling." She was "the talented young dancer [with] some new steps for your approval."[42]

Here the influence of the Jazz Age on her life showed. Mann was one of the many girls who left behind their ballet classes. Rather than promote conservatory training, she wanted to be brash and disruptive.[43] Girls her age preferred to work in the cabarets and vaudeville circuit over the legitimate theaters. They dreamed of stardom in the movies. If they trained for ballet, they would only be able to dance; but if they trained for the popular stage, they had to sing a little and act a little, which would bring them closer to stardom.[44]

Her advertisements were also appearing next to the ongoing "Starlight" adventures of Virginia Fairfax, who in February 1922 discovered the danger in being too dramatic. Later in her room, after she had left Stratton's car, Virginia thought herself foolish. She realized she was "dramatizing" her life again, which was her greatest flaw. "Since that day," she explained to the reader, "I have concluded that this ability to dramatize one self is the ability to put one's personality upon the screen, although of course, behind the locked doors of my little room I was just playing a childish game." Then, probably because this episode ran near Valentine's Day, love filled her: "He is interested in me. He is so splendid! He knows so much. He is so chivalrous and noble. He is just what I want the lover . . . coming to be. . . . Oh, how wonderful it will be when I can act with him."[45] Virginia was of two minds: one focused on her career, and the other wanted to stay in the car with her date and feel loved.

By Valentine's Day 1922, Mann was again dancing at the Point Loma Golf Club. She was the "main feature" and offered an "interpretative barefoot French" inspired dance she titled "Mon Amour" before an audience of 150 people enjoying their chicken and steak dinners.[46] For St. Patrick's Day, she again performed at the Point Loma Golf Club. Yet, though acclaimed, she was not the star. "The Point Loma Party Scene," according to the *San Diego Union*, felt revitalized by the appearance of Miss Byrd Taft, formerly of New York, who entertained at her Point Loma home, "All View,"

> with a bridge-luncheon on St. Patrick's Day. The decorations were in keeping with the occasion, and the five-course luncheon carried the color scheme in green and white,

with Shamrock place cards. Lacy ferns with snow-drop lilites were everywhere in evidence except on the mantle, where the brilliant cluster of orange blossoms was placed. The bridge tables held a variety of green playing cards, with pads and pencils to match. The hostess gave out prizes and enjoyed the attendance of the city's leading ladies.[47]

Like Mann, who was surrounded by debutants, in "Starlight" Virginia found herself surrounded by starlets. Of course, no one gave Virginia a second glance, because twenty-five other girls filled the room. "All of them beauties," Virginia complained.

The difficulty of this moment for Mann, or any immigrant youth trying to remake themselves, was what society held to be the truth regarding gender and class in America at the time. As the society pages in the paper suggested, there were few options for women; one could be a housewife, a debutant, or a star. One option presented boredom. One option was out of reach for Mann. The final option would take a miracle.

Because she lived in a fairytale, Virginia Fairfax had finally found work at a studio and discovered how hard the starlets worked. "Within their recesses," the starlets in their "repose silver slippers and stockings" were making themselves up—"the Land of Maker-Believe." Virginia realized that "even as we dance in enchanting fairylands we know, if we reflect at all, that we are working upon a schedule as fixed as the time work in a factory." For Virginia never was able to forget that "when the hour strikes we must doff our silken robes, don everyday clothes, and return to usually, sordid surroundings." She reflected on all the girls she knew in "Movieland" and realized that they all saw the directors as the princes picking up the glass slipper. To do so, of course, they had to first put down their megaphones and "haughty" manners. It made Virginia uncomfortable to realize how much they all needed the directors. Their chance came from the directors, who were the only ones able to make a girl into a "movie Cinderella." If selected the girls would then have "the chance to live happily ever after."[48] Virginia's story depicted a young woman looking for moral guardians rather than the reality of sexual modernism and free expression in a Hollywood at odds with a national culture of censorship and bigotry.[49]

In reality, the chance of Mann becoming famous in pictures was one in tens of thousands, while the chance of becoming a "moral wreck is in inverse ratio," according to writers in the prominent women's magazines. Young people spent weeks wandering from studio to studio. Once they were penniless and alone, they became prey. Easily, they fell into the hands of human traffickers and other unscrupulous exploiters. The enormity of the problem required Los Angeles to have a special court and judge that managed the troubles associated with fallen youth. Social reformers also invested in a reform school for girls that institutionalized young women, particularly women of color and immigrant women, from throughout the city, often at the request of parents. When the institution worked as intended, the young women learned a vocation, overcame starvation and eating disorders, and moved past the sex-trade part of their lives. When the institution failed, which it did consistently with the Latinas in its care, girls were incarcerated in closed wards for patients with STIs or fell into the hands of new abusers among the staff. Hollywood, then, did not create immorality; it inherited the nation's problems. Though known as the "movie colony," a better name for Hollywood would have been the "port of disappointed youth." Looking past the social issues, the interest in moving to Hollywood suggested that the myth that actors and actresses were ordinary folk swayed the youth. The celebrity's average origins meant that anyone could be a star. All it took was to become famous.[50]

While Virginia was realizing what it meant to be "Cinderella," Fritzie was becoming increasingly exotic. She added to her "French" dances several "Spanish" style performances. Each performance, "in spite of the inclement weather," brought strong reviews. "The Spanish dinner-dance at the Point Loma Golf Club last night was declared a great success," the *Union* acknowledged. "About 200 members and guests enjoyed the atmosphere of Spain, which was cleverly put over by the costumes of the orchestra, the lady attendants, the Spanish dinner and the music conducted by Harold Donaldson. . . . The dance by Fritzie Mann . . . won much favor, Miss Mann being encored several times."[51] Reviews of this show appeared in a column next to a chapter of "Starlight" in the *Union*.[52]

In May, Virginia Fairfax did not end up with the film director she had a crush on; she instead returned home and introduced her father to a man who "proffered me the honest love and devotion of his life." His name was Eddie, and Virginia had grown up with him. Having introduced him to her family, Eddie turned to leave and Virginia "ostentatiously followed." Just as they passed beyond the door, "he turned and gathered me up into his arms," she recalled. "All through the world she followed me," he whispered in her ear. This was the final chapter in the story, and it had ended not only happily but in a way that showed acceptance for the prewar family values and social respectability.[53]

In choosing personas, Mann was choosing between fictions: on the one hand, the wily Polish girl whom she eroticized in her performances, and on the other a trusting American whose character came from her conservative adopted culture. Virginia had chosen the conservative route after seeing the possibilities of life. Mann did not. As she tried to balance the extremes of her identities, her career was reaching new heights. In the early summer of 1922 she was appearing in the Shriners' parade and convention. The estimates at the time suggested that 20,000 people per night visited Balboa Park to see the Shriners' celebration. The population of San Diego was only 100,000 in 1922, which means a fifth of them saw the opening of the Shriner Circus and Mardi Gras Carnival at the Civic Auditorium; more than 20,000 people attended the last night in the park. "It was a typical carnival crowd," though the largest of its kind. "There were girls in bright-colored knit sweaters, older women in light summer dresses, men wearing neither hats nor vests, jamming and pushing their way from booth to booth, intent on seeing everything," reported the papers.[54]

Covering the walls of the big hall were depictions of desert scenes. Opposite the hall's entrance was the "Shriner Oasis." A person "for a nominal sum" purchased a little light refreshment and could dance between bites. To add to the excitement, the Shriners had placed several dancers on the stage to entertain the crowd. It was here that visitors could find Dorothy Armstrong and Fritzie Mann.

Armstrong and Mann were also riding in the Fashion Parade at Coronado "as queens should in highly decorated cars: amid much pomp and display. The decorations of these cars caused much favorable comment among the onlookers." To their great delight, if one were to judge by the smiles on their faces in the newspaper photos, Mann and Armstrong, friends and competitors, wore the latest styles from a local department store. They had achieved what *Harper's Bazaar* termed "the real standard by which a woman's elegance is measured" in that they managed to look "perfectly stunning in an absolutely plain and unadorned hat, completing a very simple costume." To be sure, "it, of course, requires an artist to design such a hat, perfect in line, perfect in material and finish, producing a result even recognized by mere men as smart."[55] Still, one had to admit that the beauty and personality of the woman mattered just as much. The photos also capture a glimpse of Mann's internal self. She understood, as did her peers, that beauty was a quality capable of manipulation, a palimpsest that could be vested upon persons of any background or rank. Beauty was not a privilege available only to society women. Glamour could be learned; so too could etiquette, presences, style, and elocution.[56]

Performing for the Shriners brought Mann better bookings in the spring and summer of 1922, and in each one she seemed to become increasingly exotic. At the start of the year, she billed herself as classically trained. In early spring, she was performing French and Spanish inspired dances, like the kinds in the Valentino films. By summer 1922, she was describing herself in advertisements as being of Turkish descent and having gypsy blood, like Nazimova. Fritzie had joined the realm of the exotic.[57]

Mann, in her life as Frieda, still lived at home with her mother and brother. She also had her practiced-self of Fritzie. In creating the myth of Fritzie Mann, she progressively opted for the mysterious and exotic. Moreover, her performances promised adventure and forbidden pleasure. Her romantic involvements had the tinge of passionate liaisons unacceptable in regular society.[58]

The body itself is neutral because anatomy is mute, as anyone at her autopsy could attest.[59] What mattered was not her body itself but what she did with it and of what she could convince audiences. Her photos demonstrate her understanding that the symbolic decoration is easy to wear. Nevertheless, becoming a completely different person is difficult to make into fact. With the symbolic as the core of her performances she could reflect deeper meaning, about who she wanted to become or whom she wanted to be with, as well as simpler ideas, like attempting to mimic an image in a magazine.[60]

Though her lovers, like Louis Jacobs, may have fantasized about sex with a gypsy, Spaniard, Turk, or geisha, with Fritzie sexual transgression was only playacting. Her performances could not negate her identity as Freida. Since Jacobs was also Jewish and the child of European immigrants, no racial taboos were broken in their relationship. It was all just an extension of her performances.[61]

Though Mann could redesign herself and her identity into performance props, she could not resolve the conflict her performances suggested.[62] She could wear the costumes. She could pretend to be whatever exotic, foreign, sexual creation her imagination might concoct. She might possess the "heightened sensitivity to the promise of life," "a romantic readiness," or "an extraordinary gift for hope," which is how Nick Caraway described Gatsby in Fitzgerald's novel.[63] Her body and sense of self were so malleable they were practically made of plastic. However, no matter how hard she tried, ultimately she would always be Frieda, because class and background mattered to the larger society.[64]

"There goes The American Beauty, the most dangerous vamp in town!" With this first line, the story that replaced Virginia Fairfax's "Starlight" opened with a scandal at the beginning of the summer of 1922. "Look!" the new narrative began. It promised readers "a romantic story," "a wonderful analysis of men and maids and marriage."[65] The advertisement for the new serial helped fill out a front page that also announced the arrival of the national PTA convention and revealed that a millionaire was the blackmailer/killer rampaging through White Plains, New York.

Again, the newspaper paralleled Mann's life. In the summer of 1922 she juggled boyfriends and became pregnant. To anyone wondering about their future and their lovers, the newspaper provided an explanation, in dramatized serial form, of what men thought and what they wanted. In the new story, "Love's Masquerade," the male lead contemplates "Love" by asking, "If any young man has a settled idea of the girl he wants to marry, I did not. In fact, I did not want to marry anyone; yet I found in many girls the woman I thought I loved—at the moment." He knew he was a bit of a scoundrel, but he suspected that women were worse than him in terms of morality. To him, women were fickle. After all, "she was always changing her home and I was always seeking her, never quite satisfied, because—as I believe now—no one woman can be all things to one man. . . . men seek the thrill of desire that love gives and when from satiety or any other reason they find they cannot get that thrill from one woman they seek it in another." "This is the history of all the great lovers in the world. It is not woman that man wants to hold." What he truly wants is "Love," capitalized. He wants to hold it, to keep it. To do so, he must hold and keep many women.

Sometime in spring or early summer, Mann was selling tickets in the lobby of the US Grant Hotel, and he saw her for the first time. Months later the police would haul Rogers van Buren Clark in and question him regarding her murder. On this night, though, he elbowed his friend and said he would pay $1,000 to meet Fritzie, and others said he joked about the money as proof of his desire to bed her. In this moment, the aspirations of the fictional Virginia and all the magazine articles about what men wanted that had punctuated Mann's last year of life suddenly collided with reality.

When Fritzie saw Clark for the first time in the hotel lobby, maybe it was as *Harper's Bazaar* described such a meeting in one of their stories from September 1922: to look at him "was to think confusedly of evil. There was about him a precision of elegance, so that his clothes no less than the expression of his dark, sardonic face become part of a mask." Mann's friends liked to chide her and claim that they were more experienced, so they might have said what the magazine suggested: "He makes love amazingly, but his kisses are like epigrams." Did he seem too "languidly at peace with his destiny, ignorant of yesterdays and oblivious of to-morrows"? Did the summer night stir a "lace of sound through the lobby" as "tongues were wagging an obbligato of gossip?" As she approached, this man seemed to possess an "intangible lure." To be sure, the magazines educated the girl to remain aloof because the man might see her as "disposable."

Romance was a "stupid game, but what would you do? We live in an inarticulate world," the magazine's romantic hero explained.[66] His justification for physical action could mar them both, a hint at the dangers of pregnancy before marriage. Both the "girl" and the "man" had reputations to protect. The magazines were selling readers on the new virtues, saying, "There is no higher incentive in human endeavor than the reward of reputation—and no greater responsibility than the responsibility which reputation compels all of us to assume." Reputation was a "reward[,] and out of that responsibility" came "the heart and mind and soul of man," or so promised an advertisement for Packard automobiles.[67]

Looking at each other across the lobby, a man and a woman both knew that they could not escape a "frank, unspoken comment that is born in the mind of every person you meet," explained an advertisement for Woodbury's Facial Soap. "All around you, people are judging you silently." Friends, strangers, "each of them is storing up impressions."[68] In the case of Clark and Mann, the people in the lobby of the Grant Hotel were jealously whispering, as they would later explain at the trial. They had watched Fritzie walk across the hotel lobby to what she thought was her destiny—a Hollywood film director. Mann was beautiful. To create his reputation, Clark had told everyone he was a film director and actor. He wasn't. Turns out, he was inventing himself too.[69]

Her physical appearance was not, however, all that one should focus on. The social status of the woman mattered too.[70] Those of the upper and middle classes spent their days learning to arrange flowers, host parties, and court reporters in the hope their names would appear in the society pages. The guest list for every event imaginable, the state of private gardens, where to buy the best silk, and what constituted modern beauty—all appeared in the paper. Mann's name showed up in advertisements and reviews, but the other types of woman—the wealthy, the smart set, the ones who would marry well—occupied the rest of the paper.

While dating Fritzie, Clark was also chasing Gladys Flowers, the daughter of a prominent Los Angeles businessman, whom the newspaper wrote for in their society pages. Flowers spent her days attending "delightful holiday dancing parties" at the Grant Hotel.[71] She appeared at bridge parties with the other respectable young women who would progress through society one tea party at a time.[72] She also materialized at the Gamma Sigma Kappa sorority's dances, where nearly every young woman seemed to be accompanied by a Navy man.[73] Clark's name never appeared with Flowers's in the society pages. She clearly held a different status in the city but felt drawn to him nonetheless. Just as Clark was slumming with Fritzie Mann, Flowers was slumming with Clark.

Not to be outdone, Mann juggled both Clark and Louis Jacobs that summer. For his part, Jacobs entertained Ella Worthington, upper-class matron who spent her time at Coronado planning the construction of her house at 1020 Encino Row.[74] Mrs. Worthington liked being escorted by handsome young men, but her main priority was status. She was keenly interested in her daughter, also named Ella. Just as she built her house, Mrs. Worthington built her daughter. The younger Ella went to France to be cultured and to the Bishop School to be finished.[75]

For all those concerned, the summer of 1922 was a tangled web of uncertain loyalties and twisted ambitions. In all these activities, Mann was denying a fundamental truth. As she rose up through the social scene of San Diego, she was never the guest. She was always the servant. She performed for the wealthy and well-to-do. Fritzie Mann was rented, whereas Ella Worthington and Gladys Flowers were man's aspiration.

Her reality must have become very clear in November 1922, when she performed at a Chief Petty Officers Club stag party. Though it seems hard to believe, given who was throwing the party and the type of party it was, the celebration featured "fine music" and dancing, according to the *Union*. The CPO Club hosted the party that began, oddly enough, with Miss Marjorie Tittle, professional whistler. She "whistled her way into the hearts of the 100 men present, with all latest songs. Her act is much better than the average whistling number because of the clear bird-like notes she emits rather than the shrill notes of the ordinary whistling performer." Following the whistling was Miss Ruth Oldham, professional jazz pianist, who played "a number of jazz numbers between the dancers." A "number of sensuous" "Oriental Dances" performed by various groups of women followed. The newspaper reported that the treat of the event, however, was two interpretive dances: "The Bat," in a specially designed costume, and "The Lure of Jade," by Fritzie Mann, now fully personified as the exotic performer. The reporter concluded, "Her efforts were so pleasing that she was required to respond to several encores." A buffet followed.[76]

5

FLAPPER

On January 16, Chief Patrick was in his office when Leo Greenbaum, local greengrocer and leader in the Jewish community, and Louis Jacobs arrived. "Greenbaum brought Doctor Jacobs into my office and introduced him," recalled the chief. The grocer, according to the chief, said "that Doctor Jacobs had come into his store with the afternoon paper and remarked about Fritzie Mann—the finding of Fritzie Mann's body." At that point, Dr. Jacobs said he thought he needed a lawyer. Greenbaum explained, "Why see your attorney? Go down to the station and see Chief James Patrick." Together, they did.[1]

The newspapers ran these same details repeatedly. Consistently, the press overlooked one person. They rarely mentioned the presence of Leo Greenbaum at the first three interrogations, including the visit to the alleged crime scene. His name regularly appears in the court testimony. It is apparent that many of those called to testify connected to each other and to the case through him. Yet he did not play a prominent role in the newspaper coverage or the court case.

In a disorganized society with no clear sense of authority, a man who can think and act decisively can be king. This might be how Greenbaum amassed social capital. He grew up in Cleveland,

Ohio. Like many of his peers, he worked as a newsboy. In Cleveland, the boys sold papers before and after school hours. They experienced a degree of oppression in this profession. Greenbaum, as a teenager, helped to unionize them. According to his family, Greenbaum moved to San Diego for health reasons. Once there, he began to make a living selling vegetables from a pushcart.[2]

The first sign of his power came in 1914. A San Diego policeman arrested him for peddling without a license. The arrest caused a clash within the police station as the arresting office discovered resistance among his colleagues. One colleague even went as far as to issue Greenbaum the missing license in hope that the arresting officer would remove the charges. The chief of police ended up having to investigate. Greenbaum settled the argument by volunteering to appear, despite the chief's objections, in Police Court. He was found not guilty. Greenbaum was arrested again in 1919 for profiteering. Accused of stockpiling corn during wartime, he would be found not guilty. It might seem unlikely, given the nature of the two arrests, but by 1923 Greenbaum was becoming significant in the San Diego area. He acted as a philanthropist serving on community boards, raising money to construct a temple, and building personal wealth through his wholesale produce business. His life had changed. At the exposition that promoted a modern city, where Fritzie Mann performed for the Shriners, he had met the love of his life, and they eventually married. He knew Mann before he reformed, and the cast of characters who traipsed through the courtroom were a hardened reminder of just how dark San Diego nights could be. Greenbaum illustrates what life was like in the border city. A person could change their fate quickly, and social power could help shield a person from scandal.

In that first meeting with Jacobs in January 1923, the chief asked how long he had known Fritzie Mann, and Jacobs explained that it had been since July 1922. "I asked him when he saw her last," the chief recollected. "He said he saw her Friday afternoon— the 12th, I believe. I asked him where he saw her. He said he met her at the Maryland Hotel by appointment and they went out for a ride in the direction of La Mesa and returned about 10 o'clock at the home of Fritzie Mann—Spruce Street." Patrick inquired if he had any other conversations with Mann. Jacobs admitted

to telephoning, on Sunday evening, from Camp Kearny to ask
about her condition. He said he went to Tijuana Sunday afternoon with Miss Worthington of Coronado, returned to Coronado
from Tijuana, then left Miss Worthington's and came over to San
Diego. "I asked him where he went to," the chief asserted. "He
said he went the Depot—that is, the the Santa Fe Depot." The
chief asked why, and Jacobs answered, "to meet the 6:30 train."
The chief asked, "Who was he to meet." Jacobs replied that he was
to meet two friends from Kalamazoo, Michigan. What were their
names? Jacobs deflected, saying he did not know their names.
"I asked him how or what information that he received that these
two men would arrive at this time from Kalamazoo, Michigan,"
said the chief, now feeling he had caught Jacobs unprepared. "He
said he received a postcard." Then Jacobs had to admit that the
two men, whose names he did not know, had not arrived. Where
did Jacobs go after the strangers did not arrive? The answer was
that he had been in one of the busiest places in town: the Harvey
Restaurant. He had something to eat. Then he returned to work
at Camp Kearny, directly.

The morning of the eighteenth, Greenbaum and Jacobs
returned to see the chief. At that time, Jacobs gave his official
statement, which was the same as on the sixteenth, with the
exception of some letters. Patrick showed Jacobs his letters to
Mann and asked who wrote them and whether Jacobs was aware
of Mann's "condition." Jacobs admitted that he knew of her condition and had known since October. Then Jacobs also had to
admit to sending Miss Wilma Miner, a mysterious woman who
arranged abortions, to Los Angeles to meet Mann.

The chief and Jacobs met again on the twenty-fourth at the
city jail. Again Jacobs relived the timeline. He left from Coronado
on the evening of the fourteenth. He went to the Santa Fe Depot
and met the 6:30 train, and from there he went to the Harvey
lunch stand and had something to eat. He made an appearance at
the Golden Lion. He went to the Grant Hotel, known for its luxury and its speakeasy. At this detail, the chief must have paused,
because it was new information, something Jacobs had not mentioned previously. What did Jacobs do at the hotel, he asked. Jacobs
explained that he saw a patient. When asked for the patient's
name, Jacobs could not recall. What business was the patient in?

Jacobs volunteered that the patient worked as a dispatcher for the Owl Taxicab Company. How long was he at the hotel? Jacobs estimated about two or two and half hours. Where did he go after leaving the hotel? Directly to Camp Kearny, Jacobs indicated.

Jacobs's mention of the Grant Hotel as his alibi for the night Fritzie Mann died illustrates just how intertwined vice and respectability were. In most cities, the places of vice were on the periphery or in the shadows.[3] What if an entire city was on the periphery?

For decades, San Diego had been in competition with Los Angeles for dominance in southern California. If history worked logically, San Diego would have been the victor. It was next to the international border with Mexico, which made it an ideal center for shipping and commerce. Unlike San Pedro, the shallow and windy port of Los Angeles, San Diego's harbor was deep and serene. Furthermore, Los Angeles was too far inland and its farmland was not as prosperous as that surrounding San Diego. Yet San Diego did not achieve its destiny. Founded by the Spanish, in the mid-1800s it had been a port for shipping tallow and animal hides. Thus, it smelled and attracted few people before the American conquest of the region. Even after California became a state, San Diego received little note. It lost out when Congress decided the course of transcontinental railroads would be to San Francisco, and that though the tracks would reach San Diego they would first stop in Los Angeles, obviously. Though there was hope that San Diego might be connected to Texas via the railroads, the stock market crash in 1873 rendered financing that project difficult. By the time financing became available, Collis Potter Huntington, who would build the first version of modern Los Angeles, won Congress's approval and funding. Courting the competing railroad companies, he argued that no one went to San Diego for anything, whereas the location of Los Angeles would link the farmland to the markets of northern California. At one point, he and his supporters suggested that San Diego had a great port and Los Angeles had nothing of the sort; therefore, Los Angeles was the underdog and deserved greater congressional investment. Los Angeles won. San Diego seemed destined to be an economic and social outpost on the southern tip of civilization—until World War I changed everything.[4]

The US Grant Hotel in 1910, looking north over the Hor-
ton Plaza fountain, designed by Irving Gill. The hotel still
stands on Broadway between Third and Fourth Avenues.
Courtesy of the San Diego History Center.

Where once San Diego had jobs at the harbor and a few bars
and hotels, suddenly there where palatial hotels, like the US
Grant, with lobbies made of Italian marble. There were speakeasies, ballrooms, and dancehalls too. These places became the
cultural centers of the city because of their architecture, jazz,
and the freedom a city on the periphery could offer.[5]

What did her calling card mean: "I am Fritzie Mann"? Maybe
existing at the boundaries is where some of Mann's power
derived. She, like the city, was without restriction and thus free
to create and live as Fritzie.

The US Grant Hotel is nine stories high and stretches almost an entire city block in downtown San Diego. In 1910, at its opening, the walls were the first thing a visitor approaching the city would see. At night, the lights illuminating the rooftop garden were bright enough to be seen from the harbor. The rooftop garden offered views of City Park, fourteen hundred acres cascading down flowering slopes toward the hotel. On the west was the bay and out beyond it the Coronado peninsula. Every sunset was glorious because of the ocean view, and every sunrise breathtaking because of the purple-crested mountains that stretched from the border with Mexico around to the foothills that divided the valleys on the eastern slope from the tree-filled canyons that slowly reached northward into distant mountains.

However, few went to the US Grant Hotel just for the views outward. The best reason to go was to see and be seen in the lobby, lounge, ballroom, and speakeasy. The vestibules leading to the main lobby and Ladies' Foyer were cool like a tomb, made of black onyx and Italian marble. Pillars of marble with low panels of onyx separated the lobby from the side lounges, providing privacy for those in the lounges without completely obscuring the view of the lobby from them. For the masses who had hurried to the city or grown up there, there was a need to "take life vicariously as readers, spectators, listeners, passive observers."[6] For its part, the lobby was said to be Spanish Renaissance architecture, but it was pure Jazz Age opulence.

Under the chandeliers walked all of San Diego's residents at some point. The hotel was just too beautiful to not visit. It acted as a crossroads. To understand the city at that moment, it is important to imagine what it would have been like to watch all the different people in Mann's life and death as they encountered one another in that lobby.

It is easy to imagine the gossipy conversations of the society matrons perched in the lobby watching the flappers come and go, because all anyone at the time seemed to be talking about was the problem with young people. More than one of those women must have clucked their tongues at the sight of the girls like Fritzie Mann sashaying through the lobby in their jade earrings, formless dresses, and corsetless bodies. There were Jewish girls, like Mann,

Balboa Theater marquee and crowd, San Diego, 1923. The women in this photo are displaying the flapper attitude, arm in arm with their friends and hands on their hips, as well as the flapper fashion of big smiles, short hair, short skirts, and heels. Courtesy of the San Diego History Center.

Mexican American girls, and upper-class white women all embracing the same identity of the flapper because they wanted freedom from traditional notions and repetitive gender norms. To the older women, it was obvious the girls had multiple lovers. At the time, one mother noted about her own daughter, according to the *New York Tribune*, that "she never has less than eleven callers a day." What made matters worse was that each boy had "the privilege of 'petting' or 'recking' her."[7] To the onlookers, there was something disturbing about the girls. "Those girls," Zelda Fitzgerald wrote, mocking mothers who worried about their daughters, "think they can do anything and get away with it."[8] Courtship, once a private act, had entered the public world. "Those girls" provided proof that the evolution of courtship into dating depended on the use of public spaces, such as hotel lobbies and parking lots, because being in public, instead of the parlor, removed the intimate acts from the oversight and control of the family.

Today we call them "flappers" in part because it is what they called themselves, but in 1923 "flapper" had not yet become the accepted term. The original hardcover version of the *Reader's Guide to Periodical Literature,* an index compiled at the time of all the articles published in American magazines, shows that at the start of the decade "flappers" was a subordinate term under the larger heading of "girls." "Flapper" was not the common term at the time. Indeed, it seems celebratory by comparison to the diminutive "girls," which could so easily be turned into a slur whispered in hotel lobbies.

"Those girls" were different, not just because of the number of young men they kept company with in hotel lobbies and automobiles but because they did not act with discretion. "All the boys know that all the others are among the privileged. Nobody seems to mind," one mother wrote. For this mother, the flapper undermined and poisoned the virtue of her son. Her actions and whims, the mother believed, were "the strongest factor in the development of this child of mine."[9]

The flapper's perceived power multiplied the perceived social problems because she exercised the greatest control over the son. She had replaced the mother, the family, religion, and custom as the fountainhead in the lives of boys. "Is it possible for my boy to hold the respect for womankind?" And to this question the answer would have been more than apparent, because the young men openly discussed the "characteristics of the girls with the same frankness and impersonal manner they use in discussing the qualifications of a ball player," suggesting that they did lack respect for the flappers. The older women were as dumbfounded as the rest of society as to the flapper's motivations. "She has thrown a shadow over our understanding. I cannot 'get' his point of view—his emphatic approval of all and anything a flapper may do," mourned the mother. After observing the shifts in their sons and the way in which the boys seemed to idolize the flapper, the parental lament rang out, "Where does the acceptance of the manner of the flapper lead?"[10]

What did the sons say about the modern girl? They said that a condition of "unrest" defined her. They called the girl "superficial." They hated how the inane chatter, the conceit, and her ability to "pervert herself into the externally attractive almost empty mentally, neutral nonentity she so frequently becomes." To phrase it more kindly, one wrote, "She is on comparatively untried ground."[11]

A twenty-six-year-old bachelor, exactly the type who hung around the Grant Hotel lobby, "earning $8,000 a year, with an enviable war record," reported, "I find myself shocked by the youngsters of to-day. . . . These girls who smoke, drink and dance like demi-mondaines are really the 'nice' girls. My lord! If the nice girls are like this, what can be expected of girls who have had far fewer opportunities in the world?" His rant continued, "The chaperone thing, too, is a joke." For the chaperone too was a "good natured, unseeing person taken along who is safe and who lends a shade of respectability to things which otherwise the girls would draw the line on. The responsibility becomes hers."[12]

The real joke was that the bachelor imagined the girls wanted him because he was a masculine achiever who could provide, did not cry, was tough, a man of character, and independent.[13] Dorothy Parker, famous New York writer and social satirist, explained the truth of the matter simply: "I hate men. They irritate me." She hated the men who thought they were "serious thinkers." She hated their shell-rimmed glasses, the kind Louis Jacobs wore, and how they talked about humanity "as if they had just invented it." She hated men who read Russian literature as though it were more than just "the sex best sellers." She hated the "Cave Men," those "Steeped in Crime," and "the Sensitive Souls."[14]

Ellen Welles Page, famous for being a flapper, seethed at the critics who seemed to think the girls were feather-brained narcissists: Everyone must recognize that to be a successful flapper takes "brains" and "cleverness." "It requires self-knowledge and self-analysis. We must know our capabilities and limitations. . . . I suppose I am a flapper." After all, she loved to dance, she spent a lot of time in automobiles, and she wore her hair short. She also pointed out that there were varieties of flappers and degrees of variations. She considered herself a semi-flapper in that she was not as cliché as "The Flapper" and not as dedicated to it as the "Super Flapper." She wrote that parents were the ones to blame for the war and Prohibition. These two forces, propagated and voted for by the parents, not the girls, had changed morality. "We are the younger generation," she wrote. "The war tore away our spiritual foundations and challenged our faith. . . . The times have made us older than you were at our age."[15]

Zelda Fitzgerald was a little more judicious. She mocked the newspaper coverage of young women when writing, "I came across an amazing editorial a short time ago. It fixed the blame for all divorces, crime waves, high prices, unjust taxes, violations of the Volstead Act and crimes in Hollywood upon the head of the Flapper." Where others saw social declination, she saw a much-needed revolution born of the rights of youth—"those rights" she explained, that "only youth has to the right to give. . . . I refer to the right to experiment with herself as a transient, poignant figure who will be dead tomorrow," like moths. Flapperdom, she declared, at its core had cynicism. Where others saw this as a corruption of youth, Fitzgerald saw it as a godsend because cynicism was "making them intelligent and teaching them to capitalize [on] their natural resources."[16] In this context, what did it mean to be Fritzie Mann?

In the summer of 1922, while Mann juggled boyfriends and jobs, those who feared the flapper imagined her moving forward so quickly that in her wake she left economic destruction. The textile manufacturers and corset engineers were at a loss. "In these days when a hem is a hem not a steel spring, covered with velveteen, no one sews on shirt bondings. Where are the manufacturers who used to make them? No one knows." Corset manufacturers had no idea what would become of their businesses because "a generation of girls was growing up who knew not stays; shameless creatures who wore their figures as God gave it."[17] It was as if young women suddenly had the power to shape their own images, personalities, and destinies. They were modern because they could choose.[18]

Worst of all, the flapperisms were contagious. The rest of society, including married women who hung around in hotel lobbies passing comments about the girls, noted *Vogue*, wanted to stay young and compete with the flapper. The married were as restless as the youth.[19] America was quickly becoming a "nation of Gatsbys."[20]

The "Wallflowers," the girls who were not flappers, understood the social shift best of all. These girls, which society seemed to be overlooking because of the distracting but radiant flappers, sent letters to their local papers explaining what it felt like to be them. "I'll try to tell you what it means," wrote a young woman named Gladys, "to be a wallflower. It means to be sitting in a beautifully lighted ballroom at your first honest-to-goodness dancing party. You cannot dance, so you just wish that handsome fellow with the 'Rudolph Valentino' smile would look your way; but he doesn't. You wish you had never come [to the dance]." An anonymous writer noted that, after her first dance, "I noticed I was not at all popular. A girlfriend confidentially told me to forget my corsets next time and notice the difference, but old 'steel sides,' as corseted women are called, will keep herself-respect and jacket on."[21]

The lack of a corset was significant to the flapper's audience because wearing that garment suggested continuing social control of young women's bodies. The flapper transformed her clothing into a symbol of freedom, which in turn made her a symbol of the changing morality.[22] Going without a corset indicated an openness and sexual confidence. According to Fredrick Lewis Allen, editor of *The World* and observer of the times, the flappers were a sign of an unmistakable and rapidly spreading trend in which long-held notions of sex and marriage were being packed away. A debate began to emerge regarding young women having premarital sexual experiences. After all, it had long been understood, if not discussed in public, that young men should have these experiences. Now, Allen cautioned, not everyone accepted this idea or practiced it, but the debate suggested that a change was under way.[23]

While social reformers blamed everything from Bolsheviks to the decline of the family for the behavior of the younger generation, *Vogue* magazine had a different take. In twin articles, one titled "The Debutant versus the Married Woman" and the other "The Debutant versus Her Mother's Ideal," the magazine dissected the motivations behind the behavior of the young debutant, whom the larger society maligned for refusing to behave modestly. *Vogue* argued that women, no matter their age or marital status, saw the unmarried woman as competition. All women were looking to behave and look younger. The magazine suggested that the older women were the ones not behaving modestly. The second problem was the girls' mothers who pushed them to go to parties and to "have a good time" because they thought that party-going was the surest way for their daughters to find a husband. The magazine chided the parents, who were not brave enough to tell their daughters that they did not have to behave as if they were "commodities." No mother ever said, according to the magazine, "I want you to be yourself." Fastidiousness was not as important as being engaged to be married. In short, *Vogue* concluded, mothers raised this "precocious modern generation" to be "desirable" when they should have raised their daughters to be intelligent, critical, and independent.[24]

There was another kind of flapper: the gold digger. At the time, torrid tales about young women filled the newspapers, magazines, films, and novels. Usually the stories were about showgirls who "treated" their boyfriends with sex in exchange for gifts and flashy vacations. Some even married knowing they would be rewarded with large alimonies. These stories tangled up the popular notions of youth, sex, beauty, and money with young women who were changing their social roles. All the fears of the flapper gold digger increased throughout the twenties because of declining family size and rising divorce rates. Women seeking birth control as well as careers did not seem to be also seeking courtship, marriage, and the traditional family. To those who loathed her, the flapper gold digger was to blame for all the changes in society because her financial ambitions undermined the romantic foundations of love and marriage.[25]

Perhaps there was nothing wrong with sexual disillusionment, as Zelda Fitzgerald quipped. "I see no logical reason for keeping the young illusioned. Certainly, disillusionment comes easier at twenty than at forty."[26] Fitzgerald was correct in the abstract sense. Nevertheless, Fritzie Mann, pregnant in the fall of 1922, found that she was no longer living in the abstract sense. There was a danger in teaching young women to be desirable without also teaching them to be judicious.

The vulnerability of the freedom-seeking girls multiplied because they were living in California in the age of Prohibition, the federal enforcement of a constitutional amendment outlawing the distribution and sale of alcohol, when a large percentage of the population decided not to follow the laws of man or propriety. What differentiated California from the rest of the lower forty-eight was its thousand-mile coastline, which was more like two thousand miles if one included islands, inlets, bays, and rivers. It was a rumrunner's dream. Bootleggers freely chose where they landed ships because the Coast Guard was too small and the local police boats too slow to mount any kind of defense. The big international ships carrying illegal liquor waited off the coast for smaller vessels to come out to meet them. The problem was not just the ships. Individuals became "mules" and carried hog bladders with liquor across the Mexican border into San Diego. Rather than bring about a higher level of morality, Prohibition made thieves, evaders, and deceivers out of millions of people.[27]

Further complicating the situation were California's inland empire, deserts, and mountains. Police and Prohibition agents had to worry about the harbors, the rural districts of ranchers, and the borders of neighboring states with large isolated and unregulated deserts. There were just too many places for the liquor to come from, and San Diego was both the entrance and the endpoint for the trade. All of these bootlegging routes distinguished San Diego from the rest of the country in terms of Prohibition.

Furthermore, farmers were still growing wine grapes, barley, and hops. Before Prohibition began in 1919, these crops were bankrupting growers. As it turned out, they had nothing to fear. Pre-Prohibition prices for grapes had been on average $10 a ton. The highest price anyone had ever seen was $20. Then suddenly the prices soared, first to $30, then $50, and finally $70 a ton. Farmers also earned 60 to 85 cents a pound for barley and hops. Californians were not only drinking illegally, they were growing the raw materials. Since it was impossible to stop the production of alcohol, California never went dry.[28]

As if the geography and agriculture of the state were not bad enough, prosecutors found it hard to win convictions in California. Judges regularly threw out cases because of search warrant violations and witness tampering. Juries were a different problem. With clear evidence of guilt, they frequently acquitted bootleggers because of fear of retribution and disinterest in enforcing Prohibition. All of this led one bootlegger to brag that he had been indicted eighty times without one conviction. In later years the policing improved, as did prosecutors. Until then, California remained wide open.[29]

Take, for example, San Diego's police force. For the city to consider itself modern, its police department would have to be up to date, which in this case meant scientific and efficient. Chief James Patrick believed that he could achieve this renaissance in policing through clerical organization. He lamented to the press that few people understood just how much paperwork and filing a police force did. He had only fifty-four officers, which he had to spread between three shifts over seventy-eight square miles and among a population of nearly one hundred thousand. Adding to the trouble were the military, two transcontinental railroads, the geopolitical reality of being only fourteen miles from an international boarder, and the fact that at that moment the United States had no extradition treaty with Mexico. Patrick saw all of these challenges within the context of logistics and clerical work. He was proud that his office maintained 114,543 complete criminal records, cross-referenced three ways. He fervently believed that his men could stop crimes before they happened because the police tracked new arrivals on and off the trains and regularly arrested individuals on the street who had no money in their pockets. Yet Ida Baily's rooming house was just around the corner from the police station—an expedient location for a house of ill repute. It certainly made the numerous police raids on the brothel more convenient for Baily to make payoffs. By 1923, the year of Mann's death, the city was an unchecked western borderland enclave where access to women's liberation and Tijuana's liquor created a metropolis dedicated to spectacle rather than substance.[30] Though it may not have been famous for a Capone or a Harlem, the area's reputation for vice took hold. There was no denying that San Diego was a Jazz Age city.[31]

Like the rest of the state, San Diego had an illicit drinking problem. Prohibition stimulated the growth of an underground network of bars in the city and openly defiant venues in Tijuana, whose bars and nightclubs were not covered by US laws. The movement of illicit goods across the border had previously been for opium. It was easy to switch gears and become a bootlegger's paradise. Soon, people from Los Angeles were motoring down to enjoy themselves.

At one level, San Diego was the kind of city where sailors drank hair tonic in the bathroom of the local skating rink, because people were willing to drink anything if it meant even a hint of a buzz. Then the sailors would stand at the door of the rink and catcall women. At the other end of the economic spectrum, the US Grant Hotel, arguably the most palatial building in San Diego, had a speakeasy. Nevertheless, arrests related to alcohol fell from 1,883 in 1917 to 322 in 1920. If the production, sale, distribution, and drinking had not decreased, as the evidence suggests, then the conclusion is that the police were not making arrests.[32]

San Diego was the perfect place for Fritzie Mann. It was a city where the nearby border, ethnic neighborhoods, and military bases made everyone an immigrant trying to reinvent himself or herself. It was a place where the city boosters and planners believed that human culture could reach a marvelous culmination in the realization of the modern metropolis. To believe this, one must ignore the grim details of the daily routine, which included wife beatings, drunkenness, and rampant prostitution. Ignore it is precisely what metropolitan San Diegans did. They lived, not in the real world, but in a shadow world projected around them at every moment by means of the paper, plaster, glass, and lights that made up the building façades of Balboa Park and the imported marble and gilt chandeliers of the Grant Hotel. In short, San Diego was a world of professional illusionists and their credulous audience.[33]

When their lack of social sophistication combined with illegal liquor, border town urbanization, and a sexual revolution, flappers, like Mann, found themselves pregnant. Where only ten years earlier young women waited for a promise of marriage before engaging in sex with their partner, for many women in the twenties it did not feel necessary to wait. To most young women, intercourse came later in dating. Many of them did not marry their first lover even if at the time they thought they might. The shift in sexual behavior was an indication of the erosion of older pre–World War I courtship habits as well as the construction of the idea that love and sex go hand in hand.[34] Though the perspective of the youth had changed, parents and civic leaders continued to try to impose the middle-class values of the prewar era. The idea that the loss of female sexual purity and modesty was the worst thing that could happen to a young woman remained standard. Anyone who deviated from this social norm was "ruined" for life.[35]

Once Mann became pregnant, according to social standards, she could never again make her body neutral or moldable like plastic. Her days as a flapper were numbered. Jazz Age artist Mabel Dodge Luhan explained "the change" this way: "The days of the pregnant woman gradually change in their outward aspects. Very gradually all the values of things change about her and while some drop in favors, others become enhanced." The strangest part, for Dodge Luhan, was that the "pregnant woman ceases to be an individual and becomes a part of the undifferentiated cosmic order about her." Quickly, the woman found that she "ceased to be." She became a "slave" to her "deeper instincts."[36] The unmarried mother, as Mann was, appeared to the outside world as entirely primal. Women in her position forfeited the support of the civilized world because they had clearly opted to not conform to the demands of that world. It was as if with pregnancy they lost their identity at every possible level, from the physical to the existential. They ceased being a girl and became a woman. It was terrifying.

Ben Shelley lived in the Grant Hotel. He knew Mann at the moment of her greatest crisis—the pregnancy. Shelley could not recall the first time he met Fritzie Mann. He did recall all the times he drove her to the Paradise Valley Sanitarium to see her sister. He had met Mrs. Mann, who did not approve of Fritzie going on car rides with men, and brother William, after her death. Shelley had known Fritzie for only eight months. One night, at a party in late October 1922, while Mann was keeping her pregnancy a secret from her family and friends, he inquired why she looked so "blue." He recalled her saying, "I just feel like ending it all." He pressed her. She told him about a supposed hush-hush marriage, which she claimed had been nullified. The entire affair had left her feeling disappointed.[37]

"I'm disgusted, disappointed. At times I feel like ending it all." As she said it, the rest of the party came into the room, and she fell silent. Shelley had tried to remember her words exactly. Like Nick, the narrator in *The Great Gatsby*, Shelley "was reminded of something—an elusive rhythm, a fragment of lost words." These words "for a moment tried to take shape in [his] mouth and [his] lips parted like a dumb man's, as though they were more struggling upon them than a wisp of startled air." In relating his story of Mann at the party, Shelley had become a narrator of things "almost remembered," and yet the words remained "uncommunicable forever."[38]

Shelley never considered that maybe "ending it all" could refer to an abortion, or breaking up with a lover, or telling the truth and stopping her prevarications. At the time, no one ever presented proof of this marriage because there was no proof to find. Shelley told the story of that night at Jacobs's trial later in the summer of 1923. He had concluded, which was the reason the defense called him as a witness, that she was contemplating suicide.

At the trial, the district attorney wanted to know where exactly this party was. Who was at the party? Where did they live? Were there any other witnesses? Shelley could never recall addresses, dates, or how often he saw Mann. He had also taken her to other parties. They never went alone. They always went in a group. The group always met up at the Grant Hotel.

"Did you go as her escort?"

"I think I did," was his answer to the district attorney. He could not recall how many times, but he did recall the exact parties. The night in question began at the Golden Lion and ended at a house party, address unknown. While everyone else was in the living room, they, Shelley and Mann, were alone briefly. She told him about her deep, ceaseless sadness without mentioning the pregnancy. Shelley, by his own admission, was not an "intimate acquaintance of hers" by any means. Still, he considered himself a close friend because he had feelings "towards her." He could not say that she had those same feelings toward him. That night was the last time he saw her.

Mann did not commit suicide. She did not seek an abortion. Instead, she did what she had always done. Fritzie made up a story. She told everyone, and even placed an announcement in the newspaper, that she was leaving for Culver City. She said she had signed a contract with a movie studio. There was no contract.[39] The truth was, the pregnant and unmarried Mann was going to the unspectacular Long Beach to stay with her childhood friend Bernice.

She stayed in Los Angeles for a few weeks. At the start of January 1923, Mann returned to San Diego and sent a final letter, written on Grant Hotel stationary, to Bernice. Mann had borrowed her friend's clothing, perhaps because her own no longer

fit, and the suitcase later found on the beach. More than anything, she wanted Bernice not to worry: "Any way, he has been
wonderfully sweet to me, and does not seem to be able to do
enough for me. He is trying so hard to make me see things the
way he does. We have been together constantly, and he's begging
me not to go back to LA." She never wrote his name.[40]

By early January, Mann returned to the Grant Hotel lobby.
Her friend Dorothy Armstrong accompanied her as she waited
for Louis Jacobs to arrive. That day Jacobs took Mann for a ride
out to National City, and all the while they talked about her
pregnancy. She also called on Rogers Clark, who was staying at
the hotel. She would meet him in the lobby too, every day.[41]

For her lovers, Mann was their pregnant, Jewish, poor, immigrant scandal. Pregnancy meant undeniable proof that she had
broken taboos. To Bernice, she summed up her belief in how to
treat men: "That's the way, tell them to go to the devil and they'll
come around all right."[42] Fed up with how she had been treated,
she wrote Jacobs, "Things are getting on my nerves."[43] From her
perspective, were she to have the abortion she would have traveled the road from dancer to harlot, because the abortion would
confirm that romantic love had not occurred. Were she to have
the child, she would never be a star. Hollywood at the time just
did not have single mothers. Up until this point, her body had
been her greatest tool. It had let her transcend so many barriers.
In pregnancy, her body became the insurmountable.

As long as she was Fritzie, she was safe. Fritzie was experimental. She was free. She also had a degree of power because
no one could catch her. Having conventional thoughts, like how
unplanned pregnancies should be followed by matrimony, would
revert Fritzie back to Frieda. She had been "determined to return
to San Diego to see Jacobs,"[44] as she had written to Bernice. In
traveling back to the city and to Jacobs, Mann was looking for a
way to legitimize herself, the act, the baby, and the possible abortion. She threatened Jacobs that she would "stop at nothing" to
get what she wanted.[45] She was telling the truth and intended to
force those around her to accept her truth. In the Jazz Age, the
most dangerous thing a person could be was honest.[46]

6

DEATH

Mrs. Spencer was a maid.[1] She lived and worked at the Blue Sea Cottage. Each day she had her work cut out for her. The bungalows were a group of twenty buildings, each containing two separate rooms, clustered together. Each room had a sitting room, sleeping area, kitchenette, and connecting bathroom. Only two had a private bathroom. One of them was number 33.

On the morning of the sixteenth, she cleaned room 33 around noon. The bed had been used and turned back as though someone had exited it. Spencer, of course, removed the bedding and replaced it with a clean set. She noticed a small spot of blood on the undersheet.

In the kitchenette, the dishes were in perfect order. Only two glasses sat on the drain board. A towel rested in the sink. It appeared to have been used.

Then she moved on to the bathroom. There was a little standing water in the tub. The water "was something near the color of iron rust, or a dark color, something similar to that—dark." She didn't pay so very much attention to water, but "it was a dark color—discoloration of some kind, in the edge of the water. Imagine a small puddle in the bottom of a 'nice, white' porcelain

Blue Sea Cottage, La Jolla, 1923. The judge, attorneys, and jury are visiting the alleged murder scene of Fritzie Mann. Courtesy of the San Diego History Center.

tub. Around that puddle's edges was the discoloration," she later explained to the police.

It was Spencer's first time cleaning the tubs in that specific cottage, so she could not say what it normally looked like. Nevertheless, she could suggest the state of the bath towels. One towel hung on the wire over the tub. The other towel lay unused on the rack. She returned to the bedroom, where she noticed the small hair net and barrette on the dressing table. Spencer did not realize fully at the time that she had discovered a murder scene. The state of the rooms did not speak to extended violence. Rather, the rooms suggested the ease with which the killer ended Fritzie Mann's life.

Drowning is complicated. There are several stages. When first submerged, the person tries to hold their breath. They fight against breathing. They struggle. Their resistance to breathing ends quickly. The body wants to breathe. It is hard to stop the body from breathing. Then comes dyspnea, or labored breathing. The lungs fight again. Only this time they fight against breathing in the water. Yet they have to breathe. Small amounts of water at first enter and then the amount overwhelms. Regurgitation follows, as does the struggle. The body realizes its error and attempts to rid itself of the water. It is unnatural to breathe water. The body wants air. Nevertheless, water goes were it wants to, and it begins to penetrate the lungs. The body swallows the water. The stomach begins to fill. Finally, the lungs give up the struggle. Until this moment, the mind is active. There is awareness. The person knows they are drowning. Then a most welcome thing happens: they lapse into unconsciousness. Irrevocably, it is over.[2]

Drowning had a very specific place in Jazz Age culture: it is how the killer in Theodore Dreiser's best-selling and banned 1925 novel *An American Tragedy* murdered his lover. In choosing drowning, the killer, Clyde, thought he could make the death look like an accident, and Dreiser hoped to use drowning to illustrate the mentality behind the hateful violence against women. The killer's compulsion to do away with the girl he once desired seemed unquestionable. He wanted to do more than kill her. He wanted to deracinate, tear up everything they had been and done by the roots. He had fallen in love with a wealthy debutant and had to be rid of this factory girl, her unborn child, and the taint of working-class poverty to which he was born. Dreiser explained that, "unless he could speedily and easily disengage himself from her, all this other splendid recognition would be destined to be withdrawn from him," meaning that he would lose access to the gilded world of the upper class. "And this other world," the one of tuberculosis-filled tenements and factory work, "from which he sprang, might extend its gloomy, poverty-stricken arms to him." He could feel it as it "enveloped and almost strangled him from the first." As he plotted the murder, the killer reflected on all of his choices. "It even occurred to him, in a vague way for the first time, how strange it was that this girl and he, whose origins had been strictly similar, should be drawn so to each other in the beginning. Why should it have been? How strange life was, anyway?" Hatred, the easiest of all emotions, drove him to kill. "As instantly sensing the profoundness of his own failure," Clyde yielded "to a tide of submerged hate" for himself, "his cowardice or inadequateness," and his lover because he felt "her power" over him and her power "to restrain him." Dreiser imagined the killer thinking intensely about hate as he looked upon his lover.[3] Dreiser had created a killer who embodied all of the turmoil of the larger society when faced with the new woman. In short, the killer hated what he imagined was her power over him and saw her as trying to restrain him.

In trying to explain the deepest flaw in humanity, Dreiser accomplished what all the newspapers and medical examiner reports could not: he dismantled the paradox of the Jazz Age by invoking the justification of the age: "Repressed desire to do—to do—to do yet temporarily unbreakable here and now—a static between a powerful compulsion to do and yet not to do." "And in the meantime in his eyes" the killer felt himself change, and his victim could see the change. His pupils grew "momentarily large and luridly—his face, body, and hands tense and contracted—the stillness of his position, the balanced immobility of the mood more and more ominous, yet in truth not suggesting a brutal, courageous power to destroy, but the imminence of trance or spasm."[4]

When the time to act came, the killer fortified himself with his revulsion for the woman he once loved and found himself "willing only to say that never, never would he marry her—that never, even should she expose him, would he leave here to marry her." He pushed her under the water; "she sank and then rose for the first time, her frantic, contorted face turned" toward her lover. "For see how she strikes about, she is stunned." Dreiser's words were short and clipped, just as the victim's breaths were growing shallower. "She herself is unable to save herself and by her erratic tenor. . . . Wait, Wait ignore the pity of the appeal," the killer thought. "But there! Behold. It is over. . . . You will never, never see her alive anymore—ever."[5] In only imagining the killer, Dreiser forgot what death would be like for the victim.

For Fritzie Mann, death was different than Dreiser described. She had been happy and drinking. She was struck on the head and no doubt meandered somewhere between consciousness and stupor. She had struggled only briefly. According to the autopsy surgeon, she was pushed under the water in the bathtub. Perhaps he, her killer, had held her head down to make sure it, the drowning,

happened because she was the girl that was never what she was
supposed to be, but this time was different because she was supposed to be dead. Her death came quickly like extinguishing a
light. Then he wrapped her in a blanket. The murder weapon
slipped down the drain. She was small, only around 130 pounds.
It would have been toilsome, yet not impossible, to carry her
body, wrapped in a blanket, out to the car and then to the beach.

In the previous hours of the day, Fritzie had been frenetic. She
had left her house around five o'clock wearing her brown beaded
dress, a brown velvet hat with a tan plume and ostrich feather, a
barrette in her hair, and an electric blue coat. She carried a small
suitcase. She told her mother she was going to a party between
Del Mar and Los Angeles. Later that night, she called home to
let her mother know that the party would be in La Jolla. Her
mother said, "My child, you know the best where you are going"
and lamented that her daughter did not want to say who she was
with. "She told me always before, but this Sunday she don't she
says, 'there is a man from Los Angeles that will take us,' she says
'Tell me what is that name of the man.' She says 'I don't know.'"[6]

Amelia Mann was never "pleased" about her daughter dating. She was against all of it. "I don't want her to go out, because
we are strangers, and I don't know the people—I never liked—I
would not say I was glad, I was against—because we were strangers, and I don't like her to go out." Yet Fritzie persisted. They
had actually quarreled over Rogers Clark. He was taking her to
Tijuana, and her mother, rightly given the reasons people from
San Diego traveled across the border, protested: "I don't want
you to go out with him until I see the man, and I don't like the
idea of a man who takes a young girl to Tijuana." Fritzie replied,
"Mama, it is day time; it is a friend of mine, I can go with him.
Don't you trust me?" He mother replied, "Yes, but I don't like
you go with any man." She forced Fritzie to take her with them
on their date. After Fritzie returned from Los Angeles, men began
calling at the house again. Fritzie always rushed to the phone and
answered before anyone else had the chance.

"She was always happy; she was always happy; she never worried," her mother recalled. Even on the day she died, "she was just
as she always was. She fixed up her things, she curled her hair, she
ironed her silk gown, she was happy; she took her bath and made

fun all day; she was happy. . . . She was the happiest girl in the world." Amelia Mann sat with her daughter the whole day. She watched her dress. She watched her pack. Then she walked her daughter, from their home at 2923 Spruce Street, to wait for the streetcar to downtown. All the time Fritzie refused to tell anything more than it was "a man from Los Angeles that will take us."

The "us" she insisted to her mother was a group of girls. "Always you told me with who you go; and this time you don't want to." Fritzie replied, "It is a man from Los Angeles; he will take us from downtown."

"That is all she said," her mother wept. "It was funny to me, because she told me always, and this time, and I don't think— what man she don't tell,—she does not know maybe." "I suspected maybe some secret marriage, or something, she don't want to tell me."

Of course, Fritzie was happy. She had spent the past two weeks in Long Beach with her childhood friend Bernice, where her mind began to clear. She realized she was angry with Jacobs. "Have gone through enough these last two weeks on account of you to embitter me more than ever," she wrote after Jacobs told her to meet Wilma Miner, who would facilitate the abortion. "If I do not hear from you in the next two days will come to San Diego immediately and stop at nothing," she wrote Jacobs.[7]

She was frustrated. It was January 6, and she knew she had been pregnant since October. She had received his telegrams and had tried to meet Miner at the hotel. "This is the second time I have tried to get Miner," she would have yelled if telegrams had been audio recordings, "and have failed. Cannot understand the whole thing. Things are getting on my nerves. Whole matter looks very funny to me." Then she wired Bernice to say, "determined to return to San Diego to see Jacobs."[8]

On the twelfth, three days before her body was found on the beach, Mann again wrote her friend Bernice. This time she sat down and, using stationery from the Grant Hotel, she seemed calmer:

Dear B. At last I have a chance to write you after trying to get a minute to myself for the last year it seems. Now as to the matter concerning myself, we have decided that

San Diego would be the best place, and all arrangements have been made accordingly. It will just take a few days and then I can come back and start right into everything. I do not understand the whole thing about Miner, as she was there, and in fact was until yesterday. He made me call the Lankershim, and they told me she has been there for the past two weeks. Something is cock-eyed some where and I'll be damned if I can figure it out.

Any way, he has been wonderfully sweet to me, and does not seem to be able to do enough for me. He is trying so hard to make me see things the way he does. We have been together constantly, and he's begging me not to go back to L.A. We both have gone through an awful strain, and it has brought us together much more than we ever have been and I am somewhat afraid that we've both got 'em again—and a little bit too strong, but I guess it's all in a lifetime. We've had a marvelous understanding and things are going beautifully.

So, honey girl, I will let you know the outcome, and hope to be, in fact, I am sure if all goes well, I'll be in Long Beach the first of next week.

As for the hat and dress, I am taking marvelous care of them, and am not wearing them as my darling mother has put them away and made me wear my own clothes, as she was very angry at me coming down in your things. In fact, she still raves about it, so, old, kid your stuff am more than safe in Ma's hands.

So no more this time, sweetness, and I shall keep you posted on everything.

Give my best love to Carl and tell him I'm storing up a lot good jokes for him. Ha! Ha!

My love to the folks, and worlds of it to you.

I am as ever your unforgetting Fritz.

Do not answer my letter as you know I won't be home.[9]

7

KILLERS

It was late April 1923. Reporters from the *San Diego Sun* had come to the jail to ask Jacobs his opinion on the national coverage of the murder, his first trial, and the confessions of another incarcerated man who had begun to claim that he had killed Fritzie Mann. Jacobs "cheerfully" stepped out of his cell wearing a blue bathrobe and smoking a cigarette. At the sight of the reporters he exclaimed, "Visitors. . . . Well, what do you know—that's new." He had been indicted for murder in late February. By the end of April, he had been tried once and was awaiting retrial after the jury in the first case deadlocked after thirty-five hours of deliberation.[1]

When told of the news that a convict in Texas, who had read about the case in the newspaper and formed the impression he was the killer, had confessed to killing Mann, Jacobs said:

> No! I'm getting so I can't believe anything any more. Everything I hear or everything I say seems to become exaggerated. Did you just now tell me somebody has confessed he killed Fritzie Mann? I wish, if she was killed, whoever did it would come through. . . . You know that old saying, "Murder will out." I believe that. I believe, if

Fritzie Mann was murdered, the man that did it is going
to have to tell it some day.

He smoked vigorously, the reporters noted, and finished two
cigarettes in less than five minutes. Then he asked the reporters
to repeat the details of the news:

Circumstantial evidence! But of course this may not be
true. But say, if it is true! When I'm freed I'm never going
to believe in circumstantial evidence again! Just suppose
this lad is telling the truth. I've heard of things as strange.
There was the Mary Page Tucker case in Massachusetts.
A man was convicted, on circumstantial evidence, of
murdering her. Fifteen years later—the old story, Another
Man! I don't want to talk too much. It seems like everything I say comes back to hurt me in someway.

He continued anyway: "The truth is going to come out about Fritzie Mann some day, if it was murder. You wait and see. I know it
will." Then Jacobs left for a long conference with his attorneys,
to discuss if the unfounded confessions of the convict could be a
possible new strategy for his upcoming retrial. His attorney, Louis
Shapiro, publicly announced that he did not believe the convict's
confession because he, the lawyer, maintained that Mann had not
been murdered.[2]

Troubling details of Jacobs's relationship with Mann had
emerged during his first interviews with Chief Patrick. Everything was in his letters. Chief Patrick asked why Jacobs had
sought to employ Miss Wilma Miner. Jacobs admitted he sent
her to Los Angeles to make arrangements for the abortion. As
to why he would do such a thing, Jacobs told Patrick that it was
"more of a sympathy—to that effect—sympathy with her." Miss
Miner, Jacobs explained, was acquainted with *certain* parties in
Los Angeles. Jacobs also said he had met Mann at the Grant Hotel
on the eight of January when she had returned from Long Beach.
Dorothy Armstrong, friend and fellow dancer, had been with her.
After Dorothy left, Mann and Jacobs went for a ride to National
City to "talk over her condition." Jacobs would call his interest,
during his first police interviews in January 1923, "purely altru-
istic" and labeled himself a "damn fool," Patrick recalled.[3]

After that interview, Jacobs, the chief of police, the county detective, detectives Sears and Chadwick, various newspapermen, and the greengrocer Leo Greenbaum went to the murder scene. As they walked the grounds of the Blue Sea Cottage, Chief Patrick asked Jacobs if he had ever been in number 33. Jacobs was no longer willing to share details: "I refuse to answer that question."[4] The killer's car had been parked near the office of the Blue Sea Cottage to the left of the main driveway and crossed a portion of the grass, cutting rather deep into the ground. The little group of investigators, the suspect, and his friend the grocer could still see the tire tracks.

Despite these details and the evidence of the letters, Jacobs's first trial had ended in debacle. The jury had become locked in controversy and given up. As the summer of 1923 approached, the city, the Mann family, and Jacobs all prepared for the second trial. For a man waiting in jail, the newspaper debate over the death penalty, the constant growth in crime, and the memories of the life he left behind must have weighed on Jacobs's mind. Meanwhile, out in the nation a fear began to grip the public. It was becoming apparent that enormous prosperity and previously unimaginable violence would define the decade, making the Jazz Age distinct and Jacobs rather ordinary.[5]

During his time in jail, the press relayed the stories of the outside world to Jacobs. His grasp on reality became the depiction of the world provided through the newspapers. Those same newspapers provide a way to assemble and connect the details of the national context to the very personal crime that resulted in the death of Fritzie Mann.

The people of San Diego had no way of knowing Mann's murder was at the beginning of a national trend toward violent killings. Statistics gathered by social scientists and insurance companies throughout the Jazz Age indicate that the homicide rate had risen. In 1910 the murder rate was 5.9 per 100,000, and by 1923 it was 10.2. In twenty-eight American cities with a total population of over 20 million, there were 1,877 homicides (around 9 per 100,000). In Chicago there were 53 killings per 100,000. Memphis had a rate of 67.4 per 100,000 in 1922.[6]

The increase in crime was so great that one Missouri newspaper, the *Chariton Courier,* declared in August 1920, "Daily

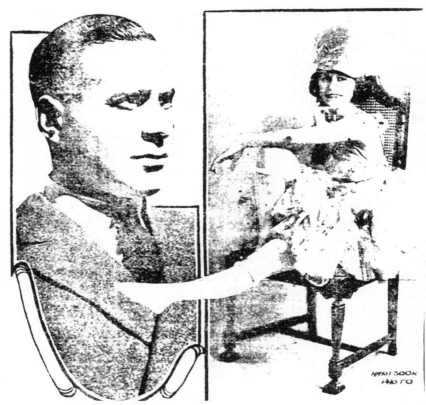

Louis Jacobs and Fritzie Mann, from "Dr. Jacobs Held without Bail for Death of S.D. Girl," *San Diego Union*, February 18, 1923. The caption under the photo reads, "Dr. Louis L. Jacobs, Camp Kearny physician, is held without bail at the county jail following his arrest yesterday morning on an indictment returned by the San Diego County grand jury charging him with the murder of Miss Fritzie Mann, pretty dancer of San Diego . . . whose almost nude body was found in the Torrey Pines beach." Note that the photo of Mann was taken at the Hartsook Studio.

accounts of murder, holdups of messengers with money, bank robberies, wife and husband homicides, abductions, burglaries and deaths from abortions indicate an increase which cannot be accounted for on the theory of general unrest altogether." Indeed, "millionaires have been put to death in their own homes by women or their paramours or both." "Torsos concealed in trunks . . . babies and children kidnapped . . . Negroes shot or hung ... bandits killed in unsuccessful raids ... suicides and infanticides galore." In the end, the reporter offered no statistics, interviews with authorities, or anecdotes to prove all of these things had happened. There was also no analysis of events, just the appalled and overwhelmed exclamation, "The time is out of joint somewhere about its machinery, prohibition to the contrary notwithstanding, what is it all about?"[7]

Those trying to explain the increase fell into two groups. One blamed the American gun culture rooted in the frontier mentality, the moral damage of World War I, and the lawlessness of Prohibition. For the other, the problem was the loss of the past. They lamented what they imagined to be the disappearance of core values that had once defined life, family, and larger society. America was separating itself from its historical roots—be those roots Puritan or Victorian, the nation could not agree. Still, they, the social scientists and laymen, were quite sure that the decrease in church membership, permissive parenting, the automobile, industrialization, and vulgar popular music, books, and movies were all to blame.[8]

Despite the differences between these two groups, they did agree on one thing—that there had been a loss of social coherence. "Capital punishment is evidently not in itself a sufficient deterrent," the *Literary Digest* asserted. "Prohibition has not helped; the war cannot be blamed[,] for the increase was constant before 1914. The growth of huge cities and the cheapening of life by the modern industry cannot be held the sole cause. ... Crime is often of social origins and the social origins of the last twenty years have been great,"[9] which was a nod to the social changes since the start of the war.

Social disintegration was a process, not a condition. Americans saw themselves as moving through a kind of twelve-step program that ended not with salvation but with perdition. They felt powerless to stop the process; even the greatest attempts to stop it, such as Prohibition and the growth in various kinds of institutionalizations of undesirables, all seemed to be failing.[10]

There was no greater indication that the end was nigh than the growth of the youth criminal. There were the romanticized killers like Richard Reese Whittemore, the Candy Kid, who ran a gang of diamond thieves and enjoyed a kind of public fame in which young women gathered outside the jail to weep over not being near him.[11] In California there was Dorothy Ellingson, a San Francisco flapper who at sixteen shot and killed her mother because she forbade Dorothy from going to jazz clubs. In a statement to police, the girl admitted that her love for the nightlife had led her to murder.[12] In the Midwest there were other flapper killers, such as Olivia Stone. She had killed Ellis G. Kinkead. She claimed to have been legally wedded to Kinkead and that he had deserted her to marry another woman.[13] When the jury found Stone to be not guilty, men in the courtroom threw their caps in the air. Women wept and rushed over to her. Yet Stone never found freedom. Instead, a few weeks later, she took bichloride of mercury. She did not die quietly. Stone confessed that she had of course killed the "only person I had to live for," so the remaining choice of suicide seemed clear to her. Doctors asked if she regretted the murder. "No," came the reply. "I would do it again if I had to. I killed him because I loved him. If I could not have him, then no one else was going to."[14]

The kings of this entire social decline were Nathan Leopold and Richard Loeb. In May 1924, the pair picked up Robert Franks from a schoolyard in a prominent Chicago neighborhood. While one drove, the other forced a chisel into the boy's brain. Later they dumped the boy's nude body into an Indiana field. They partially concealed the body in a storm drain and, just in case the body was discovered, poured acid on him to obscure his identity. Later, Leopold would confess that they had spent months planning the crime. The killers believed they were smarter than the average person—smarter than the average policeman too, or so they thought. Enamored by crime novels and feeding off each other's narcissism and megalomania, they schemed and plotted. Ultimately, they were undone because Leopold dropped his glasses near Frank's body. The glasses were an expensive, custom-ordered item purchased by only three people in the state. Very quickly, the police went through the list and came down to two college-age sons of well-to-do Chicago families. They confessed and Clarence Darrow, the legendary attorney, defended them. He was successful in saving them from the death penalty but not from jail. Leopold and Loeb's crime suggested an unbelievable level of depravity, and it provoked a similar level of sick interest in the newspapers and the public. The ruthlessness of this crime suggested to onlookers that sympathy, pity, and emotional sense were all absent from the killers.[15]

In response to the Leopold and Loeb trial, author James Thurber quipped:

If a fellow killed his sister
When dear old Dad was young
    A jury of his equals
Had him sent out and hung.
But the use of such rough tactics
    Is abolished in the land
And we let 'em go if they can show
    A low pineal gland.[16]

Leopold and Loeb each received the sentence of life imprisonment. Some wondered if execution was a fitting punishment, since life imprisonment did not actually last for a lifetime. Thirty-two of the states with the death penalty also gave the jury the right to choose the death penalty or life in prison. Furthermore, from 1912 to 1919, 210 of 722 people sentenced to death in twenty-three states avoided execution, which means that only 70 percent of executions occurred.[17] The crux of the whole matter seemed to be the "tender shrinking feeling" of jurors and public sentiment that caused people to "recoil from inflicting death." If the death penalty vanished, these critics suggested, the substitute punishment had to be as heinous. Life imprisonment was horrific because it stripped the individual of both freedom and hope.[18]

A year before Leopold and Loeb, Louis Jacobs was waiting in jail, chain smoking and probably wondering about the possibility of execution. He would have found no solace in the fact that capital punishment made juries nervous. Even those who did not feel fully comfortable with the death penalty found themselves advocating it, because they thought "the malignant growth [in violent crimes] must be eradicated at all costs." Moreover, if found guilty, Jacobs would have had difficulty escaping the death penalty.[19] The punishment had to be as "inexorably certain as it is within man's power to do it," jurors argued. In the Jazz Age it was impossible to argue that capital punishment deterred crime, because there had been an increase in crime in every state regardless of the presence of capital punishment. Indeed, the argument in favor of the death penalty, later fueled by the Leopold and Loeb case, concerned the degree of the penalty rather than the impact the penalty might have on deterrence. Those making this argument asserted that life imprisonment was not harsh enough, given that not only crime but the barbarous violence in crime had increased. Some began to wonder if a new era had come, one in which murder was a diversion for the newspaper readers as well as the killers. Therefore, many believed the punishment needed to match the crime.[20]

For the incarcerated man daily reading the city newspapers, it would have been hard to miss how "the crime and the trial are dramatized." To the social critics it seemed that "the public is gorged with columns of lurid and carelessly prepared material." Nearly everyone suspected that the media coverage shaped "the public mind," which no longer regarded a courtroom as "a stern and dignified tribunal where retributions descend swiftly and inevitably on the guilty, and the innocence of the unjustly accused can be established." Rather, people had begun to see the courtroom as "a sort of stage where sensational legal battles are waged, where lawyers tear their hair and deliver impassioned speeches, where fair defendants languish and weep." It seemed as though "everyone reads the newspapers nowadays, it is impossible to impanel a jury entirely free of press-imposed prejudices"[21]—a circumstance Jacobs had to fear because the press had never portrayed Fritzie Mann as the loose *woman* deserving what she got. She was forever the defenseless half-nude *girl.*[22]

In February 1923, newspapers as far away as Alaska and Arkansas reported that a grand jury had returned an indictment against Jacobs, despite the fact the police had already released him because of "lack of sufficient evidence to connect him with the crime." The indictment arrived after the district attorney had presented new evidence, which was not revealed to the press. Jacobs's arrest occurred at "Camp Kearny where he has been stationed. It came like a bolt of lighting from a clear sky," reported the *Denver Post,* "following a week in which the case apparently was dropped by the investigating authorities."[23]

At the start of the first trial, in March 1923, reporters remarked that "boyish" Jacobs had a "pallor" and looked "slightly pale" as he sat watching jury selection and from time to time cleaned his glasses, which many said he had acquired specifically for court.[24] Of course, the use of the word "pale" was important to those writing the copy because the cottage manager had described Mann's companion using the same word. Mann had registered, the manager said, with a "pale and trembling young man."[25]

Nevertheless, Jacobs, wearing a gray suit, "sat with his hands quietly folded in front of him and carrying an air of confidence in the courtroom of his trial," reported the *Union*. "He was neatly dressed in a dark suit," noted the *Sun*, "with an air of confidence." While his attorneys questioned prospective jurors, Jacobs "intently studied their faces," his chin in his hands. "Very seldom did he make any suggestions to his attorneys."[26]

The newspapers, defense attorneys, and public had transformed Jacobs's first trial in March and April 1923 into a spectacle. For example, a "woman dressed in black, apparently about the same age as the young physician, sent him a thick note from the audience just before the examination of jurors was begun." Jacobs's attorneys gave him the note, which Jacobs "tore" open "eagerly, and read the contents with a smile on his face, then settled back to await the beginning of his case." Each day, crowds gathered in the courtroom an hour before the trial began. "The room was full to the doors" before the judge arrived. Many people had to stand, and to accommodate the crowds the doors of the courtroom remained opened so that those in the hallway could hear the proceedings. "Conspicuous among the spectators in the courtroom were many pretty girls who were friends of Fritzie Mann when she was alive," which might have been heartening had they been the members of the jury or even her true friends. Dr. Jacobs continued to look pale. The reporters speculated about whether he looked more pale or less. Yet they ruled that he seemed "not disturbed over the possible outcome of his case," as the first trial was coming to a close.[27]

Jacobs was in California, a hanging state. At the time, the philosophical purpose of public execution was to reveal the truth. What each prisoner knew was that the truth in every execution was not the guilt of the prisoner but the power of the state. Executions upheld and demonstrated the importance of state power in a world gone sideways after World War I and Prohibition. It seemed that every citizen questioned the seat of power, and executions remained the last decipherable symbol that suggested nothing had changed. Those in power remained in power even if the class system, the morals, the customs, and every other foundational cinder block of society had shifted under the weight of social upheaval.[28]

Surely the thought of the noose would have been inescapable for Jacobs given that, as he was being arrested and questioned by the police in January 1923, Felipe Bisquere, a twenty-year-old Asian American man convicted of killing a lumber company superintendent in Plumas County, swung from the gallows. In April 1923, while Jacobs awaited the verdict of his first trial, Ullah "Gull" Mohammed, who had been convicted of killing his business partner, was sentenced to be hung by the neck until dead. In both cases, the press had called the killers "cold blooded."[29]

Again, in July, as Jacobs went through his second trial, another execution occurred in California. This time it was Mauro Parisi, who as he stood waiting to be hung showed no emotion. The press had called him the "coolest man ever executed." He was also a stunning example of the violence of the age. He had encountered Felix Paladino on the streets of Fresno in May 1922. Parisi took out his gun and shot Paladino. Somehow, Paladino managed to turn and run, all the while screaming for help. Parisi followed. He shot his automatic pistol and hit his target four times. The last bullet entered Paladino's back and exited through the abdomen. This shot stopped Paladino. He could no longer run or scream for help. Quickly, Parisi caught up with him and, discovering he was not yet dead, bent his victim over a street railing. Then he brutally used his gun as a tool to bludgeon Paladino's head until bystanders pulled him off the now limp and bloody victim. Reportedly, Parisi let off seven more shots. One hit a man in the crowd. Paladino, the intended victim, died two days later.[30]

The prosecution in the case had a cakewalk in convicting Parisi. There had been numerous witnesses to the sidewalk slaying. Also, the judge in the case had little sympathy for Parisi, who showed emotion in the trial only when the verdict was read. The newspaper reporters wrote that Parisi cried at that moment. "Society," the judge said, "must be protected from such acts of lawlessness." Parisi had made a widow of Paladino's wife and orphans of his children. Therefore, the judge felt that sentencing Parisi to death would serve as a warning to "men of this type that they cannot run amok."[31] Truly, hanging was a formidable threat to the criminal. After all, it could take up to fifteen minutes to die, and during that time the prisoner was conscious.[32]

In a strange way, Jacobs was lucky. He had class, race, and social standing to protect him from the death penalty, which Bisquere, Parisi, and Mohammed did not. He was also lucky to be facing a possible hanging, because there were worse ways to die. Had he been tried in Nevada and convicted, he would have been facing the gas chamber. Executioners used liquid hydrocyanic gas pumped into a stone chamber, which one critic likened to executing humans as though they were chloroforming kittens in a box.[33]

One might pause to pity the treatment of kittens in the twenties, but then one might miss the fact that New York State had adopted the electric chair as a move toward "scientific" executions. Electrocution was a form of punishment so frightful that the prisoner's body actually caught on fire at the points of contact with the machine. All the muscles in the body instantly contracted, causing sever contortions of limbs, mouth, face, and eyes. Mercifully, the witnesses to the executions did not view the ordeal in total because the prisoner's face was covered. They also may not have known that human skin offers considerable resistance to electric current. In fact, if human skin were removed and well dried, it could be used as a very good insulator—good enough that low voltage would not break down the resistance of the skin. Thus, executioners did not use low voltage. They preferred to use 2,200 volts, which was enough to cause instant paralysis of organs and to disintegrate blood. Still, it could take as long as seven minutes to kill a person in this manner. There were also examples of execution by electrocution that went wrong and necessitated that the executioners throw the switch two or three times before the prisoner died.[34] The idiosyncrasies of electrocution were enough to make a person miss widespread hangings.

Nationally, from 1912 to 1919 inclusive, 1,724 persons were sentenced either to death (272) or to life imprisonment (1,452). In the five states where the death penalty was absolutely retained, during the same period 263 were sentenced to death and 454

sentenced to life imprisonment.[35] The death penalty made
Jacobs's trial high stakes.

In the summer of 1923, Jacobs maintained to the press that
his only crime was offering Mann, lovely girl in trouble, his
friendship and help. Since he was presenting himself as a friendly
altruist, his explanation raises questions about what kind of man
he was.

Mann's collection of letters reveal his darker side. One of
Mann's flapper girlfriends wrote tauntingly to her, "I saw your
Doctor Jacobs today. . . . He sure looked fine in his Hudson sedan.
I'd like to go out with him if it could be arranged. I wouldn't let
him treat me rough as he did you. I'm pretty strong."[36] Mann
may have thought the same thing when she first met Jacobs.

Jacobs treated women "rough," and Mann, according to court
testimony, misled men. Rumors had it that Fritzie Mann either
married or had lied about being married.[37] According to popular
culture, all women lied. Why then wouldn't a man lie to them?
Everyone knew courtships were problematic. Men who regarded
marriage as a "steel trap" avoided the institution. Popular custom
held that this was exactly the kind of man who should not marry.
The girl "unfortunate enough to be preferred by him should take
care not to fall in love with him without sentiment or special
interest merely as an occasional visitor," was the advice offered
by the popular media. The magazines encouraged her to "take
any attitude except that of waiting long meaningless years for
him to 'come to the point.' . . . girls of the coming generation
will see that in cases of this sort a man isn't wholly to blame." Of
course, any girl who preferred this type of man was "at fault too"
for whatever hardship befell her, which is certainly the attitude
her friends had of Fritzie.[38]

It would be difficult for anyone in this era to argue against
the view that Mann and her friends were playing with fire when
they tried to manipulate this "type of man." Her circle of friends,
as they wrote in their letters, regarded the Navy boys, who were
their own age, as "cheap skates" and, the worst insult of all, "nice
guys." One girlfriend wrote Mann to explain, "Was awful tired
and cold coming back, but put the laprobe up around and was snug
as a bug in a rug. Eddie's a nice fellow and seems to think a lot of
me. He's all right, even if he is only an ensign." She concluded,

"Don't think I'll run around with them any more." As for riding in cars with boys and men, one wrote, "Gee! I guess I made an impression with the cigarette, but I thought it was the regular thing there." The same friend who wrote about Jacobs acting "rough" with Mann also wrote, "There's an old fellow wants to go out with me. He wants to buy me clothes and pay my room rent. The rent is $15, but I told him it was $20. He only wants to go with me twice a week. Don't think I will get into trouble because he is too old."[39] These letters indicate that Mann and her group of friends were more than just flappers, gold diggers, or party girls; they were on a treacherous path with access to affluence on one side and the potential of becoming pregnant or being beaten by angry lovers on the other. Plus, they were clearly in competition for the greatest prize, an older man foolish enough to give them money. Perhaps Jacobs refused to be that man.

Jacobs and Mann had been misleading each other. Nevertheless, few at the time believed there was gender equality in lies. To "lie like a gentleman," as one popular publication put it, "is one thing. But—to 'fib like a female' is radically another." The man's lie "is approved by the world. It moves hand in hand with romance. It is a courtly creature." Men, or at least the type of man Jacobs hoped the public would understand him to be, thought there was honor in doing the dishonorable if the act shielded the honor of a woman. The lies of a woman, though, were "trouble and treachery; disgrace; disaster; death." The popular perception of "feminine falsehoods" was that they were like "dagger points that fall from the lovely lips of ladies." The fact that the flapper always lied was the single constant running "through all her characteristics; modernism." In other words, people believed the flapper used lies like a "sudden flashing instrument of death." The flapper's lies were "vicious as the knives the most primitive of humans used to slay." Since she was presenting herself as a primitive, did she then lie to satisfy a primitive urge? "Who shall say?" However, everyone knew that "the lies told to entrap men . . . were acts of dominance" by those who were supposed to be subservient because they were female.[40]

Even more than illustrating the fear of women controlling men, lies were the things that constructed the performance. The basic problem with embroidering facts, as Jacobs had learned when he lied to the police about his letters to Mann, was that his dark secrets were in constant danger of being uncovered by the newspapers. The liar must relentlessly control information by strategically keeping secrets.[41] The urge to control information is what drove Jacobs voluntarily to place himself in the hands of the police and to welcome the reporters to his cell. Yet Jacobs was a man with too many secrets.

Jacobs had another problem. Part of his alibi was that he had been in Tijuana for several hours the day of the murder. Therefore, his alibi relied on portraying him not so much as a hardworking virtuous physician but as an active participant in the Jazz Age. Histories of the Jazz Age eagerly portray the 1917 closing of New Orleans's Storyville, the red light district, to be the beginning of a new era in American history because it forced musicians to spread out across the United States to new cities and new audiences.[42] Despite common thinking, the Jazz Age came earlier to southern California than to the rest of the nation. Legal horse racing gave the San Diego-Tijuana area a special pull that brought Jelly Roll Morton to the region as early as 1916. When he lost big at the races, he always had to find a gig in a bar or club to pay his gambling debts. Such was the case in 1921 when he was living in the US Grant Hotel. Morton went broke playing the ponies and picked up work at the Kansas City Bar in Tijuana. It was there that he wrote two of his most important compositions, "Kansas City Stomp," named for the bar, and "The Pearls," named for the waitress at the bar.[43]

Jacobs, and Morton for that matter, had to go to Mexico to misbehave because in 1909 social reformers drove the red light districts out of California south to Tijuana and Mexicali. The forced dismantling of the sex trade followed the scattering of the sex workers. Many of these women thought working in Mexico was far better than working in the United States. After all, as one woman reported, she could earn $3 "a piece," which meant that she might earn $25 more a week than a woman working in the sex trade in the United States. It was also far more than the $4–$6 a week earned by women working in factories at the same time.[44]

Mexican authorities tried to make it illegal for women to immigrate to Mexico for the purpose of working in prostitution, but the border was too fluid. For example, Chinese immigrants regularly entered Mexico and then crossed over to the United States during this period to escape the Exclusion Act.[45] Also, the women migrating to Mexico lied. On their immigration papers, they frequently listed their occupation as "waitress" or "cabaret dancer." In these jobs, they earned $30 a week and 50 percent of each drink they sold.[46] As a point of comparison, "taxi dancers" in New York City were making $25 a week in 1924.[47] Furthermore, the development of vice districts in northern Mexico, aided by American laws and money and hastened by the Mexican Revolution of 1910–20, resulted in an impressive growth in the tax base of the border areas, where creative government workers funded public works by selling brothel and prostitution licenses. Soon Tijuana boasted vice, gaming, spectator sports, and the sex trade.

By the time Jacobs was visiting, the border was changing. In the nineteenth century it was little more than a line on a map. The US government did not prohibit or regulate Mexican immigrants from crossing. They did not even keep records of entries. Officials were more concerned with collecting customs duties. During World War I there were more controls in place, but those dissolved quickly. By the end of the war, the growing sense of women's liberation and the beginning of Prohibition were all a boon for Tijuana as well as emerging cities like Mexicali and Ciudad Juárez, which all developed a "substantial and diverse" vice economy. Between 1920 and 1926, bars, dog and horse racing, golf courses, hotels, spas, and swimming pools transformed Tijuana from a border town to a destination.[48] An American visiting the border town in an attempt to escape the reach of Prohibition laws would have found huge benefits, such as the Tijuana Monte Carlo and the Foreign Club.[49] Ultimately, it seemed, Jacobs's alibi implied that he liked to party and liked to take women, in this case Mrs. Ella Worthington, with him across the border.

Moreover, he also liked to party on Coronado, the small island peninsula in the city's harbor that nature and wealthy men made into a kind of Eden. If Tijuana had all the vice and sin, Coronado was the dreamland of luxury and aspiration for Jacobs. The pinnacle of luxury was the Hotel del Coronado. Built by John Spreckels, the owner of the *San Diego Union*, the hotel hosted Hollywood stars such as Charlie Chaplin and Valentino. The hotel, known as "the Del" by locals, offered visitors the beachfront, polo, golf, and a film studio. On Coronado, a wealthy, slightly older woman, Ella Worthington, had entertained him and made him essential to her life. Coronado was the place where the weather was never too hot or too cold. The island had no slums, no filth-strewn alleys, no shacks or shantytowns. All it offered was contentedness. How perfect his life had been when he was part of that gilded cage of class and exception, which meant he was leaving behind his upbringing as the child of Jewish immigrants. He was a tourist in the elite, wealthy, smart set. His medical degree and good looks bought him that access.[50]

Jacobs's relationship to the seat of social power in the city is one of many ways he is unlike the group of youth killers for which the decade is remembered. Rather, he bears a greater resemblance to the killer Clyde, from Dreiser's *An American Tragedy*. While dating Fritzie and Mrs. Worthington at the same time, had he, like Clyde in the novel, frequently glanced at Fritzie and wondered how he could be attracted to her when she was "not of the high world" to which he desired to belong fully? Had he wondered what it was about Fritzie that enticed him so? Was he drawn to her because of a "chemic or temperamental pull" that felt so definite even as it felt a little too much like drowning?[51] How confusing aspiration is. How puzzling and irritating the contrasts between the two women were. Had he yearned for both to the same degree? Or was the relationship with Fritzie a manifestation of his physical urges and his affair with Mrs. Worthington an indication of his social inclinations?

It might be unfair to compare Jacobs to a fictional character from a novel whose proponents labeled a "veracious and significant picture of a new America" and called the author "courageous" in his handling "of erotic themes." The most negative of the reviews, that written by editor and social critic H. L. Mencken, who considered himself Dreiser's friend, called the work a "shapeless and forbidding monster—a heaping cartload of raw material for a novel, with rubbish of all sorts intermixed—a vast, sloppy, chaotic thing of 385,000 words—at least 250,000 of them unnecessary!"[52] Still, no one declared the book to be false or an exaggeration. Instead, libraries across the country banned it. Dreiser's work was the victim of what was known at the time as "voluntary censorship."[53] Social critics deemed the book dangerous because it contained premarital sex, abortion, drinking, classism, and murder. Perhaps its greatest threat was that *An American Tragedy*, at least when compared to all the seedy everyday murders such as Mann's, seemed accurate to its Jazz Age audience because of the prevalence of murder and the stark realities of class differences. In other words, Dreiser had told the truth.

In his defense, Jacobs maintained that he was not a killer and had only acted out of altruism toward Mann. Altruism was a defense buried deep in the idea of chivalrous manhood, which opens up the importance of gender to the idea of the victim and the perpetrator. True altruism, according to the prewar norms, would have been to marry Fritzie even if the child was not his. If he loved her, he would have done the "right thing." However, norms were clearly shifting. The magazine *Delineator* asked bachelors why they were not married. A thirty-year-old respondent answered, "The modern girl has no reticence; she wants only to be popular with men." This bachelor made $7,500 a year. He was conceited. He was proud to admit he had "played around" with tons of girls. All kinds of women liked him. There was not a type of woman he had not known. None of them was worthy of marriage.[54]

If bachelors in their thirties and early forties, like Jacobs, were conceited, a woman columnist writing for *Harper's* declared, it was because they were raised to be. Women created conceited men because they liked marrying financially successful men. Conceited men "bred conceited boys, whose conceit" women fostered through praise. Or perhaps, at least, the previous generation of women created the conceited men with whom the flapper now had to contend. However, the women over forty were also finding it hard to be with the self-satisfied men who believed their purpose in life should be to work themselves "bent and grey" to provide for their family. Such men believed they had to raise up their womenfolk in a glass box to protect them from the ills of the world. In protecting and providing for them, men had concluded that women were incapable of being equal. The

glass-box men provided nothing more than a prison that prevented women from developing socially and intellectually, thus
perpetuating their inferiority. What the woman of forty knew,
the anonymous author in *Harper's* argued, was that men took
credit for building civilization, with "George Bernard Shaw their
mouthpiece," without noticing that women had been growing
and changing too.[55]

If only he were female, then escaping execution and even
conviction would be far easier for Jacobs, or so the press and the
larger culture suggested.[56] For instance, giant headlines announcing the capture of Clara Phillips, "Hammer Slayer," had driven
Jacobs from the front page of the *San Diego Union*. Reading about
Phillips would have made him fully aware of the gender differences in court and in punishment. Truthfully, Phillips was bad
for every incarcerated person proclaiming themselves wrongfully
accused in 1923.[57] "I know people won't believe it," she sobbed
to the press, "but I am returning to a grim prison life because I
thought more of my honor than my freedom."[58]

When Phillips was on trial in the fall of 1922, there were five
other female killers on trial in courtrooms and in the headlines.
The *San Diego Tribune* noted what seemed to be an uptick in
women on trial for murder and asked, "Is feminine charm and
youthful beauty the best defense of fair defendants in murder trials?" Their answer was yes. It appeared to onlookers that
American juries would not convict a pretty woman, especially in
death penalty cases.[59]

The reluctance of juries to convict women was in part a
response to defense strategies. In California murder cases with
a female defendant from the 1870s to the 1950s, lawyers argued
that gender mattered because women were victims of a corrupt
male-dominated system. Part of the strategy was to suggest that
prosecutors were motivated by misogyny rather than justice. It
is important to note that as early as 1901 defense lawyers shifted
their strategy slightly. Where they had been arguing temporary
insanity, they began to connect self-defense to justifiable homicide,
saying that their clients' motivations did matter when discussing
the crime of murder. California juries accepted the argument long
before the appellate courts or the legislature. The verdicts that
resulted from this understanding of murder transformed women

into the victims of outrageous acts of violence. The murder victims—the husbands and lovers—became the guilty parties and the criminals. Quite simply, the juries came to believe that there were men who deserved killing. The women had to be seen as having enough agency to kill, but not enough agency that the jury would see them as anything other than victims. In using this tactic, the defense attorneys were constructing contemporary gender stereotypes for both the courtroom and the press. Indeed, the press and their audience preferred stories about women on the margins of society, sanity, and femininity.[60]

If there had been an increase in female killers, would society's perception change regarding women? Would women have no longer been seen as perpetually the victims? The inability of juries to convict had less to do with whether the woman was innocent or guilty. Indeed, the critics had already indicted modern women as being incapable of telling the truth and declared them ill suited as wives because of their conniving ways.[61] What happened in court had more to do with how juries and judges perceived women. In Ohio, Judge Florence Allen, the first woman to serve as a criminal court judge, argued that women understood that men, who made up the majority of jurists, were reluctant to hold women "accountable for their misdeeds." Judge Allen thought that as more women began to serve on juries there would be an increase in convictions. However, she also saw the nature of the crime as different depending on whether the killer was male or female. She noted that men frequently killed in conjunction with robberies, whereas women seemed to kill for jealousy or monetary gain from an insurance policy, which Judge Allen thought were crimes harder to prove than the crimes of men. Judge Allen also added that women were not above staging fainting spells in court, which provoked great concern among the men present and annoyed the judge. Famed defense attorney Clarence Darrow agreed with Judge Allen to a certain extent. He too detected a sense of chivalry in court and a commitment to the centuries-old idea that women were similar to children—mentally underdeveloped and so needing protection. If a man killed his wife, Darrow postulated, "he is a brute, and no sentence is too severe. But, let a woman strike her husband or nag him, or make his life unbearable," he said like an unhappily married man, "and the public applauds her conduct and says he deserves it."[62] Because of these cultural peculiarities, the law saw men and women as unequal.

Phillips's beguiling ways in the court and her claims that Peggy Caffee, the eyewitness, had killed Meadows with the hammer did not sway the jury. They convicted her of second-degree murder. Still the crowds followed her. They were there after her escape, and they followed her train as it transported her to San Quentin prison. They waited in the train stations to catch a glimpse of her, and women's societies gathered to express their support for her.[63] The crowds also waited for Jacobs. In his trial, the crowds seemed divided between the "army of flappers" and the attractive women who passed notes to his lawyers hoping their messages would reach the defendant. His notoriety had made him a celebrity.

If only Jacobs could have led a jury by sobbing as a woman could, his attorneys might have wished.[64] Or if he could have stood over the body of Fritzie Mann with a "smoking revolver" in his hand, declaring her to have been a brute, which is how the *Saturday Evening Post* chose to explain female murderers' presentation of their victims; then it would have been simple for his lawyers to win an acquittal, or so the popular press argued regarding the difference between male and female killers in court. Homicide committed in self-defense, the prominent magazines reported, was "justifiable homicide." "This also is an extremely useful defense, especially when the prosecutor has no eyewitness," the magazine pointed out in a sardonic critique of the legal system. If only Jacobs could have appeared "frail" and "shrinking," then he might have entered the witness stand and tearfully recounted how he struggled with Mann's burly form, by some miracle managing to overpower her and drown her in the bathtub, then dumping the body on the beach only by some almost superhuman adrenaline-fed effort. If he had been a woman his attorneys could have suggested all of the above, and his defense would have been an easy one.[65]

Jacobs might have wished to be back at Coronado, or to be underestimated as women were, or to just simply not be living in a state with capital punishment. Nevertheless, he was in jail, he was awaiting a second trial, and his lawyers would have to make him seem to be a sympathetic victim rather than a man who treated his lovers "rough" and liked to party with married women. He never, over the course of two trials, took the stand. Instead, his lawyers claimed that the prosecution had failed to prove that a murder had been committed. From their perspective, the only criminal in the case of Fritzie Mann was Mann herself.

8

ABORTIONIST

Wilma Miner was strangely prepossessing. In her black suit, swearing to tell the truth, the whole truth, she was effervescent and caused the courtroom of reporters and lawyers to stop breathing for just a moment. It was the summer of 1923 and Miner was more than a "beautiful woman," as the *San Diego Union* called her. She was powerful in that she had knowledge of a secret world to which only the desperate sought access. In exchange for her knowledge, or because she was beautiful, or because they wanted to legitimize an illicit woman, the press sought to conceal her secret by describing her beauty, her outfit, her walk, and by labeling her a "registered nurse." By her own admission, she was no nurse. In fact, she had no job or career per say. She was a fixer, a procurer, a dealer of information, a friend to the friendless, and a friend to the fallen. Actually, there is no good title for what she was. In short, she knew the names of abortion doctors and how to arrange for their expertise. Her testimony was the prosecution's best chance at proving Jacobs had a motive to kill Mann.[1]

Though no one was sure of her exact age, Miner, also known as "Miss Minor," was probably in her thirties in 1923. She always refused to give her date of birth and claimed her mother had kept it a secret. As she explained, "My mother had an overweening desire" to conceal her own age. For this "reason she would never give us her age nor tell me mine. . . . If my life depended upon it I could not even hazard a guess this minute as to my age."[2] She also claimed to have been born in Los Angeles and educated in a convent school. She had apparently lived in various parts of the country, including Florida and Kansas. Being well traveled was something she attributed to her career as an actress in a touring company, though it may have had more to do with her mother's frequent marriages. There are indications that Miner, who lived in an apartment on the Fifth Street hill and in a second apartment among the wealthy in Coronado, attempted careers as a dress designer and a scenario writer for motion pictures. In the mid-twenties, she found limited local fame writing profiles of celebrities and descriptions of the homes of the wealthy in "Sidelights on Life," which appeared in the Sunday women's section of the *San Diego Union*. Her greatest fame came in 1928 when she attempted to sell a set of forged love letters she asserted belonged to Abraham Lincoln and Ann Rutledge to *Atlantic Monthly*. When denounced as a forger, she claimed that the contents had been communicated to her psychically from the realm of the dead.[3]

What made her think she could pull off the scam? Perhaps it was her beauty. Nevertheless, as her contemporary culture understood it, beauty alone could not explain why some women always had lovers. It took more than beauty for a woman to find success selling "loveliness to eager eyes on some stage of the town." What Wilma Miner had was charm, "which is the genius of women." According to *Harper's Bazaar*, "These women felt their beauty, as a man of genius feels his greatness beating within him demanding expression." The magazine assured its readers that "it is not enough that one should sit and be beautiful; something had to be done about it." There was a mandate to make sure "as many men as possible" knew of one's beauty and were made "miserable" because of it. "And beauty must be served—produced, perfumed, clothed, framed—seen adored and desired. All this takes intelligence and—art. When it comes to expressing their beauty in manifold and delirious ways, the great enchantresses take, as all genius must, infinite pains."[4] Indeed, Wilma Miner "proved to be a handsome woman with a curvaceous figure, seductive gray green eyes, and an appealing ingenious manner," or so wrote a man investigating her background during the forgery scandal. Those at the *Atlantic* had no idea she had once helped women find abortions. Moreover, the public did not know about her life as a forger until the 1970s, when editors at the magazine began to publish their autobiographies.[5]

She was dangerous because she felt no shame in using her beauty. On the contrary, she knew it was her greatest power. Besides, it worked. She beguiled the editor of the *Atlantic* for almost a year, causing him to write, "Isn't it strange . . . that sometimes one feels as though they have known a person a long time, although their hours together may have been very brief." In other words, "Miss Miner's personal charm" was all the evidence he needed that the Abraham Lincoln letters were real.[6]

Thankfully for the *Atlantic,* an investigator discovered that, though she was pretending to be a "dauntless youth," by the late twenties she was in her forties. She had been married twice and was unsure of the name of her father. Her mother had at least five marriages and several cohabitations. People of Emporia, Kansas, where Miner and her mother lived for a time, remembered the mother and daughter as being "too pleasure-loving." The implications of the background check were clear: what made her untrustworthy was her sexual past. What motivated her to push for fame and social position, according to the investigator, was that she wanted to leave behind her "desultory marginal life. . . . she yearned" to be someone important.[7] Although her greatest fame as a forger of Lincoln letters was yet to come, her sexual background and itinerant life made her important in 1922 because she held the keys to the underworld.

Miner came to know of Fritzie Mann's condition when Louis Jacobs called in search of the name of the physician a "friend" of Miner's had visited in Los Angeles the previous summer. She did not know Jacobs well. She had only met him a few times at parties and through mutual friends. Though Jacobs spoke in veiled terms and offered no specifics, Miner knew he was trying to arrange an abortion. Her loyalty to their shared social network motivated Miner to help Jacobs as he sought a solution to Mann's "trouble."[8]

Meanwhile, Jacobs had kept up a correspondence with Mann, who was living at the Rosslyn Hotel in Los Angeles. His letter of

December 6 began, "Sorry—but I think the whole thing was engineered wrongly." Writing as though he did not need to explain the subject or would rather not explain, just in case, he attempted to placate Mann: "Of course—a delay—while inconvenient—should not worry you. It may be all the better for you. Will inform you as soon as I can definitely determine how to go about it." As though he were worldlier than she was, he explained, "You see physicians like to keep their business to themselves—and not allow anyone to get anything on them. Which of course is perfectly businesslike but sometimes inconvenient." Then he hinted at something larger: "The enclosed notice please return as I have to forward it to my attorneys." There are also moments where one captures a sense of just how in over their heads Mann and Jacobs were: "In the meantime keep a stiff upper life—and your courage high. I am sure everything will turn out OK. Should anyone you go to question you—you may tell them that you are an arrested case of pulmonary tuberculosis in 1916 and are worried that if carried all the way thru" the pregnancy would "re-activate the disease." "Above all," she had to tell the doctor that she was "a married woman! Yours. Louis L. Jacobs"[9]

His telegram of December 18 reveals that Jacobs's anxiety had heightened: "Expect reply to my letter which was written last Tuesday any minute. My men must be out of town if I do not hear today will call up and as soon as I hear will let you know. Hope you're getting along OK, Sincerely, Louis L. Jacobs." By December 20 he had given up on his "men" and fully turned to Wilma Miner for help.[10]

"Do you know Mrs. Miner who use to trot around with Leo Greenbaum?" the prominent grocery store owner in San Diego. Jacobs wrote to Mann repeatedly and described Miner as "the soul of discretion and a good sport." Then came the proposition: "How would you like her to take you to a specialist she knows in LA? Of course, I mentioned no names but the best way to accomplish results rapidly is to go with her. I am sure she can be trusted." His manipulations of Mann to protect himself always made it sound like it was in her best interest. However, Jacobs could quickly turn on a dime and seem almost jovial: "I am learning lots of things but then that's the way things go. Let me know immediately and I will forward full instructions."[11]

In sending Wilma Miner to Los Angeles, Jacobs was attempting to limit Mann's choices.

Throughout the entire history of Fritzie Mann, there were many women. The flappers, her mother, her sister—yet none of them had the kind of power Miner had. In the twenties there were two kinds of prohibition. One concerned alcohol. The other concerned information on sexuality, contraceptives, and abortion. The latter prohibition assumed that anything concerning sex would cause temptation and lust. The laws against abortion forbid the procedure while also making discussion of it an obscenity. In a world where nothing could be published or shared,[12] Miner's power came from knowing people and informing. In this instance, what she knew was that, although he was a doctor, Jacobs could find a solution to his problem only by speaking to a woman. He was thrusting Mann into a secret world where only desperate women lived and where no one seemed comfortable saying the word "abortion."

As it turned out, Miner's "friend" had also once been in a "delicate condition," already had a family, and was married. She had not felt "strong" enough or "equal to going through it," which could be inferred as giving birth "again, and she sought the services of a physician for that reason." Miner had helped her "friend" make contact and work her way through the maze of illicit southern California.[13]

Miner explained to Jacobs, during one of their many phone calls, that she did not recall the name of the doctor but knew where he worked. She went to the Los Angeles telephone directory and looked through the list of physicians, hoping to find a name that seemed familiar. A few days later, Jacobs called again. She gave him the name of Dr. Frank E. Young.

Jacobs wrote to Mann on December 5, 1922: "Now read carefully—Go To see Dr. F. P. Young, Black Building. *Tell him you were sent by Miss Miner* (if he asks you) of San Diego—who saw him a few months ago with a friend and who recommends him most highly." Then he shifted into his paternalistic tone: "Be diplomatic—tell him that they have stopped for two months and that you are feeling terrible—intense nausea—much vomiting—dizziness—unable to hold your job if things are not remedied—etc. He is a good man—so don't worry—and write me the results."

Jacobs's anxiety was in full view at this point, and he did not hesitate to remind Mann of the most important part: "Don't call up—because I am moving and don't know where I'll be. Above all *don't tell him you were sent by a doctor!* Best Luck."[14]

It was not until the third call that Jacobs explained to Miner that he wanted the name of the physician for a "friend" in Los Angeles who had been secretly married and been deserted. "She is ill and badly in need of medical attention. She is a very nice girl, a nice family, and she has appealed to me, and I would like to help her out and do all I could for her. I gave her the name of the physician, and the address, and she went there, and was unable to find anybody by that name." He suggested that Miner was mistaken about the name of the physician. He went on to explain that the woman was a dancer and "had quite a career ahead of her," but only "if she can get on her feet and get all right, she can go to the physician in San Francisco."

All of their subsequent phone calls followed the same "theme," Miner said. "About the young lady, and her condition, and how anxious he was to help her out." Miner found it "peculiar" that the "young lady" could not reach the physician. After all, she had the address, name, and phone number. Jacobs persisted, she said, and he continued to say, "If I could see you and talk with you personally . . . I could tell you what a worthy case this is." To Mann he wrote: "The lady in question has just informed me that she will be glad to go up—and will let me know when. I told her as instructed that you were secretly married and that your hubby left and that you were feeling frightfully on account of the whole thing. I mentioned no names. Will let you know when to meet her. Hope you are feeling better."

Jacobs's pleading suggests anxiety and desperation, but buried in his instructions to Mann is also the idea that only the earnest, well-intentioned girl should have access to the special knowledge of the secret procedure. Only the innocent girl could justify this action. An experienced woman was a different matter altogether.

In trying to shape Miner's perception of Mann, and in scripting Mann's hoped-for interaction with the doctor, Jacobs revealed that the idea of the "fallen girl" was a widespread notion in the early twenties. Even social crusaders trying to help these girls reported that three types of women were the patients of abortionists and midwives: rich women and the girls who worked in department stores; women whose husbands were out of work or had too many children already and could not support an extra child, and "the betrayed girl." The reformers were unsure if the largest group of women seeking abortions were the wealthy women or the department store clerks, but they were sure that these women sought abortions because they felt having a child would ruin all of their fun and force them to settle down. The demographic that provoked the greatest sympathy was "the betrayed girl" because love had led her astray.[15] The alternative to abortion was one of the numerous maternity homes and hospitals in the nation where "good girls" were "herded together . . . with girls of other classes—bad girls who are sometimes so tough that they glory in their badness." Opponents objected to the hospitals because they were "a melting pot," which was not a term of endearment in a Jazz Age America, which had a growing Ku Klux Klan and frequent race riots.[16]

Maternity homes were places women went to have their children in seclusion, under the guise of putting babies up for adoption. Some were "secret"; others functioned openly by calling themselves hospitals, but they refused oversight from medical boards and nursing organizations. Still others were legitimate charity homes run by the Salvation Army.[17] In San Diego, maternity homes frequently assisted women in finding abortions.

If events in other cities are any indication, some women who used maternity homes discovered that their babies were sold rather than legitimately adopted. In some places women paid to have their children sold, but not in all cases. In other homes, the receiving families paid for the children. Moreover, the women in the hospitals had to pay for their time in the ward, which led to the sale of babies. It was a growth business for the proprietors, who justified their actions by saying the "traffic in babies" was defensible if one could find "people decent enough to take illegitimate children."[18] However, public health officials were frequently unable to trace such infants. In Chicago, when they followed up on some addresses subpoenaed from maternity homes, they found the addresses to be false. In Los Angeles health officers concluded, "It would be impossible to say how many babies vanish each year leaving no clue to their fate. Many babies are taken for adoption" and then sold.[19]

San Diego's Coroner Kelly is a vital source for understanding abortion, the illegal system and the procedure, in the twenties. He saw that the real crime of the maternity homes was not that they were creating social leveling. Rather, he denounced the maternity homes by writing an open letter to the press in which he declared San Diego a place where "life is held too cheap." He went on to explain that the county maternity homes, facilities where unwed mothers could seek care, were trafficking in abortions. The maternity home employees would take women to Tijuana to have the procedure and then return them to the home for convalescence. According to Kelly, this illegal system resulted in lives being "needlessly and wantonly sacrificed by the criminal recklessness or carelessness" of those administering the abortions and those who ran the maternity homes. Routinely, he autopsied the bodies of women who had died from the illegal procedure. His denouncement was on behalf of the women who died because their only choice was to trust their lives to a medical shell game in which illicit entrepreneurs profited.

Recall that his office had death by abortion on the list of possible explanations of Mann's death. Evidence of the procedure was one of the first things they checked. Many opposed abortion because of the rumors they heard; Kelly's opinion came from seeing the bodies of the women who perished. His experience made him one of the few people willing to acknowledge how the system of abortions actually worked.[20] Abortionists were bold. Basically, they placed classified ads in newspapers advertising their services under the guise of being a hospital, which suggests how hard it was to prosecute them and how few were prosecuted. Nevertheless, what is known about being in this situation is how difficult it was to be an unwed mother in the Jazz Age.[21]

The move to connect abortion to vice and immorality culminated in the Comstock Laws, starting in 1873, which made it illegal to send "obscene, lewd or lascivious," "immoral," or "indecent" publications through the mail and made it a misdemeanor for anyone to sell, give away, or posses an obscene book, pamphlet, picture, drawing, or advertisement. The act gave the federal government control over sexual and family matters via the post office, whose job it was to inspect the mail for "obscene information." Information on abortion and contraception came to be included in the final bill without debate or discussion. No one in Congress dared to speak out against the legislation, because the congressmen were too afraid of being labeled immoral.[22]

There is evidence that people who wanted information about contraception found it. For example, the average number of children born to white women declined from 4.4 to 2.1 between 1880 and 1940. For African Americans the decline was a dramatic 7.5 to 3.0. Those against the Comstock Laws ran ads in newspapers about how to prevent pregnancy. For the poor and working class it was essential to limit the number of children, through contraception or abortion, in order to feed the family. Smaller families also meant that these groups would have some protection from those social crusaders who supported sterilization campaigns against the poor and immigrant classes or preached that laws were needed to force "egotistical" women to have maternal responsibilities and to fulfill their "obligations."[23]

The common perception of abortion was that the procedure existed outside the realm of regular family planning and that midwives were to blame. This idea stemmed in part from the fact that social reformers rarely asked women if doctors performed their procedure. Instead, they would specifically ask about midwives. Likewise, the question of abortion rarely appeared in surveys asking doctors about their services. The available information about abortion comes from mortality and conviction reports as well as a few university studies. A 1917 study of women who came to the Washington University Dispensary in St. Louis found that physicians and midwives performed, on average, the same number of abortions. Of the fifty-one women in the study, 24 percent had seen a doctor and 24 percent had seen a midwife. A larger study in New York City reported that between 1925 and 1950 midwives performed abortions in 22.5 percent of cases and physicians in 27.9 percent of cases. Since most health care happened at home, either the home of a physician or the patient's home, it would be difficult to fully know the rate of abortions. Beginning in the twenties and thirties, larger numbers of physicians opted to become part of hospitals and began to create oversight boards. As they did, health care shifted away from midwives and homecare into institutions. This shift made it easier to control women's access to birth control information and to abortions.[24]

By the twenties, the original Comstock Law and the subsequent state laws that echoed and built on that act had suppressed the availability of contraceptive materials as part of a crusade to enforce female sexual restraint and men's virtue. Women's sexuality became part of anti-vice laws and policing, which placed it in the realm of prostitution, alcohol, drug use, and porn mongering. Moreover, the Comstock Laws warped the distinctions between the medical uses of contraceptives, the information concerning contraceptives, and erotic publications. Medical textbooks, for example, could be censored if they discussed condoms, medicated sponges, or abortifacients.[25]

Those who spoke against women managing their own reproductive health made two primary arguments, which quickly formed social barriers against women controlling their own fertility.[26] One argument was that any woman who attempted to reduce or negate pregnancies failed to meet her responsibilities within her marriage and her duties, if she was a white woman, to the white patriarchal state. This argument drew on the social fears of young women being seduced away from purity and family by men they encountered in the shops and mills where they worked. Sexual assault was no doubt responsible for some seeking abortions. In Alameda and Los Angeles County courts between 1910 and 1920, 28 percent of the statutory rape cases were forcible assault. Of the female victims of sexual assault, 43 percent were attacked by male relatives and 27 percent by neighbors or close family friends. Rape in the workplace accounted for 17 percent of cases. Most victims were employed in offices, shops, or factories; only one was a domestic servant.[27] When women sought abortions, the laws transformed them from citizens, to victims, to criminals.

The second argument contended that contraception and abortion were dangerous to a woman's mental health. There were doctors who supported these claims.[28] The arguments drew out the fine line that distinguished the progressive woman from the delinquent girl. The women writing about abortion and the rights movement did not tell maudlin stories of working-class girls, low wages, broken families, and urban decay. Instead, they did surveys and collected data. With thousands of respondents, this generation of social crusaders believed they truly understood the circumstances of youth. Often their conclusions suggested that the sexual energy of young women be redirected into religion, athletics, education, and marriage.[29] Progressive crusaders were contributing to the process that transformed girls like Mann from women asserting agency into girls who were objects in the debate.

Nevertheless, many women still sought the information and means by which they, and not the state, could control their bodies. For women in Jazz Age San Diego there were options—and not just in Tijuana. The police did arrest licensed physicians in San Diego for performing the "illegal operations" in places ranging from maternity homes to hotel rooms. One poor woman was even drugged by her husband and transported all the way to Imperial Valley, where an abortionist performed the procedure against her will. Each operation occurred under the shadow of potential death. Women succumbed because they received too much anesthesia. Hemorrhaging was a possibility, as was blood poisoning resulting from infection.[30]

For a point of comparison, it is useful to turn to New York City and Chicago reformers and their numerous studies of perceived social ills. Before the war, reformers estimated that there were 30,000 abortions conducted in Chicago each year. Skilled abortionists charged $50 to $100 for the procedure, which was too much for working-class women, who had to turn to lesser-trained midwives for assistance.[31] A study of New York City conducted in 1917 revealed that, of a sample of 464 women, 192 knew of no contraceptive methods. The remaining 272 women knew of one or more methods, more or less effectual, for the prevention of conception. Of the 192 women who were ignorant of the use of contraceptives, more than half (104) had a history of abortion. In other words, these women averaged two abortions each. In contrast, of the 272 women who knew of one or more contraceptives, only a fourth (72) had undergone abortion.[32] For those who knew about contraceptives and used them, condoms were the favored devices. Clinics in the twenties and thirties reported that the number of couples using some kind of family planning had almost doubled since the turn of the century. Men had learned about prophylactics while serving in World War I and brought those lessons into their homes. The use of condoms to prevent disease meant that condoms were exempt from laws outlawing other forms of birth control. Still, abortions remained common, with 19 percent of Jewish women and 16 percent of Italian women in one New York City study reporting having had an abortion. Moreover, 45 percent of Italian women and 54 percent of Jewish women noted that they knew someone who had an abortion.[33] In the years after World War I, women faced a stark reproductive reality.

Reflecting the unfairness of society at the time, one's reproductive options depended upon one's status. Reformists wanted the establishment of "state institutions where afflicted girls could be taken care of in privacy." They believed "this would do away with the private sanitariums, which now are said to care for the girls and get rid of the babies." Poorer women had more difficulty receiving care from a doctor in general, let alone when seeking illegal abortions. They tended to visit midwives. Because midwives were women and seen as having a lower level of education, social reformers charged them with performing the majority of abortions; in Chicago this was estimated to be three-fourth of abortions, a statistic proposed by the male-dominated medical establishment. In many states there were no training facilities, licensing, or regulation of midwives. Reformers argued that, if midwifes improved their skills, the number of abortions and deaths from abortions might decrease.[34] This might hold true, if midwives were performing the abortions.

For those with money or status, the world of the illegal abortion was very different. Wealthy women could check themselves into legitimate hospitals where their physician would list their procedure not as abortion but as "appendicitis," which shielded the physician from prosecution should a wealthy woman die.[35]

Even knowing that there was a spectrum of patients seeking abortion and an illicit system that stretched from the tenement midwife to the concierge physician, social reformers still targeted those who came from poverty and the "fallen girl," saying, "The only way to eliminate abortionists was to fund lying-in hospitals to care for unfortunate girls." They went on to explain, "The cause and cure for the abortion was in the status given an illegitimate child and until this was changed . . . girls would seek out criminal abortions rather than face the world in shame." They feared there were criminal syndicates in the major cities that, when not running rum, were offering abortions, as though the two kinds of prohibition went together.[36] Therefore, they concluded that "new legislation to revoke licenses of those who perform abortions and to force midwives to record births and deaths" was necessary, as was establishing schools of midwifery within the established hospitals and medical schools.[37]

The perspective of the abortionist differed from that of the reformer. "I am getting too old to stand any more trouble," said Lucy Hagenow, the most notorious of all Chicago's abortionists. In 1922 she was again under arrest for "murder by abortion," meaning a patient of hers had died from the procedure. "I have seen too much of it." At the time, she was nearly eighty, and the newspapers seemed to delight in calling her "aged." "And why do they come to me in the first place?" she demanded of the journalists who had asked the question. "Money, money—that's it. They don't want to spend any money. Of course, they do not want the stigma that attaches to the unwed mother—if society knew no such thing as the illegitimate child this cause would be removed—but greater than this social question is the economic one." The issue of class and money was one everyone seemed to be aware of; still, Hagenow added an uncomfortable dimension to it: "They tell me: I can't afford to go to a hospital and have my baby. I'll lose my job. I'll lose my pay, and I have my mother to support." Money could buy a great deal, she argued. "Most of them," she said, "the ones who have money take their troubles to their family physicians. Those are the cases you never hear of."[38]

Most of the patients who visited Hagenow in the early twenties were like Fritzie Mann. They were working class and young. She summarized for the press: "Their age? Most of them are under thirty—around twenty and even younger. Yes, they have come much younger than twenty. But the older ones come too—mothers of four and five children who are too poor." Though poor, "none of them are ignorant." From her perspective on modern youth, she saw something different than the flapper's critics saw: "I tell you the girl of today is wise. They know every remedy. They have tried them all before they come to me." She claimed that the patients died because "these girls first start out by taking pills—bushels of them. They go from drug store to drug store, buying patent remedies, medicines that ruin their health. In a very few instances, these drugs work but more often they fail."

Indeed, most abortions began not just in secret and in isolation. Some women wanted to conceal more than the fact that they were seeking an abortion. They wanted to hide the truth of having even conceived a child. If there was no one around to witness the birth, then no one could prove there had even been a pregnancy. Such women took ergot, a fungus that could cause poisoning, as an ecbolic. Symptoms of ergot poisoning included madness. It also opened the uterus, caused hemorrhaging, and could kill both the mother and the fetus. In addition, they took lead, which speaks to their desperation. They took tansy, arsenic, colocynth, phosphorus, hellebore, and pennyroyal. Some drugs caused the opening of the uterus, some caused menstruation to begin, and others were simply caustic. All of them were highly poisonous.[39]

Desperation, in Hagenow's perspective, and not stupidity, drove the girls to "try more violent methods, swallow huge quantities of more violent drugs." Still, there were things worse than pills. As she explained to the *Chicago Tribune*, "Finally they try to operate on themselves. Blood poison is the inevitable result." After desperation came disgrace as "they rush to a doctor, who often refuses to treat them." When all else failed, "then [they go] to a midwife who has little or no knowledge of medicine or surgery and who only aggravates their condition," which was Hagenow distinguishing her profession of abortionist from the midwife. "Then to me. They come to me weak and fainting and miserable and pleading for me to help them, as a dope fiend" begs a doctor for more drugs. Hagenow saw herself as the last recourse of the desperate girl.

"I do what I can for them," she said as she stroked her white hair and rubbed her wrinkled hands together. "Most of the time," she concluded, "antiseptic solutions do the work and they recover, but sometimes they are past medical aid." Those were the times when Hagenow's patients died.

How might society stop the increase in abortions and subsequent deaths from abortions? Hagenow brought forth the only answer there was: "How can they be stopped? They can't be."

What she understood, and no one else seemed to, was that "they can be materially reduced by legitimizing every child, by providing retreats for the unwed mother, where she can give birth to her child without economic loss to herself and those dependent upon her, by impressing upon girls the necessity for consulting reputable physicians and educating them to the dangers of home remedies." However, in Hagenow's perspective, it would be impossible to ever completely stop the girl determined to end a pregnancy.[40]

Cases of abortion rarely found their way to the courts unless the procedure proved fatal to the mother. The reason for the lack of court cases was the simplicity of concealing the operation. Also, the woman solicited the operation in secret. Death resulted from recklessness or carelessness. Obstetricians rarely performed the operation, and they were generally the only ones with enough knowledge to be successful. If the abortionist thought they only had to puncture the fetal membranes to cause the expulsion of the uterine contents, then most likely the patient would die. The puncturing did not always cause the abortion. When it did not happen, all parties involved thought they had to take more active measures, sometimes leading to abortion attempts over several days. The woman would eventually hemorrhage or develop septicemia.[41] As it turned out, abortions were as difficult for the layperson to perform as they were to procure.

Still, reformers focused on the patient and the midwives. Society held that the majority of (male) doctors "disliked and hesitated to even trifle with" those seeking abortions, which were "illegal, dangerous, invoked little or no pay as a rule and the sentiment of this local world was all against them," according to novelist Theodore Dreiser. "Besides," as Dreiser imagined a physician thinking in his controversial *An American Tragedy*, "he personally was more or less irritated by these young scamps of boys and girls who were so free to exercise the normal functions of their natures in the first instance but so ready to refuse the social obligations which went with them."[42] Dreiser's account brought the reality to his fiction, but it also offered insight into the larger problem.

For the girl approaching the physician alone, it was a dreadful experience. Dreiser summarized the young woman's emotions: "At the same time, startled by the fact that at last she had reached the place and the moment when, if ever, she must say the degrading truth about herself, she merely sat there, her eyes first upon him, then upon the floor, her fingers beginning to toy with the handle of the small bag she carried." In even approaching a physician, the young woman opened herself up to being morally judged for her sexual activity and for asking the physician to compromise himself. The young woman became, in the eyes of the physician, arrogant and selfish. "In the first place," Dreiser imagined the physician saying, "the thing you want done is something my conscience would not permit me to advise." Then the physician feigned sympathy, "I understand, of course, that you consider it necessary. You and your husband are both young and you probably haven't very much money to go on." Though he was rejecting her, he wanted to be sure to maintain his moral and social position over her by explaining, "Now I know the tendency of the day in some quarters is very much in this direction. . . . There are those who feel it quite all right if they can shirk the normal responsibilities in such cases as to perform these operations, but it's very dangerous . . . legally and ethically as well as medically very wrong." For a moment, he may have felt empathy. Perhaps he desired to protect her from her worst impulse by frightening her because he believed that the woman sought "to escape childbirth die in this way." Yet, no matter how much he tried to make it about the young woman, the physician always came back to himself and limited himself because "it is a prison offense for any doctor." Still, he knew the procedure happened under certain circumstances. "The only excuse," in the mind of the physician " is when the life of the mother, for instance, depends upon such an operation." In summation, the physician felt stuck, "not wishing to enter upon any form of malpractice and at the same time not wishing to appear too discouraging to a young couple." There truly was little he could do for the girl. "Nevertheless," explains Dreiser's omniscient narrator, "this business of a contractual operation or interference with the normal or God arranged life process, well that was a ticklish and unnatural business at best," which physicians wished to avoid.[43]

The problem of doctors—both locating an amenable physician and negotiating the moral terrain—was a perplexing one, which is why Wilma Miner was a necessity. Miner understood the system so well she suggested that she visit Los Angeles to help Mann. At that time, mid-December 1922, Jacobs said to Miner, "I don't think that young lady would welcome any assistance of that nature." Instead, he asked for the name of another physician. Miner volunteered that her "lady friend" had another doctor, a Dr. Bassett.[44]

Jacobs was nervous. He desperately tried to convince Mann, via telephone calls and telegrams, to have the procedure. He was, when faced with this crisis, as Dreiser would describe his fictional character Clyde, "as interesting an illustration of the enormous handicaps imposed by ignorance, youth, poverty, and fear as one could have found." No doubt, Jacobs went through a similar set of problems as the fictional Clyde despite the fact that Jacobs had education and was a physician with professional status. Both came from poor beginnings and both had acquired professional standing. Jacob's family were Jewish immigrants, according to census information. Like Mann, he was trying to escape his immigrant background. At a certain point, Mann became a thing holding him back. As did Clyde in the novel, Jacobs sought out an abortionist. "One thing, however, which caused [Clyde] to pause," Dreiser wrote, "before he ever decided to look up a physician was the problem of who was to approach him and how. To go himself was simply out of the question" because this would implicate him in a crime and potentially tie him indelibly to the pregnant, low-class girl.[45]

Clyde, like Jacobs, attempted to force his girlfriend to go alone. "That leaves me sorta stumped now, unless you're willing to go and see a doctor," Clyde said. "But the trouble with that is they're hard to find—the ones who'll do anything and keep their mouth shut. I've talked with several fellows without saying who it's for. . . . It's against the law, you see." Clyde wondered aloud if his lover would have the "nerve" to go alone. "He paused because," Dreiser wrote, "as he said it, he saw a flicker of shame, contempt, despair at being connected with anything so cheap and shabby, pass over" his lover's face.[46]

Jacobs went through the same system of manipulation as the fictional Clyde but was saved having to look at Mann while he did it. His correspondence was careful. He never made romantic overtures to her or was specific about what kind of procedure he was arranging for her. The message that came up again and again was: "Above all avoid mentioning that a doctor sent you because they will absolutely turn down anything if you say that."[47]

"I think I have found just the woman to help you. . . . She is a good sport."[48]

"Tho I was shocked at your outburst I can scarce blame you," he began in his letter of January 5, by which time Mann was staying in Long Beach with her friend Bernice,

> for I realize your point of view far better than one usually does. However I hope you will soon be well and recognize many things that you have failed hitherto. Miss Miner will meet you at the Hotel Lankershim at noon on Friday. She's registered there. She will make all arrangement. You wired me something about returning one hundred dollars. Please don't do that—but use it to cover incidental expenses. In the meantime I shall wire you to make sure that you will get the right steer. Of course I told her that you were secretly married and that he has left you or you left him—I did not know which, that I was interested in you—professionally—I hope everything will turn out OK—because Miss Miner is a peach—and she'll help you as much as she can. Lot's of luck![49]

His letters detailed how she should approach certain physicians to gain assistance by telling them "you have suffered from pulmonary tuberculosis and if something isn't done it may come back again."[50] In another letter he upbraided Mann for complaining about her health, saying, "I'm surprised at your outburst. But don't think you are the only one who has been sick." Moreover, he wrote, "I have been suffering from the 'flu' myself." He advised her not to mention his name or to even mention that a physician had referred her; after all, he had a reputation to protect.[51] Sadly for Jacobs, Mann resisted and refused to comply with his plans.

Two weeks after their conversation in which Jacobs asked by phone for the name of a second doctor, a "mutual friend," as she referred to greengrocer Leo Greenbaum in her court testimony, called Wilma Miner and asked, "Are you contemplating—are you still contemplating that shopping trip to Los Angeles after the holidays?" She answered in the affirmative and then Dr. Jacobs took the phone. "Well Miss Miner," he said, "could I get you to see this young lady while you are in Los Angeles?" Also, "Would you try, while up there to really find the name and address of this physician and give it to her when she calls?"

Then Jacobs said, "Her name is Miss Mann."

Miner replied, "Not Fritzie Mann?" She had seen Mann perform and had met her the previous summer. "I will know her when I see her."[52]

To Mann he wrote, "I shall know definitely by Monday when Billy," Wilma Miner's nickname, "can come up. She is surprised that you cannot get in touch with Young—as someone else shared his office and would know of his whereabouts. In the meantime [I] have moved and they have disconnected my phone—I do not intend to have one at the hospital as I don't know how long I'll stay. So if you need anything in a hurry wire me. Hope you are well and taking good care of yourself."[53]

To Miner he offered, "Can't I help defray your expenses, since you are doing this favor for me?"

"No, thank you; I am going up any way." Miss Miner loved to shop in Los Angeles. "As you know, and I wouldn't think of such a thing." After that conversation, the only communication she received from Jacobs was a letter. "I destroyed it," she would later tell the police and eventually the court. She explained it contained a check for $35 and one line: "Just a token of appreciation."[54]

In an undated note, Jacob's correspondence with Mann became clipped: "Just returned to the hospital and found your telegram. Wrote you to tell me all particulars but have not heard one word." Again he made himself the center of attention: "Am just recuperating from an attack of influenza and am pretty low in every way." Then he pleaded, "Let me know what happened. Hope that you are recovering rapidly. . . . Sincerely."[55]

Miner did indeed go to the hotel, the Lankershim, between noon and one on the fifth of January, ten days before Mann's body was found on the beach. However, Mann did not show. Miner, always dutiful, sent a wire to Jacobs: "All arrangements made. Party did not arrive. Wire them to meet me Lankershim Lobby Saturday noon." Jacobs obediently did so. Again, Mann did not appear.[56]

Jacobs's persistence was unflagging, and he made a long-distance call to press Miner. Since Jacobs had not provided Mann's address, Miner could do little more. He acquiesced to Miner's suggestions that she needed more information and gave up Mann's phone number in Long Beach.

Fritzie Mann had already left town.

9

RABBIT

A. F. Wagner, the autopsy surgeon from Los Angeles, testified on behalf of the defense regarding whether or not sand would enter the lungs of a person drowned in the ocean. To do so, he ran a test to simulate drowning. He went to Fisherman's Cove at Laguna Beach, located halfway between Los Angeles and San Diego, where there is plenty of sand, he testified, around five in the afternoon. The waves were coming in. He recalled for the court that the waves "pretty near broke us up—threw us—we got saturated with them. . . . Anybody that drowned in there would surely have sand" in their lungs. He used a rabbit, a large rabbit, as a test subject. "They have the same windpipe," he justified, "bronchi and lungs, larynx, as a human being." Recalling that day, "There was sand in the water and on the beach, yes; so much so that shoes were just covered with sand, and the rabbit's fur was filled with sand—everything was sand."[1] By making Mann's drowning analogous to the drowning of a rabbit, Wagner aided the defense in their magic trick of transforming Fritzie Mann from the victim to the fiend.

The rabbit test was a sleight of hand in which they surrounded the jury with medical jargon and replaced the facts of her death with assumptions about her life. The first step was to discredited Kelly, Shea, and Thompson, who had ruled Mann's death a drowning and murder the cause of the drowning. To their credit, these doctors never waivered or changed the facts they presented regarding Mann's body. Nevertheless, their science, their procedure, and the faith they placed in the corpse revealing the truth were all on trial. The next step was to challenge the validity of Mann's body and thereby disgrace her life.

In the pages that follow, Wagner speaks for himself. His words are important. He was following a script that began with the rabbit and ended with discrediting Mann on the basis of her gender. By the end of his testimony, she was no longer the victim of a murderer. Wagner made Mann out to be the killer of herself and her unborn child. His testimony attempted to declare Fritzie Mann guilty of being a neurotic woman.

Pretending the rabbit was Fritzie Mann, Wagner submerged the rabbit for two minutes, until it died. Submersion eventually causes asphyxia. There is at first an attempt on the part of the animal to breathe. Then the animal senses danger and struggles to escape. At the same time, the animal fixes its thorax, which happens voluntarily. The animal suspends respiration in order to prevent the water from entering the air passages. Soon the respiratory centers move beyond the control of volition. Involuntary respiratory movements are set up by which the lungs draw in the water. The water penetrates the alveoli. The trachea opens. The glottis no longer has control. One might assume that upon submersion the lungs draw in water. That assumption is false. The air passages resist.[2]

Having killed the rabbit, Wagner waited until the next morning to dissect it. He wanted twelve to fifteen hours to lapse. Wagner reported to the court, "A great deal of the experiments that are pointed out in our authorities are based upon animal experimentations such as this." He had opened up the larynx and the trachea, run his finger along the inner portion while wearing a glove and found nothing.

Though the rabbit version of Fritzie Mann may have drowned in two minutes, when a person drowns, unassisted, it rarely happens from continuous submersion. Even when a person falls from a great height above the water level and consequently sinks to a great depth, they generally return momentarily to the surface.

The involuntary movement of the limbs helps to bring the body up into the air. In general, it would have taken longer than two minutes to drown.[3] Had the rabbit Fritzie Mann been unconscious and left to bob about on the surface until it drowned, maybe a comparison could have been made between the flapper and the unfortunate lapin.

Even when he took off his gloves, Wagner found no sand. He saw no sand either. Then he took the scalpel and scraped at the congested mucous membrane, "which should be there in all cases of drowning,—the mucus membrane congestion gets thicker, and the little grains of sand that are not washed out by the current, as the water comes out of the lungs, will then bury themselves in that mucus, sticky material." The aspiration causes a secretion of mucus in the bronchial tubes. The mucus blocks the finer bronchi. Even if the victim dies of prolonged submersion, the heart keeps beating. The heart remains hopeful even though the mucus continues to flow.[4] Nevertheless, despite the viscosity of the mucus, Wagner saw and felt no sand. It was only when he used a microscope, a piece of equipment Shea did not have when examining Mann, that Wagner found the sand. Then he asserted that rabbits and humans were similar in his experience, saying, "I found that the rabbit's lungs in general corresponded exactly with my experience in examining human beings, and that is that I didn't find any free water in the bronchi or in the air passages." He based his conclusions on his experience rather than on multiple test rabbits drowned in various ways. The rabbit confirmed what he already believed. Thus, there was no need for further scientific inquiry.

Wagner also asserted that the bodies of victims could not be trusted because of the postmortem treatments. The water with sand he explained, "runs out—as the body is turned over, and especially an embalmed body that an undertaker prepares for burial—they get out all that water; and when they draw off the blood all that water that would remain there is absorbed into the circulation so that your air passages are practically empty." What he did not tell the jury was that a human being begins to experience asphyxia one to two minutes after submersion, but death usually does not occur for five to six minutes. Some people last longer than others because they hold their breath.[5]

"Now, in the lungs, however, on sectioning the rabbit's lungs, I could squeeze out not only froth, I did find froth, and you always find froth—but also fluid, liquid water, in sufficient liquid form to recognize it as water." Had he drowned a second Fritzie rabbit in a bathtub, he could have compared the water in the lungs. The water would have contained soap.[6] What the rabbit teaches us about the experimenter is that Wagner saw all experiments as limited. Once the conclusion he sought presented itself, no other tests were needed. "Now you can only go so far in dissecting a rabbit's lungs with scissors or a knife. I didn't make microscopical sections of the lungs because I had demonstrated the sand was in the mucus membrane of the upper air passages by microscope." Then he reminded the jury that Shea had not used a microscope, saying, "and it showed you could not tell it by your naked finger, by rubbing it over the air passages."

What all involved were neglecting was that in a case for drowning there is also the problem of shallow water. Most adults do not drown in shallow water. The reason is obvious: they would just stand up. Drowning by placing the head in water contained in a bathtub usually indicated suicide or murder. In these cases, intoxication or other causes could assist the death. Epilepsy might play a role in this type of death. Helplessness could be a factor, which is the reason so many babies died of bathtub drowning at the hands of adults. Such murderers might then throw the body of the infant into a pond or river, hoping to obscure the real cause of death, which of course was impossible because forensic doctors could tell the difference between pond water and tap water. In the case of adults who died in this way, investigators had to examine the body for marks of foul play, such as the bruises and abrasion on Mann's forehead, because, much like rabbits, a person needs assistance to drown in shallow water. Except in the case of the very old, the very drunk, or the very young, it would be difficult to murder anyone in this way, unless the victim was rendered incapable of resisting.[7]

Wagner, who spoke so fast the court reporter did not bother to insert punctuation into the testimony, finally paused to breathe. In that moment the lawyers failed to notice the flaws in the experiment. It was faulty. She did not die at Laguna Beach. Mann's beach was not some beautiful soft stretch of sand. It was hard baked. It was solid enough to park a car on. It was rocky and covered in weeds. It was firmament. For the experiment to be valid, the surgeon would have needed the same stretch of beach.

The specifics of the beach had been lost to time and poor evidence management.[8] The judge, attorneys, court officers, and jury had all traveled out to the Mann's beach to see the place where her body was found. The whole point of visiting the beach was that this specific stretch of sand was important, but as they wandered no one seemed to understand why it was important. "Now," Judge Spencer Milton Marsh began, "is it stipulated that this is the vicinity of where the stake was?" He meant the stake the police set the day after the discovery of the body. They had not thought to do it when they found Mann. Thus, the next day they tried hard to remember where everything was, to draw a map and place markers. In answer to the judge's question, defense attorney Paul Schenck had to reply, "Some place here, yes, your honor."

It was past 3:30 in the afternoon, and they were all standing on the beach. The judge asked, "It is agreed that some of the witnesses at least indicated that the blanket was found on the bank about a third of the way up from the end of the rail, where our car stands,—about a third of the way up to the grade there; and that in the same vicinity, somewhat further away from the bank, that the vanity case and handbag were found?" Mr. Schenck had replied, "None of us know exactly where it is; but they know what the testimony is." In this moment, he was both a member of the defense team and a man willing to accept that there was no evidence. Mr. Selleck, from the prosecution team, admitted that he did not know for sure, either.

As Wagner explained to the court, he attended the University of Pennsylvania medical school and had specialized in forensic medicine since moving to California in 1905. He had also obtained a position of great renown as a professor of pathology and bacteriology in the Dental Department of the University of Southern California. Though his background was dentistry, he still worked as an autopsy surgeon for Los Angeles County.

His claim to fame was his participation in the 1918 Gibbons case. Mrs. Gibbons had admitted to buying the cyanide and giving it to Mr. Gibbons. She also admitted that she married

Mr. Gibbons without securing a divorce from her first husband. The district attorney put aside the bigamy charges for a while. The real problem was whether Mr. Gibbons died from poisoning. Professors of pharmacy, toxicology, and chemistry all concluded that they had not found cyanide in Mr. Gibbons's tissues. However, other experts said that cyanide was present. The district attorney had a choice to make. Was he going to charge Mrs. Gibbons with murder? The Los Angeles coroner stated that he would sign a death certificate declaring that Mr. Gibbons came to his end from natural causes. Supporting the coroner's position was Wagner's finding that Gibbons had died of pulmonary hemorrhage due to tuberculosis, of which he was already dying before his wife allegedly began to plot his murder. The police suspected cyanide poisoning, but Wagner had found no evidence. The grand jury refused to indict, and Mrs. Gibbons went free.[9]

In his capacity for the county, Wagner did not regularly appear in the newspaper coverage for the higher profile cases in 1922. Instead, he did turn up as the only witness called in a pool hall murder. One man killed another man over the placement of a cue ball. The men fought. The fighting subsided. Then one man shot the other in cold blood.[10] Wagner also worked a suicide of an automobile salesman. Powder burns indicated that the salesman had killed himself. However, before the salesman did the deed, he went to the trouble of shooting up his own car on a deserted road. He used several guns to make it look like a gang slaying, but he forgot that he had placed one of the bullets from the "unrelated" gun in his pocket.[11] Both cases required no special forensic skills to solve.

In the San Diego Jacobs trial, Wagner was a paid expert for the defense. Being from Los Angeles, he was acquainted with attorney Schenck, the lead attorney for the defense. As did Shea and Kelly, Wagner had to work out of mortuaries.[12] He had to testify in court. He saw a great many victims of drowning. He estimated that he had done a total of nine thousand autopsies in his career, and those who died from drowning were "about 35, 40, or 50, as near as I could get to it." As he recalled for the court, all but one had drowned in the ocean.

"Doctor," the defense began. "Assume the postmortem performed over the body and the card," a reference to the cards kept by Dr. Shea as he autopsied Mann's body. "What would you call the cause of death from that statement?"

"Well, I couldn't arrive at any intelligent cause of death, unless there was some other facts brought out," replied Dr. Wagner.

"Then, so far as that that I have read being the contents of the card, it would not enable you to determine any cause of death?"

"It would not."

Was froth in the mouth or lungs "peculiar to any cause of death, any sudden cause of death?" Wagner answered, "It is not, except as a class of deaths; it is not peculiar to any form of death, that is, it is not peculiar to drowning, and it is not peculiar—it is not the only symptom and important symptom of any one cause of death." Did Wagner have experience with this type of frothy mucus, which is a reference to the findings of Mann's body? "Many times," Wagner indicated but could not give an estimate because of the nine thousand bodies he estimated having seen throughout his career. Most recently, he had seen it in someone who was hit by a truck.

They then moved on to his knowledge of water deaths. The questions were general so that he could be an expert but without specific knowledge of Mann. The doctor explained that he did not always find water in the stomach, at least not invariably; sometimes he did and sometimes he did not. In the case of an ocean drowning, Wagner said that there would be sand, undetectable to the naked human eye, in the air passages. The doctor prevaricated: "Well, no, I really never looked for sand in the stomach. If I had water in the stomach and wanted to know whether it was salt or not, I merely put it in a test tube and put silver nitrate—very simple test—and showed the excess amount of chlorides." All of this was speculation since he had not examined Mann or similar drownings on the same beach.

Wagner's testimony was not the only time generalizations were essential to the case. To discredit the prosecution's criminologists who specialized in handwriting and fingerprints, the defense called bank clerks to discuss the signatures on the Blue Sea Cottage register. The bank clerk swore they saw handwriting all day long and could tell if the signatures from the hotel matched.[13]

The defense's goal in calling Wagner down from Los Angeles was to suggest that Shea, Thompson, and Kelly had not looked for evidence of poisoning because the body was embalmed before they could. The implication was that the San Diego team was insufficient in their knowledge and tactics and the defense's Los Angeles surgeon the better, more knowledgeable scientist. "Well, we have frequently found cyanide, where the body has been embalmed," Wagner began. "Of course, it was just a small dose of cyanide of potassium, only enough to kill, had been taken, and no more, and then the body thoroughly embalmed by formaldehyde, it might even then make it impossible to get tests for cyanide; but most cases you can find cyanide even after the body has been embalmed."

Yes, of course cyanide could be found after embalming. However, Shea, Thompson, and Kelly were not in the habit of looking for poisoning after embalming when they saw no evidence before the embalming. Cyanide causes the tissue to swell and the blood to disintegrate. A consequence of the poisoning is that the blood presents a brownish-red color. As a result, the appearance of the stomach at the necropsy, in a case of typical potassium cyanide poisoning, was stunning. The autopsy surgeon would see an organ with generally contracted walls. To the touch, it would have felt thickened. Inside would be a large quantity of soapy, slimy, hemorrhagic mucus. The mucous membrane throughout would be a diffuse blood-red or brownish-red color. It too would be markedly swollen. The crest of the rugae would appear transparent and again soapy and slimy to the touch. These alterations would be apparent through the mucous membrane and inside the submucosa.[14]

On the use of cyanide, Wagner was in disagreement with a significant number of scientists and autopsy surgeons of the time. Victims of cyanide generally vomited. Lesions appeared in the esophagus and the pharynx after death, which was one motivation for continuing an autopsy over several days. Unfortunately, the poison, if given in small doses, could break down in the body, making detection difficult, which was why autopsy surgeons also paid attention to the smell of the body while they waited for the other effects to emerge.[15]

Schenck continued to ask Wagner to speculate—and implicitly to submerge the jury in what must have sounded like facts but were merely his musings. "Eclampsia," for example, "only occurs in women that are pregnant. We don't call those convulsions that occur in other conditions eclampsia. Eclampsia is a term that is partially limited to convulsions that occur in pregnant women, or women who have just been delivered of children."

"With reference to the susceptibility to it," asked the defense, "is there any difference between legitimate and illegitimate pregnancies?"

"Why, we have good authority for saying that is more frequent in illegitimate—those illegitimately pregnant, and that is simply because of the anxiety that is connected with the condition; but any anxiety, due to any other cause—financial trouble, or family troubles, of any sort—any anxiety, would hasten the condition that is called eclampsia."

Dr. Wagner's next trick was to suggest that Fritzie Mann killed herself. At that moment, Fritzie Mann became a rabbit of folklore. They knew so little about her, because she was so successful at obfuscating, that in place of facts they had to speculate. In African and Native American tradition, the rabbit is a trickster figure that outsmarts all the other animals. Given her love of costume and self-mythologizing, one might associate Mann with these legends. On the other hand, in the early twentieth century European children's stories told of how the moon punished the rabbit. The rabbit ended up with a split lip and a fear of the moon. The rabbit "had been brave before, but now he is the most timid of animals, for he is afraid of everything and everybody." In Russian and Yiddish folklore, the rabbit is always a coward. It was easy for Wagner to see Mann this way. After all, he emphasized, she was pregnant and had no means. He thought she had walked out to the beach that night and ended herself. From Wagner's perspective, it seemed a logical conclusion to the life of a girl.[16] For anyone familiar with Mann and the details of the case, it was problematic to hear Mann reduced from victim to criminal. If she had drowned in the ocean, how did she manage to keep her shoes on? These small details were inconsequential to the defense, which wanted to depict Mann as the criminal in her own death.

"Now, on the question of anxiety you speak of," began the defense, "is there any difference, according to your experience or the authorities, or both, in the mental state of a woman during the period of gestation, or while she is pregnant?"

"Well not in all women, but, then, we have the tendency toward neurotic conditions in pregnant women." The "we" was probably a slip of the tongue; a Freudian might have said that Wagner was revealing his own bias. By "neurotic" he meant that a pregnant woman's "nervous system is not well balanced. Their tendency is toward insanity; their tendency is to do things that they would not do in other conditions,—the tendency is to eat things and have appetites for unnatural articles of foods." The pregnancy so altered women that even their minds were lost to the condition.

Given that the defense's case depended so heavily on proving Mann at fault for her own death, it is surprising that Wagner did not cite the common theory of the age that women experienced "anger-neuroses." The etiological factors of this issue were "domestic." Such women, usually married women, had a "strong element of dissatisfaction in their minds regarding their conjugal relations." Doctors concluded, "It does not appear to matter very much as to the precise cause of their discontent; the essential fact being that such discontent is felt and is strongly resented." Husbands "took" their wives in a "matter-of-fact way" rather than by offering romantic solicitations. The wife became annoyed. For other women, the infrequency of sexual relations was the problem. No matter which group the women fell into, all of them felt they were not "prized" but rather "used." Consequently, their resentment grew into anger. They knew it was impossible to effect a change in their husbands' or lovers' temperaments. They also knew openly expressed anger would not change the situation, so they suppressed their emotions.[17] According to this hypothesis, woman feeling this way might become melancholy and contemplate suicide. However, to call upon this theory, Dr. Wagner would have had to consider that the relationships in Mann's life shaped her anxiety rather than placing the blame on her womb.

"And what have you to say with reference to suicide?" the defense asked.

"Suicide is one of the neuroses," Dr. Wagner paused. "Suicide and homicide, and anything that is unnatural or—criminal or unnatural." Basically, pregnant women were more prone to violence against either themselves or others.

In 1923, 4,316 of the 12,948 suicides nationally were women. The Save-A-Life League speculated that the "leap" in "self-destruction among the women" was doubtlessly "due to the women's newly acquired personal liberty." According to the League, joining "the fast set," as Fritzie Mann had, "with its endless social whirl, dinners, dances, and cigarettes, which often cause physical collapse and nervous breakdown," could end only one way. What was more troubling for these social workers was that young people were so easily led astray—especially away from chasing after the heights of achievement propagandized in the cinema by fictional characters. They concluded that disgrace and death were what awaited a woman living such a life. The League went further by suggesting that insanity caused a third of all suicides, and "sex trouble" was the cause of another third. The "decay of American home life" and the disquieting "jazz spirit of the times" were laying waste to American youth. In conclusion, according to the League, "life was held cheaply" and the only solution was to preach the "sanctity of life."[18]

As a conclusion, suicide was as troubling as murder in the case of Fritzie Mann. By discussing whether or not she took her own life by drowning, and then in speculating on the possibility of pregnancy-based neurosis, the defense forgot that Mann was a human being. In understanding her to be a human being, the lawyers, Dr. Wagner, and Save-A-Life would have had to understand her as possessing a choice about her pregnancy. Even though society offered the unmarried mother little, Mann was a woman who saw herself with choices. She had evaded Jacobs and Miner. She had returned home to demand the outcome to which she believed she was entitled. To recognize all of this would be to understand that her life had a context. The problem was that in admitting the context they would have also been shining a light on the lack of education available to women about their bodies, the special barriers they faced when seeking employment and supporting themselves, and society's expectation that they accept all blame for the pregnancy—which unlike Mann's death was an accident. In doing so, they would have linked Jacobs to

Mann, because he represented the Jazz Age custom of both celebrating and devouring transgressive women.[19]

Their rabbit test was more than bad science; it was indicative of the tragedy of the 1920s. Most people seemed dedicated to covering up the truth that they were living in chaotic times. No wonder the jury, the reporters, and those called to testify had difficulty deciding if Jacobs was guilty. For in condemning him, they would have been condemning themselves. In *The Great Gatsby*, which Fitzgerald set in 1922, the killer is never revealed, but everyone knows why Gatsby died. In *An American Tragedy*, Dreiser indicts society because, rich or poor, everyone is equally guilty. What the two great novels of the Jazz Age teach is that the entire nation shared in the illusion of normality.[20]

10

ARCHETYPES

Though she may have tried to usurp it, Fritzie Mann lived in a world governed by men. Her death did not free her from them. Instead, it increased the power men had over her life. They were no longer just brothers, boyfriends, and killers. Now there were newspapermen who published her private letters. There were coroners who peered into and disassembled her internal secrets. There were police detectives measuring her beach by putting one foot in front of the other. Worst of all, there were lawyers who suggested she had killed herself.

During Jacobs's second trial in the summer of 1923, the adulteress, the matron, and the widow took the stand. In this chapter, these archetypes speak for themselves, as do the men who questioned them, and their words illustrate the underlying tension between women and the unfulfilled social revolution of women's equality in the Jazz Age. The women's testimony lays bare the reality for women at the time. At first glance, it may appear that the story of Fritzie Mann is a story about women fighting to free themselves from prewar values. After all, at the heart of her story are the flappers, modernity, and abortion. Look again, for it is just as much a story about men attempting to assert or recapture their social power after the upheaval of World War I and the

success of the suffrage movement. In their discussions and delib-
erations about Fritzie Mann, the men revealed that their power
came largely from controlling and defining women.

Hyman Strunsky, writing for *Vanity Fair* in 1915, reported
that an "odd creature has lately made its appearance: woman."
Strunsky pointed out that previously no one really took note of
women or considered their place in society, because they were
women. If they were poor, they were slaves who lived in hovels,
and like all other slaves they were invisible to the society that
lived off their labor. If they were wealthy, they lived in doll-
houses, no doubt a nod to Ibsen's play. Suddenly everyone—and
to Strunsky everyone included H. G. Wells, George Bernard
Shaw, May Sinclair, W. L. George, and other "literary lights"—
was taking notice of women. Daughters were no longer obeying
their parents. Women no longer supplied or demanded marriage.
Why? Women were willing to work, they were willing to serve
in the war effort, but they were not willing to surrender their
souls. "She has discovered that there are other vocations besides
being a wife," Strunsky declared. Her predilection for freedom
over marriage made the modern female "odd." She could have
been protected and taken care of for the rest of her life. Marriage
could have saved her from seeing the horrors of the world. Yet she
refused. She was no longer willing to feign passivity. She wanted
to be active in society.[1]

Despite all of the changes and the clear view of what women
could accomplish, there were those who still doubted them.
Women's detractors couched their criticisms by saying that no
one wanted to take away from women the valor they earned during the war. The social truth these critics maintained was that
women could never be politically equal to men because men
were oaks and women were vines.

The main problem with women, according to men writing at
the time, was that once they had an idea they became "thoroughly
imbued" with it. Thereafter, women were incapable of having any
other idea. For Irvin S. Cobb, it was as if "everything else on earth
is subordinate to the thing, cabal, reform, propaganda, crusade,
movement or what not," women wanted at that moment, following their whims. Everyone else who fought in the war had made do
with "the palms of victory," "the sheaves of glory," the "crosses

of sacrifices," and "the thorny diadems of suffering." Women, not satisfied with these totems of triumph, wanted too much for their sacrifices. In Cobb's opinion it did not matter if society gave "freedom or let her take it, her course will be the same. Free-love hampers itself, and while woman talks of independence, demands and obtains the Franchise, punctiliously joining all freedom leagues, her feelings make freedom impossible. . . . The more a woman changes, the more she stays the same."[2]

All of these prejudices against women are essential to understanding the story of Fritzie Mann after her death because so much depended on the production of truth in the court trial. Women would be witnesses. They were going to be key to the narratives that the men—the lawyers, the judge, the doctors, the press, and the accused—were constructing not only of Mann but of society. It is essential, then, to understand that for social critics of the time a woman, "it must always be remembered, is as yet only half-educated in the principles of law." The problem was not a woman following the herd and being easily misled. Rather, man feared the supreme individuality of woman. They feared that a woman juror would base her judgments, as she did her acts, on a code of right or wrong specific to each individual case. They refused to believe that she had any public conscience and saw no difference in the behavior of the average female citizen and the average female criminal.

The evidence for the claim of universal female willfulness was the crime of shoplifting. Petty theft was believed to be a female crime, just as burglary and forgery were male crimes. All were crimes against property. However, a man became a burglar in order to make a living, which at its core was a respected impulse and key to the role of masculinity in society. Woman stole "for sheer covetousness, for the sheer furtive desire to possess some gew-gaw or trinket." They gave no thought to the principle of private property, or so critics such as Cobb thought.

In this way, the psychologies of the female criminal and female citizen were the same because selfishness was the root of both. To be sure, the wisdom of the age declared, it was not the fault of woman. After all, man had "caged" her "for a thousand years," which robbed her of the ability to empathize with the view of the people outside the cage, meaning men. A man, having been free to take part in society, naturally approached crime and citizenship differently because "for generations he and his fore-bears have possessed citizen-rights under the law, he knows both consciously and subconsciously that if he infringes that law . . . he will go to prison, that if he commits murder he will hang." Even the most perverted of male criminals still possessed a sense of public consciousness, or so went the theory of those trying to understand women and their changing roles in society. These rhetorical acrobatics failed to recognize that men were not just outside the cage; they were also the producers of the of the cage because they controlled the legal system. Women were not just challenging the law when they shoplifted, for example, or their traditional gender roles when they served on a jury, for instance; they were obstructing the right of the producers to dictate and predict outcomes.[3]

The men who authored the popular culture magazines clung to the age-old idea that women were all mad, as in unstable or crazy. For example, if a woman, any woman, was in a court-room—whether she had engaged in shoplifting or murder or was a juror—her "individual want" would "dominate" all her actions. The male observers thought this was why women were so prone to "that pitch of madness where even the commonest concepts of right and wrong blur to an indeterminate haze through which" women see only their own desires.[4]

In the context of imagined and imminent change in gender roles, male writers interpreted any deviation among women as a manifestation and the cause of social anarchy. As women joined the public sphere, they became even more subject to men's attitudes than when the vast majority of them were defined solely by their role within the home. While women were attached to the home, white men in the United States saw themselves as having detached their minds from their bodies' needs. They saw their minds as ruling their bodies. By separating their body from their mind, they believed they had placed their minds in charge of their destinies. White men, who were the power holders, judged all others, including men of color and all women, by their ability to do the same. They believed that the habit of dividing themselves in two was a necessity if they were to distinguish themselves from women and men of color because they felt these "lesser" groups needed subordination. When these men met women like Fritzie Mann, they found themselves no longer able to separate their urges, their thoughts, and their power.[5] It was not so much that they had repressed women. The arising conflict was more than just men controlling women, because women wanted more than equality; they wanted the ability to define themselves.

Because of the massive shift in social relationships, the women in the jury box, for both his trials, made the outcome of Jacobs's murder trial unpredictable. Female jurors were new, and no one had quite figured out what they would do when called on to *reason* their way to a verdict.[6] There were those who thought, "If women are really intending to make a better first at their political and social responsibilities than men have done," they should begin by working to end capital punishment. This perspective, put forth by the magazine *The Freeman*, concluded not just that capital punishment was a social evil but that in no other area had men "bungled . . . their responsibilities" more than in the administration of that punishment.[7] At the other end of the spectrum were those who feared that the thousands of years women spent as "chattel" made them psychologically unprepared for the responsibilities of citizenship.[8] In the case of Fritzie Mann's death, the defense attorneys hoped the female jurors would understand that a pregnant, unwed, woman was a desperate person capable of doing anything, even killing herself. Could female jurors do this, or would they see Mann as their avatar?

Many lawyers and judges, primarily men, argued that women should not serve on juries if the case centered around a woman, such as in divorce cases, because it seemed obvious to them that a woman could not be objective.[9] Women writing about the issue in the press seemed to believe that their peers were less likely to allow wholesale dismissals and acquittals, which appeared to be true in cases involving liquor laws, due to the involvement of women in the temperance movement.[10] Women of the press also argued that women of leisure and education had, relative to men with an equivalent level of education, more free time than anyone else in society. These women would surely be filling the jury boxes in no time, even in states such as California that did not require women to serve on juries.[11]

The reason behind women's service was the feeling of democ-
racy. They had fought for the right to vote, and jury service was
a responsibility tied up in their expectations of equality. "The
Woman," pseudonym of an anonymous author who reported for
Outlook, presented her jury service as the first time she had been
treated as an equal citizen. She was eager to make sacrifices, to do
her duty. Whereas men, particularly businessmen, tried to "get
out" of their service and many juries composed entirely of men
were thought to have a "mean character," women were conscien-
tious in their duty and "should set an example for men to follow."
She acknowledged those who argued that feminism was killing
chivalry and causing undue deterioration of social norms. To
these critics she suggested that, if chivalry died because women
were "assuming their new role," then no one could "deny that
women are receiving more practical respect and administration
from the men than ever before." She asked, "What matter if the
men fail to give us their seats in a streetcar . . . if they have a sufficient regard for our minds to value our opinions?" If the women
writing on the topic of female jurors were correct, the attorneys
of the nation had reason to fear verdicts as much as they feared
women as witnesses and criminals.[12]

Indeed, the second Jacobs trial was much the same as the
first—until the day Blanche Jones took the witness stand to assert
that Jacobs had the means and opportunity to kill Mann. A former nurse at Camp Kearny, Jones was the bombshell hurled at the
defense. With her testimony, the trial became more about men
and women than about murder. The prosecution claimed that
Jacobs took Mann to the Blue Sea Cottage, where she later died.
He then took her body to the Torrey Pines Grade and returned
to Camp Kearny, a distance of ten to fifteen miles, directly from
the top of the Biological Grade. It was on his journey back to the
camp that Mrs. Jones claimed to have seen the doctor at about
9:30. She had parked her car near the intersection of an old dirt
road and the Escondido highway. Her testimony revealed that, as
San Diego urbanized, a network of dirt roads that circumvented
the modernization of the area still existed. Though there were
squabbles between the attorneys and judge as to what the roads
were called, Mrs. Jones explained that she remembered the exact
intersection where she stopped the car because "the Escondido

highway was under construction."[13] Her eye-witness testimony, and the corroboration from her passenger, had the potential to discredit Jacobs's claims that he returned to the camp before 9:00 and remained at the hospital all night.

"Did you see any machines there that evening?" asked the district attorney, meaning any automobiles.

"Yes," she replied. "I saw a machine on the Linda Vista road fast approaching the Escondido highway. It turned and passed near my machine."

How did she know it was Jacobs's automobile? "I could see his outline. . . . The lights were on in my car. . . . I could see into the other car. . . . I could see it was a man alone in the car," and it looked like Jacobs's "outline." She had worked with him at the hospital. Plus, the automobile was "new and shiny and it was a Hudson coach." Thanks to the two trials, Jacobs was now the most infamous owner of the Hudson coach in southern California.

The defense asked, "What did you stop at the right of the road for?"—a question that caused laughter in the court.

"We decided not to go to Escondido." The "we" was Mrs. Jones and a hospital patient she was taking for a ride that night. Their relationship, she reported, was that they were just friends. "I liked to talk to him. He was a patient, and I took him for a ride in my car. I never took anybody else for a ride. We drove down the road, then stopped by the side of the road and talked." Notably, it turned out, when the two returned to the hospital, the patient insisted that Mrs. Jones let him out of the car before she entered the hospital gates.

Blanche Jones was the best eyewitness the prosecution could offer. She had not come forward during the first trial because she was married and had a twenty-one-month-old child. Had she come forward, she feared, the "shadow of rumor and suspicion" would fall upon her and "possibly cost" her "future happiness" as well her husband and her child. Her fear was credible. Even leading feminists demanded that the newfound role of women in society, which included working outside the home and voting, was not for self-satisfaction but for the betterment of their "eternal vocation" of mother and wife.[14] Here too we see the tension of maintaining prewar values while trying to increase the personal freedom of women.

The courtroom did "titter" and whispered as the defense—
Schenck along with Clifford Fitzgerald of San Diego and Louis
Jacobs's uncle Joe Shapiro from Detroit—dragged out what she
had hoped to keep secret about her own life. Her husband was a
disabled veteran living in a "soldier's hospital." Why, when her
husband was convalescing, was she traveling the countryside at
night with a man?

"It was just a visit, and that was all."

If it were so innocent, then why hide it?

"I never dreamed it would turn out to be such a terrible thing
as it has been made to appear. It would probably cost me my
happiness."

Was she seeking fame?

She explained, "I have no interest in the Jacobs case. I wish
I had never seen the man that went driving by in the car, for if I
had not I would not have been called in to testify in this case."
But she had, and eventually her story would need to be revealed.
"I tried to keep out of it," she testified, and in so doing she publicly exposed her sense of self-loyalty. "I didn't want to testify,
but in some way they found out I had seen the man who drove by
and compelled me to become a witness."

"When they called, me as a witness," she said as though she
knew what people thought of her, "I determined to go through
with it and tell the truth. They asked me all sorts of questions,
but I gave an absolutely truthful answer to each one. . . . I did
write a letter to the man who was with me," she admitted.

That letter, and its subsequent reprinting in the newspapers,
was a stark indication that the relationship of women to the world
had changed forever. Before the Jazz Age the intimate depths of
the female soul were, like the female ankle, more a discrete and
pleasurable suspicion than a blunt reality.[15] The San Diego newspapers held Blanche Jones out for the entire city to see. The letter
began, "Mac: No word from you, Looked for a letter yesterday,
Wanted to see you and talk over this affair we are perhaps unwill-
ingly thrust into." Then she softened her approach and expressed
a degree of resentment: "You, at least, are." She begged, "I do
wish you could see it differently and not withhold what evidence
we have." She called out to him, "Why feel that way?" and then
turned to use his own words against him: "'A life' you said, yes, I

know, but think of the lives cut off overseas, for what? This man should not go free, if guilty, should he? Why should the woman always pay," she asked, and then demanded, "Stand by. It's not so hard. It's principle, dear, that counts with God, not money. I beg of you, to be and do what is right in these matters, and I know you will, at whatever cost, because I believe in you. Of our personal interests, whatever happened will have to be." Like a woman in love with someone she knows is lost, she pleaded, "I can only hope it may eventually mean happiness for us both together. Yours Always, Blanche."[16]

There was a degree of disloyalty in her statement. She and Mac had clearly come to an agreement concerning what course to take. Their consensus was only a coating facilitated by each of them, concealing from the other their own wants behind assertions that seemed like values: telling the truth would ruin her marriage, telling the truth would drag their lives through the mud. They obligingly nodded at these prewar values, all the while knowing they did not truly cling to this set of morals.[17] To admit otherwise would be to admit to being immoral people. Still, there was the greater immorality, the murder. To not give witness, for Blanche Jones, would be a sign that she was a far worse person than she had ever imagined she could be.

"I am sorry everything has turned out as it has," she told the court. "It is going to cost me much. I have done my duty, but it seems at a cost that is out of proportion to the results. I have done nothing to deserve the trouble that it has brought me."[18] Despite the fact she had risked everything in her life to deliver evidence to the court, her claims were not valued. She had not realized that the means by which she witnessed the event and the means by which she arrived at the conclusion to tell her story made her testimony untenable. She may have been offering valuable facts, but the attention drawn to the context of the facts disrupted and discredited the impression she had hoped to foster.[19]

Mrs. Jones had not understood that there was more to justice than telling the truth. Justice was like mathematics. In a death penalty case, is a single testimony enough or must there be other testimonies? Are two partially true testimonies equivalent to a completely truthful testimony? Are there clues that become evidence only for certain crimes, in exact circumstances, and in relation to specific persons? Can the eye-witness evidence offered by an adulterous nurse be disregarded if it is contrary to that of a nonadulterous, and thereby virtuous, nurse? Can the word of a nurse be trusted if that nurse is speaking out against a doctor? Can a woman be believed over a man? Justice in the Jazz Age was an algebra hardened by sophistry whose function was to define how lawyers constructed reality. Nevertheless, truth in the age of abstraction, which was the Jazz Age, was loyal to artifice and dominated by supplanted realism. This system of "legal proof" makes truth in the justice system the result of complicated maneuvering and strategy. In every case, justice derives from rules known only to specialists. Consequently, the lawyers could use evidence to corset the weakest truths.[20]

Mrs. Jones saw a man so closely resembling the defendant that she was sure it was Jacobs himself, "driving from La Jolla to the hospital reservation late Sunday night, January 14th," was how the papers summarized her testimony. According to the newspapers from Los Angeles to San Diego, "This evidence, not heretofore given, is regarded as knocking out a number of props from Capt. Jacobs's alibi." Even more than the damage to the alibi was the fact that her testimony was the "first definite indication that the physician may have been in the vicinity of the scene of the asserted crime at a time when the defense maintains he was elsewhere." The newspapers practically rejoiced at the news. "They," Jones and the patient, Mac, "were so close to the road that she said she recognized the passing auto as similar to one owned by Jacobs and that the outlines of the driver also strikingly resembled the doctor." "Mrs. Jones then said that she and her companion returned to the camp following the other automobile and saw it turn into the reservation."[21]

On cross-examination, defense attorney Schenck—who had defended film star Roscoe "Fatty" Arbuckle by focusing on deadlocking the juries or proving jury tampering rather than the innocence of his client[22]—asked about the details of Mrs. Jones's life. She explained that she had been living in east San Diego for the previous two months and that before then she was stationed as a nurse at Camp Kearny for seven months. She was married. These details mattered because they informed the jury of the veracity of her statements. She was married, and yet she kept time with men in cars. This made her disloyal. The men she accompanied were also her patients, which made her unprofessional. Where she lived in the city indicated that she was poor and lived in the heavily immigrant precincts, which made her the "other."

Beyond the details was the establishment of power. The attorneys were performing for the jury. Their performance was different from the witness's. For example, of primary concern for Blanche Jones was whether the jurors would believe her or not. Quite easily, her desire for credibility twisted into an investment in defending her public standing. Because she became interested in saving her own public character, her interest eventually moved away from the conviction of Jacobs and the redemption of Fritzie Mann. The defense attorneys needed to establish an asymmetry in which they had an advantage over all of the witnesses because their responses to the witness testimony provided the jury with meaning that could then become narrative. Moreover, narrative could resemble truth without necessarily being truth.[23]

Mrs. Jones knew what was happening to her in court. She sensed that the construction of the narrative damned her rather than Jacobs. For this reason, she emphasized in a low-toned voice, "I know I was on the highway on Sunday night, January 13 about 9:30." Her tone, which accentuated her frustration, was so noticeable that many people in the courtroom gave added interest to her words. Even so, she was unable to state whether she had been in an automobile on the highway or out riding on other nights a week or a month before or after January 14. She seemed to remember only one night. She could not explain why she could fix the time so accurately in this case but repeatedly said, "I know it was the night." Again and again, she repeated her original statement that she "knew" that was the night. Dr. Jacobs displayed the deepest interest in Mrs. Jones's testimony. He frequently whispered to his counsel and more "than once moistened his lips," the newspapers reported.[24]

Mrs. Jones was the eyewitness. Mrs. Worthington was the alibi. She resided at 1020 Encino Row, Coronado, so her life was set in the Eden to which Jacobs longed to belong. She had lived there a little over a year. She had known Jacobs since April 1922, which was about the same time he met Fritzie Mann. In making Mrs. Worthington the key witness, the defense was admitting that what could save Jacobs from the taint of a working-class immigrant girl and an adulterous nurse would be the mantle of an upper-class woman.[25]

Mrs. Worthington recalled well reading in the papers of the finding of the body of Fritzie Mann "on the beach some place here last winter," for she had spent the weekend in Jacobs's company. On Saturday, January 13, they had left for Tijuana around 1:30 in the afternoon and crossed the border to visit the racetrack. Jacobs drove his Hudson. After the races, they drove around the border town visiting first the Foreign Club and then the Sunset Supper Club. They had hoped to find her daughter, who was keeping company that afternoon with a Lieutenant Chapman. While searching, Jacobs cashed two checks and received a traffic ticket. Mrs. Worthington paid little attention to all of this. They spent the day together and returned to her home around eleven in the evening. They came by way of the Strand, a silver stretch of beach beside the road that connects Coronado to San Diego, and on straight to her home, where she was also entertaining her sister and another female houseguest.

The next day was much the same. Again, they left for the racetrack. Jacobs drove. They returned a little after six in the evening. Then Jacobs said his good-byes. She did not see him again until Tuesday night. The news of the murder had broken that morning, but she would not read about it until the next day. She and Jacobs met up at the US Grant Hotel, which suggests that they were at the speakeasy where everyone seemed to meet, and then on to dinner at the Golden Lion. Jacobs departed because he had to meet "friends from the east" arriving at the Santa Fe depot at 6:30.

Mrs. Worthington's testimony seems mundane, which was by design. After all, it was an alibi for a man who hoped to be mundane. She was a brilliant alibi, for she always remembered to check the time and noted what everyone wore and where they were standing when she had conversations with them. Still, her testimony exposes the details of a life of leisure in which a married woman could be driven about the countryside, for she did not drive, by younger unmarried men. She had no occupation other than entertaining and presented herself as a damsel in need of men. Because of her exquisite mind for details, the majority of her testimony dealt with travel itineraries.

Only a woman above the age of forty could have offered such an alibi, that is, if one holds to the wisdom promoted in an anonymously written essay that appeared in *Harper's*. Society forced women to take note of everything. Women had to "take account" of other people, whereas men were expected to live independently and to remain unshaped by the personalities of others. Women had to be able to talk to anyone and everyone at dinner parties. Women had to be charming; they had to furnish a home with elements of beauty and offer men a sense of leisure.[26] It was a strange division of labor in which grew the domestic establishment. The gender roles were not just tasks. On the contrary, they were important performances that gave meaning to the otherwise meaningless. It was Mr. Worthington's job to acquire wealth and thereby socioeconomic status. It was Mrs. Worthington's job to display his acquisitions.[27] To be clear, she began as one of his objects and slowly, if she were charming enough, became his hostess.

At the same time, she had to avoid being too charming and thus risk being thought manipulative. Once a man saw a woman as "parasitic," he would seek to exploit her, as he believed she exploited him. For men, as the woman of forty understood, saw their injustices as chivalry and their instincts as reason. Therefore, she had to tread carefully through the world, noting everything.[28]

Though one might think the relationship between Mrs. Worthington and Dr. Jacobs fascinating, it raises a few questions. "Was he a frequent visitor over to your home, was he not, during the summer and fall?"

"Yes, he came there frequently . . . sometimes twice a week, and sometimes maybe once a week but I think we saw him on an average of once a week and sometimes oftener for I came into town in the earlier months, because I had some one driving for me, but if we happened in to town, we would see him."

They saw each other at parties because she had a lady friend keeping company with a doctor friend of his "and we went out in parties of four, frequently."

"He was for a long period a very close friend of yours?"

"Friends, yes."

Note in the final interchange the use of past tense by the attorney and no use of a verb from the witness. Jacobs had fallen out of favor. Even if he escaped conviction, it was unlikely he could ever return to his previous position; he no longer held an active place in Mrs. Worthington's life.

In contrast with the testimony of the nurse, Mrs. Worthington's virtue was never in question. Was it her beauty? Was it class? Was it that she lived on Coronado and had important friends? Or was it because she was over forty and therefore more detached from the sexual urges that governed the relationship of women and men of a younger age? Most women enjoyed the company of men, or so the anonymous author writing for *Harper's* suggested. Men led fundamentally different lives from women. Men had a "free economic existence, and active, full and stirring lives." The result was that women sought out men because "their experience is far richer than ours." Men marched "cheek by jowl with events," whereas women of the upper class came in contact with the world only through their relationships with men. The woman over forty was not like the flapper; she needed men. In Mrs. Worthington's case, she could not even drive. Or, maybe, the lawyers never asked her to detail her relationship with Jacobs because everyone already understood.[29] Whichever was the plausible explanation for the difference in treatment between the nurse and the upper-class matron, Mrs. Worthington was the perfect alibi.

The attorneys had not finished placing womanhood in all its various archetypes, from fallen woman to matron, upon the stand when they dismissed Mrs. Worthington. There was still the matter of the widowed mother of the victim.

There were many kinds of widows. One group was only interested in money, or so the *Ladies' Home Journal* purported. Another group was "self-made," a hint of the realities of World War I. These women applied to the courts to be declared widows. Some widows were temporary and made public the fact. The final group, like Mrs. Mann, were the "durable" Victorian widows who seemed to be judging the shift in morals and the men who benefited from it.[30] No matter the type, all widows were dangerous, according to popular culture, because they knew too much. Unlike the young woman or the married woman, the widow was capable of considering questions of principle without emotion. They also understood that questions of emotions were without principle.[31]

In her testimony, Mrs. Mann was answering the same line of questioning as always, and the questions tried to imply that she did not know her daughter. She took the stand in July 1923 after Wilma Miner's testimony about abortion.[32]

"And of course, as her mother, you knew about what time she got back?" asked the defense.

"Yes, always."

"And every time she went out with Dr. Jacobs, she always got back very early in the evening along ten or 11 o'clock, or earlier, didn't she?"

"She came home 11, sometimes 12."

"And I believe you said to Dr. Jacobs that you liked to have him go out with her, or her to out with him, because he always got her home so early, didn't you?"

"He brought her home."

"I say, you told Dr. Jacobs you were glad Fritzie went with him, because he always got her home early?"

"He bring her home at 11 or 12 o'clock."

"But I say, you told the doctor you were glad Fritzie went out with him from time to time, because he got her back so early?

"Can you tell me this in German? I cannot understand you in English."

Judge Marsh, a former district attorney and bank president, interrupted. "I think you can understand. You know what 'glad' means?"

"Yes."

Then the judge asked, "Did you tell Dr. Jacobs you were glad he took her out because he got her home so early?"

"I never said a word—I never talked to him—just once."

"Well, as a matter of fact, you were pleased?"

"No, I was not pleased—never. If she went—with whoever she went out—I was all against the boys—I never was this time."

"You did not want her to go out with anybody?"

"I don't want to go out, because we are strangers, and I don't know the people—I never liked—I would not say I was glad, I was against—because we were strangers, and I don't like her to go out." Here Mrs. Mann revealed the dangers for immigrants. There was the unkind treatment she received in court, but there was also the fear she held of American society in general. She had seen war and violence in her life in Galicia. She had saved her children from it by immigrating. At the moment she was sitting on the stand she had no husband, she had one daughter dying from tuberculosis, and her other daughter and unborn grandchild were dead.

Had she been a good widow, the *Ladies' Home Journal* suggested, Mrs. Mann would have shown more deference to the men around her. The assumption was that her husband had taken care of everything, and that Mrs. Mann had led a cloistered-by-marriage life. In the place of a husband, she would need to rely on men of status and knowledge. Since she had clearly resolved to be a "permanent" widow, she had to continue to be the "dutiful wife" to the masculine leaders of society with all the burdens of "obedience" demanded by the culture. "If your husband dies," the magazine reported, "you lose your identity. You are not only a widow." She had become the figure in "black," referring "to the fact that your husband is no longer living." Sardonically, the *Ladies Home Journal,* by drawing on the name of a law degree, called it the "LL.D degree of bereavement conferred upon you; and it sticks" to women. Men who had lost their wives were not held to these same standards. The widow had to strike a balance. She had to be "intelligently faithful to a husband's memory without yielding to disintegrating emotions." "Recall," the magazine evangelized, "how many times you questioned his judgment."[33] In court, the defense attorneys sought to blame her for her daughter's death. She was the one who had raised Frieda and had not stopped Fritzie.

In telling Frieda, what she always called her daughter, not to go out, she was attempting to teach her daughter not to be helpless. It was possible to control one's need for affection. The popular depiction of widows was that they saw no need for any girl to be a victim. They understood, or so mass media would have the public believe, that any girl who is hurt by the social ills is not without blame if she figures as a victim. Bringing out this point was the goal of the defense attorneys. Yet widows also knew that it was "impossible for men to be virtuous." The self-knowledge and the knowledge of society made Mrs. Mann powerful and weak simultaneously.[34] "Do not ask for sympathy," the *Ladies' Home Journal* demanded of the good widow, "nor complain of how the world takes advantage of you in your defenseless condition." In other words, be a realist. "That is the way the world makes its living. You cannot expect it to make an exception in your case." "Besides," there was hope: "You are not defenseless," the magazine reminded the reader; the widow still had her "wit."[35]

"And you pleaded with her and begged with her, even up to the time that she left the house?"

"Yes, I walked with her to the car line."

"And even went down to the car."

"She didn't want to tell."

"And all the time she refused to tell—or said she didn't know the man's name?"

"She says 'He is a man from Los Angeles, that will take us.'"

"She told you, didn't she, that it was Louise Garrison?"

"Yes."

"She didn't mention to me more than—I said, 'Tell me which is the girls that will be on the party?'" She wrote down on a piece of paper, "Louise Garrison."

"Did you know Louise Garrison?"

"No."

"What did she say about the other girls?"

"She just said a party, and they take us—she don't want to say anything, because she was teached not to tell."

"I think that should be stricken out," said the defense. "I didn't even hear it myself, in fact, I won't pay any attention to it. It was not responsive." Judge Marsh agreed.

At this point, the threat Mrs. Mann posed had become clear. True, she was a foreigner without social status and all the protection social status could afford Ella Worthington, for example. Nevertheless, Mrs. Mann was "what no woman except a widow ever is—a free agent." The "maiden" like Frieda, no matter how mature, lacked the widow's "subtler knowledge and experience in dealing with men." The married woman like Blanche Jones, the nurse, can "never exercise" her knowledge or will because "no woman can live in love and charity with her husband and be a free agent." Man was made first, according to popular belief, and "given dominion over all things." Without man's dominion, there was nothing left for the widow besides being "durable."[36]

"Did she tell you during the course of that afternoon that this man was coming down from Los Angeles in the automobile? She didn't tell you that?

"No, she don't tell me that."

"Did she tell you where she was going to meet the two girls and the man?"

"No, she don't tell—she just said, "He will take us from downtown."

"But she didn't say automobile?" He asked, "Or whereabouts downtown?"

"No, she don't want to tell me anything."

"She didn't want to tell you?"

"And I asked her, 'Always you told me with who you go; and this time you don't want to.' She says 'It is a man from Los Angeles; he will take us from downtown.' That is all she said." The shift in her daughter's behavior was enough to make Mrs. Mann nervous. The unsustainable reality Fritzie was trying to manage was her pregnancy. Her mother only suspected that Fritzie was hiding something. To her mother the inner self, home, and family were the most significant things. She did not trust the outside world. Yet Fritzie's inner self was porous. Her family was separated from the outer world to which she directed her attention. She felt herself only when she engaged with that outer world's meanings and frameworks. She came to understand herself only in terms of the outside. She comported herself to things, to choice, to love, and finally to regret. She relied on being open to the world precisely because being open meant being transfixed, engaged, and dependent on the context she had created rather than the one her mother offered.[37] How terrifying it must have been for her mother as they walked to the bus stop. The daughter was heading out into a world Fritzie thought her mother did not understand because she did not accept it, but Mrs. Mann understood it well enough to know to be afraid.

"You say you asked her all the afternoon?" the defense attorney pressed.

"No, a few times I asked her; it was funny to me, because she told me always, and this time, and I don't think what man she don't tell, she does not know maybe."

The judge interrupted, "It does not do any good to talk, unless you talk loud enough to be heard."

"It is my voice."

"You speak loud enough," the judge said, "to begin with, and then you sort of run down so we cannot hear what you say. It is better not to talk at all."

"I will try my best." Mrs. Mann was stuck. In death, her daughter had become part of competing discourses dependent on the vagaries of language put forth by the attorneys as they attempted to make her real, but only in relation to their respective narratives. However, for Mrs. Mann, her daughter's life resembled a kind of topography within which her daughter struggled for social capital. Mrs. Mann understood Frieda's life outside the home, her life as Fritzie, as a series of social gatherings, dinners, and dances. She comprehended that those who attended the events composed a world that existed between two fields of power. There was the familiar and the material, which reduced the world outside her home to an abstraction with embedded meaning in everyday events, such as walking her daughter to the bus, and objects, such as the hairpin Fritzie left on the Blue Sea Cottage nightstand. Then there was the world of those with power: the attorneys, the judge, the jury, and the newspapers. Her understanding of the world was at odds with the attorneys' understanding. For her, social and economic conditions were at the heart of the matter rather than at the periphery.[38]

The defense continued to repeat the questions that had already been asked: "You mean always in her whole life before, she told you the man?"

"Always."

"This time she wouldn't tell?"

"Always, and I take a pencil and paper and write down the man's name; and this time she refused; I suspected maybe some secret marriage, or something, and she don't want to tell me." "She said, 'Mother.'" Mrs. Mann tried to continue but the judge interrupted: "You have answered the question." Mrs. Mann attempted again, "She said 'Mother.'" The judge interrupted, "Wait a minute. You have answered the question."

In their treatment of Mrs. Mann, the men of the court seared into the minds of all those in attendance the fact that she was not just the untrustworthy widow; she was also the foreigner. Add to this her Jewish background, and Mrs. Mann's experience becomes a demonstration of nativist power in the Jazz Age. Why did they fear immigrants? After the war there was an enormous influx of European women to the United States. From the conclusion of the war to 1921, 500,000 alien women had landed on American shores. Immigration officers expected the number to grow to a million by 1922. In San Diego specifically, the population had almost doubled from 1910 to 1920, and there were fears that most of that increase had come from immigrants. The rumor was that the primary reason the women came to the United States was to look for husbands.[39]

"By the way, talking about secret marriages," the defense began, "had Frieda a marriage annulled in Denver?" The defense threw this question in as a way to pique the jury's interest without having to present evidence of a marriage. Ben Shelley, who claimed he had gone to parties with Mann in Autumn 1922, had mentioned a supposed secret marriage in Denver. Also, Jacobs had instructed Mann to lie about being married while seeking an abortion. The defense attorneys offered no proof of marriage. Since marriages are a matter of public record, it would not have been difficult to present the court with facts. Questions were easier than facts. Questions simply introduced the idea to the jury.

The defense also hoped to challenge the testimony of Mann's neighbor who recalled Mann bringing Jacobs home to meet people in the neighborhood in October 1922. "Well, how do you like my doctor?" Mann asked and then announced to the women present they would all be maids of honor and flower girls in her wedding. Jacobs reportedly stormed off and was overheard saying to Mann that he would never marry "anyone"—that he would "assist" Mann, "but I will never marry you." Mann yelled back, "You will marry me!"[40]

"No, she never was married," Mrs. Mann told the court.

"You used to live in Denver?"

"Nobody can say in Denver, the child was married—nobody can say this, she was engaged once, but not married." The questions were orchestrated to cause Mrs. Mann to have an emotional response that would make her seem hysterical and dishonest to the jury. The defense could not cross-examine Fritzie Mann and prove her to be a gold-digging liar. So they settled for destroying her mother.

"There was no court procedure there to annul a marriage?"

"No, nobody in Denver—she came there a little girl—was there ten years." Mrs. Mann testified in such a small quiet voice that the judge and lawyers constantly asked her to repeat herself. Her voice failed her the most when she tried to give the basic details of her daughter's life. She was twenty years old. She was unmarried. She was always happy.

"When did you, if at all, did you become acquainted with the defendant, Jacobs, in this case?" She had met him in town in May 1922. Her family was still living on Twenty-ninth Street then. They had lived there only four months. She remembered the date by the fact that they did not move to A Street until July.

"Always the whole day," while she watched her daughter pack, Mrs. Mann recalled, "it was in my mind why the child don't want to tell." Her date went unnamed.

"Every way I tried to find out who is the man."

William Mann, Fritzie's brother, substantiated his mother's testimony. He recalled first meeting Louis Jacobs in the latter part of April 1922. William lived at home with his mother and sister. Jacobs had come to pick up Fritzie and was waiting in the living room. On average, he saw Jacobs a few times a month. He merely sat in the car and honked the horn. Fritzie would run out to meet him.[41]

On the day she died, he remembered, his sister was extremely cheerful. She ironed her dress, and he remembered watching her being all dolled up to go out. She was "chaffing gaily with the rest of the family and telling us she was going to knock us off our feet." She hinted at marriage, and her brother thought she was planning an elopement.

Like his mother, he next saw his sister at the undertaker's on January 16. He had read about her death in the *San Diego Union* because the coroner had failed to notify the family first. It fell to William to identify the body and her possessions. He had been the one to suggest that she have the calling cards made up that read "I am Fritzie Mann." "She was away so much," he lamented. "I asked her to carry an identification card, as I thought it was necessary." She had started to carry them in September.

Like his mother, William did not know for certain that she was pregnant until the autopsy. He knew her period had ceased, and it "had been attributed to some local cause." "I don't think she herself was aware of her condition." The lawyers kept his testimony brief. For their purposes, Mrs. Mann was the more suitable spokesperson.

"Did she tell you when she would be home?"

"No," Mrs. Mann answered. "She don't told me—she said she would call me up and then she will tell me everything, when she will be home, and don't worry."

"Didn't she say, now, "Mother, I think I will be home by noon, or early in the afternoon, but if I don't get home.'"

"No."

"Don't worry, because I will be home by night, and way."

"No, she don't told me."

"You say that she was always, not that she was never worried?"

"No, she was the happiest child in the world, she never was worried."

"Is that true, October 15th or from the first of November, on—is that true during that period, that she did not worry about anything?"

"She never worried."

"You knew that she—knew or thought she was in a family way, didn't you?"

"What did you say?" Mrs. Mann demanded. "I cannot say what you mean—'family way.'"

"I mean that she was going to have a baby?"

"You can tell that to me in a different language as an educated man," she asked.

"I tried to use the word 'family way'—I thought probably that would be enceinte," the defense answered, using the seventeenth-century French word *enceinte*, which can mean pregnant or refer to a walled castle, when explaining his question to the court.

Mrs. Mann understood exactly what was happening. "Insult me," she said, "I would not take from you—"

"What?" The defense replied with a degree of surprise.

"I would not take insult from you. I am a heart broken mother—you shall tell this to me." Finally she was speaking at a level Judge Marsh could hear, and he interceded: "Never mind, Mrs. Mann, the question really is, did you know she was pregnant from October on?"

"She don't told me," Mrs. Mann began. "She don't know it herself." But being a concerned mother and living with the grief of having another child sick with tuberculosis in the sanitarium, she sent Fritzie to the doctor.

"Just a minute," the defense interrupted. "Did you know or believe from October on that she was pregnant?"

"No, I didn't know—I didn't know it until I find out—then she was in the Undertaking parlor—then I know. I didn't know it."

"You knew did you not, that she had ceased to menstruate in October?"

"From October on, it was her sick time, and I asked her 'What is the matter with your sick time?' She says, 'Nothing,' and I was a little worried, and I sent her to Dr. Butterfield, and he said, 'There is nothing to worry—it often happens with girls, the climate is so here, so I was not worried."

"You appeared before the grand jury in February of this year, and testified?"

"Yes."

"I will ask you if at that time and place you did not state that she was a pregnant, and that Rogers Clark got her some medicine," a reference to the possible use of an abortive medicine, "to make her sick time come, and it made her so sick that she had to go to bed, or words to that effect?" In asking this question, the defense lawyers did not read from a transcript. They were not quoting testimony from Clark, who was only called to the stand to restate his alibi.[42] The defense team's strategy was to prove Mrs. Mann untrustworthy, which they hoped would make her daughter seem less like a victim.

"No, nothing of the kind. I don't say this, I never said this."

"Well, did he give her some brown colored medicine?"

"She been up to the doctor." Her frustration showed as her answers became more clipped. Mrs. Mann had come head to head with the issue of who is permitted to create public knowledge. She was not. The lawyers were, and had the power to confound the distinction between culture and science, factual and artificial, authorization and authority.

"No, I mean Rogers Clark?"

"No, I don't say Rogers Clark, no. Why shall I lie? I never said it. She went to a doctor."

"I think that is all," the defense said, and then added, "Did you not testify there under oath, that after Fritzie came back from Los Angeles, arriving here on January 8th, Rogers Clark took her out frequently until the latter part of that week?"

"Not when she came back. Before she went. He was acquainted and he took her out a few times, but not when she came back—he never called her up—no, sir."

Eventually the lawyers asked Mrs. Mann if she cried the night Fritzie left. "No, I don't cry, no, no. Why should I cry?" Wasn't it obvious? "I should cry if I know where she goes."

11

CLOSINGS

In his closing arguments in Jacobs's second trial, District Attorney Chester Kempley pointed at Jacobs to say, "Fritzie Mann knew who was the father of her unborn child and this man here was not man enough to marry her." According to Kempley, Jacobs's interest in Mann had not been altruism, as the defense claimed. If it had been altruism, Kempley asked the jury, why would Jacobs demand Mann keep his involvement with her secret? Mann "was a good, pure girl when he met her," but "when he had accomplished" what he wanted "with the little girl who loved him," then "he destroyed her life" and "he also destroyed the life of her unborn child." The prosecutor held up Mann's purse and declared, "She was not a gold digger. Do you think that the little girl who carried this tattered old handbag along with her on her last trip from home was a gold digger? Did they find any rings on her fingers or anything else to indicate she was a gold digger living off the money of men?"[1]

Kempley's speech reveals a critical facet of how the evidence was presented and interpreted. The case had come down to a trial of Mann's morality against Jacobs's public position. What the jury held as true depended on how they defined virtue and honor. Many statements of fact became qualified by the perspective of those involved. They were not "true" in the strict scientific sense. Any hope of basic agreement was doomed. The only verifiable truth was that Mann was dead and there was a fetus, because these certainties had their own kind of validity; they could be seen and thus not disputed. Because the criterion for truth in the two trials of Louis Jacob was not the scientifically verifiable ideas put forth by Drs. Wagner, Shea, or Kelly, "truth" as a concept became simplistic. Everything depended on scope, precision, and coherence of what was knowable to the greatest number of people. Any number of valid theories could become self-consistent, applicable, and relatively adequate to explain what led to the death of Fritzie Mann.[2]

The diversity of theories made the lawyers' task—both defense and prosecution—difficult, but not impossible. It is conceivable that they saw the shifting nature of the "truth" as an advantage. Their first step was to find a frame of reference simple enough to be managed yet flexible enough to translate as many "facts" as possible into a single, smooth narrative.[3]

The final plea from Paul Schenck for the defense struck immediately into the theory of the death of Fritzie Mann, declaring that this was only the second time in thirty years of practice that he had made a final plea to the jury without knowing what the prosecution believed had been the cause of the death in the murder charge. The other occasion was in the first trial of this case, which occurred a few months earlier in April. "As a matter of fact, I do not know how to address myself, what argument I must answer. None has been advanced. It is indeed a handicap not to know what the prosecution thinks as to how, when, and where Fritzie Mann died. Their own surgeon named nine possible causes. Mr. Selleck," the assistant district attorney, "said he could give you five. If they and their own surgeon do not know what was the cause of Fritzie Mann's death, how can I know, or how can you determine it?"[4]

The defense wanted to sweep away the narrative ground the prosecution had hoped to gain in the trial. Schenck planned to do so by embracing the politics of truth. He silenced witnesses, asserted doubt, and suggested that the jury forget certain things they had heard over the course of the trial. Within his narrative, Fritzie's mother was not to be trusted because she clearly did not know everything about her daughter, and thus knew nothing about her daughter. She also bore a grudge against all the men her daughter knew. Blanche Jones, the married nurse who testified as an eyewitness, was also to be forgotten, because she was of dubious character and thus untrustworthy. He called witnesses who had been part of the grand jury. He asserted that the authorities had amnesia and had not maintained the same story throughout from the grand jury to the first trial and then the second trial, which meant that none of their stories could be trusted. His was a radical reformulation of how to speak about violence. He was willing to draw on the illusions of monster, victim, inferior, martyr, and celebrity, but his goal was to discharge this imagery at the victim rather than the defendant. By challenging the power of the police, the knowledge of the surgeons, and the innocence of the victim, he positioned himself in the dual roles of interpreter and advocate.[5]

The defense then proceeded to classify the evidence and questions at issue, primarily the issue of corpus delicti, that is, whether a murder had even been committed. Schenck put all of the 106 witnesses into seven categories. There were, for example, those who testified to physical facts, such as the condition of roads, tides, and winds; others who testified to the motive of witnesses, such as Wilma Miner and William Mann; and "opportunity witnesses," such as the handwriting experts, whose evidence showed the defendant had the opportunity to commit the crime. He eliminated all those whose testimonies for lacking in material facts or direct proof. His denunciations were frequently scornful.[6]

"Who is the criminal?" the defense was asking. Can those guilty of ethical or moral infractions really speak to the truth of another man's actions? Schenck's argument rested on generalities that cast doubt as a punitive function. He was attempting to appear as though he was rooting out illegalities. From his role in the case, he took control over who should be punished by the crowd. He made the jurors, the people in the court, and the population of the city, via the newspapers, feel as though they had the power to determine the course of events, both those before the death of Fritzie Mann and those after. In reality, he was the one

with the power, or at least the one with the possibility of grasping power.[7]

Feeling that sense of power, Schenck became declarative:

> But all this, has nothing to do with whether a crime was
> committed or whether Dr. Jacobs committed a crime. It
> is merely evidence that he may have had both a motive
> and opportunity. I want you to remember always that the
> burden of proof throughout this whole case rests with
> the state. They have to prove everything. I don't have to
> prove anything. The only evidence on which they have
> based their claim that a crime was committed was that
> the hands of Fritzie Mann were folded on her breast and
> even their own witnesses do not agree as to that.[8]

The witnesses had disagreed about the placement of her
hands, if her eyes were shut, if there were footprints around the
body, if her arm fell from the coroner's stretcher. Members of
the grand jury were called to testify about changing police and
coroner statements. Mr. Kerns, the proprietor of the hotel, had
consistently changed his story as to whom he saw with Fritzie
Mann throughout the two trials. Mr. Miller, a hospital colleague
of Jacobs who claimed he had seen Jacobs burning letters, had
changed his testimony and in the end claimed he had not seen
Jacobs burning the letters. There were no photographs of the
crime scene. The morticians processed the body before the com-
pletion of the autopsy. Moreover, the police had mislaid many of
Mann's letters, items of her clothing, and even the card that read
"I Am Fritzie Mann."[9]

Of supreme importance was the fact that Fritzie Mann had
called her mother on the telephone about 5:15, the afternoon of
January 14, and notified her that a contemplated house party had
been changed from Del Mar to La Jolla. "At that time," a member
of the defense team, Clifford Fitzgerald, famous for his work in
military courts, had asked: "Dr. Jacobs, according to testimony of
the Defense witness was in Tijuana. Who did Fritzie Mann meet
that caused her to change her plans? It was not Dr. Jacobs. Who
was it?" It could not have been Jacobs, according to his attorneys,
because he was an innocent man who had voluntarily cooperated

with the police. His attorneys denounced the prosecution for suggesting to the jury "that no matter how the dancing girl met her death, it was as the result of criminal agency."[10]

According to Schenck, a member of the defense team from Los Angeles, the San Diego police were inept, simpleminded, and bumbling. They could not keep evidence straight, they could not read a map, and they could not tell time. All of the evidence against Jacobs was circumstantial, the defense attorneys claimed. Fritzie Mann's *condition* could not have been motive for her alleged murder by Dr. Jacobs. If he had been responsible, he would have either married the girl or denied he was the father. Trying to help her was not proof of guilt. All Jacobs was trying to do was what any man might have tried to do for a friend. In making this argument, the defense attorneys made it clear that they did not intend to trample "on a dead girl's grave." All they were saying was that, if Dr. Jacobs had been responsible, and if he thought himself too socially above Fritzie Mann to consider marriage, all he had to do was deny responsibility. Obviously, the only reason Jacobs was on trial was that he went voluntarily to the chief of police to explain his relationship to Fritzie Mann, which was the act of an innocent man. No guilty man would go to the police and offer information. In making this argument, the defense neglected to remind the jury that Jacobs had actually lied to the police in his first meeting with them. He had known Mann for far longer than he was willing to admit and had tried to arrange an abortion for her.[11]

Though it will seem strange to modern readers looking back on the case, the prosecution did not make much out of the letter from Mann's friend that indicated Jacobs treated women "rough." Here was the hint at violence. But this was not the kind of violence they were prepared to talk about. They showed the murder but opted not to discuss the private, domestic violence, which was a pervasive part of society. In not discussing one type of violence and preferring another, those involved with the case revealed a tendency to connect certain types of violence with certain types of guilt and innocence, which were determined by the virtue or moral status of the victim and the social status of the killer. In making the choice in narratives, the police, lawyers, doctors, and journalists revealed that they expected a certain amount of conflict and violence as normal as long as it was within certain limits.[12] In not pointing out the possibility of domestic violence in Mann and Jacobs's relationship prior to her death, the prosecution gave the defense a free hand to argue that Jacobs was a good guy caught in the net of inept policing.

As the *Union* reported, the defense launched a sustained drive against the testimony of the coroner, Dr. Schuyler Kelly: "I am not calling any witnesses liars, but a lot of them are mistaken. Remember that you are determining whether you will hang that boy by the neck until he is dead. You should be as careful of the evidence as if your own flesh and blood were being tried."[13] Schenck was suggesting that, because lay people believe scientific voices bring truth-telling, transparency, and authority to a case, mistakes by those scientific voices lead to a cascading problem of detectives building off that original mistake. The focus then shifts from science to law as detectives announce criminal charges. Reporters project the detectives' work. The tension rises and the climax in the story arrives when the cunning police stamp out the defendant's lies and the confession provides the resolution. There is a difference between a crime story and a criminal act. If no one notices the difference, then a man might be executed for that story rather than for an actual crime.[14]

The defense asserted, and the *Union* chronicled word for word, that there was no conclusive evidence to demonstrate what killed Mann. In arguing against the medical evidence, they demanded that the jury understand that Kelly "and the other two surgeons who examined her did not make one conclusive finding as to the cause of death, and Dr. Shea said so himself. The district attorney can only say, 'I want you to guess, to guess my way and then hang a man.'" In declaring the intentions of the prosecutor, the defense sought to negotiate, through hyperbole, what could be seen and what remained in the shadows. "Why, they haven't proved anything," Schenck affirmed in a vainglorious moment of oratory. "If I hadn't stipulated it, they wouldn't even have proved that Fritzie Mann is dead."

There you see before you . . . the man charged with this murder that has not been proved. There is the fiend described by the prosecution. Look at his face in evidence

there before you. It is the face of an educated gentleman, a
face for a mother to love, for a sister to idolize, a face that
reflects every heartthrob of goodness. Look at him, ladies
and gentlemen, and decide whether he is the fiend who
committed this murder—if murder was committed.[15]

In making this argument, Schenck was playing with the jurors'
understanding of their place in the complex system of permission
and prohibition that constituted the legal system. In actuality,
this argument was an attempt to pervert the jurors' place within
that system by arguing that in this moment they could see and
know all things. It was not a leap to believe this, given the focus
on consumerism and media visibility that characterized much of
the twenties. Schenck wanted them to believe that, because of
failures by the medical examiners and police, neither the body
nor the crime had any meaningful value: "Remember that you
are determining whether you will hang that boy by the neck until
he is dead, you should be as careful of the evidence as if your own
flesh and blood were being tried."[16]

Defense attorney Schenck was moralistic. He spun a narrative with events in the spring before Mann's death, when she
was juggling boyfriends. This narrative insisted that Mann was
a bit of a tramp. It was a parable of how not to live if you were
a girl. He was teaching the jury that interpretation is more than
attempts to recognize details; it engages the participants in the
process of divorcing meaning and truth. Jacobs could keep company with multiple women, and this did not make him immoral.
Yet Mann could behave in the same manner and receive a different coding independent of Jacobs.

By simplifying everything in Mann's life, the defense team
was attempting to perform a trick of perception. They made the
evidence seem transparent, which prevented the jury from seeing through the façade to some truth. Instead, he looked to the
experience of the viewer. He made the jury feel that they could
see the truth. The trick was that in giving the jury this privilege
he was removing their ability to find a single truth at the heart
of the matter. The jury willingly slipped back into the old comfortable fictions of transparency, the idea of a single truth, and

failed to notice that they had moved in the opposite direction from reality.[17]

> In conclusion, ladies and gentlemen of the jury, I want to remind you that if there is any reasonable hypothesis under which Fritzie Mann came to her death, beside by murder, you must acquit the defendant. If you think this evidence satisfies your minds that Fritzie Mann was murdered, and that Dr. Jacobs did it, I want you to do only one thing. Hang him as quick as you can do it. Either hang him or turn him loose. But if there is one reasonable doubt either as to whether the crime was committed or that he committed it, then you must turn him loose.[18]

Though he seemed to offer two options, the reality Schenck had composed for the jurors was inescapable. He asked them to confront mortality without asking them to confront the problems of their own modern society. He coded and encoded the evidence. He wanted the little voice inside each juror's head to focus not on the crime already committed but on the possibility that they themselves would become murderers. He asked the jury to believe there had been no murder. The exclusion of Fritzie Mann's death from his case became the exclusion of the killing as well as the terror of state-mandated execution, which if applied to an innocent man would make murderers of the jurors.

It was the strategy of the defense to depend on the assumption that human nature, with all its passion and irrationality, is fundamentally the same everywhere and among everyone. Schenck operated as though the shared opinions and feelings of humankind constitute the most reliable of outcomes. Basically, he was betting that the jury would not convict because they would see themselves as smarter than the experts.[19]

In painting her death as suicide, the defense lawyers were offering a denouement to a narrative that seemed to them tragic and self-deluding. Their plan, as lawyers, was simple: they were going to make the trial a "moving-picture of drama." They had brought in the wealthy, dignified, respectable Mrs. Worthington. They had found the autopsy surgeon from Los Angeles who talked about drowning rabbits. When the prosecution brought in handwriting experts, they had brought in the bank clerks to analyze the same handwriting. Browbeating the witness would count against them, unless the reason for so doing was clear and convincing, such as when they were terse with Mrs. Mann and implied that she did not know her daughter.[20] They could not afford to offend the jury or allow them to feel that they had treated any of the witnesses unfairly. So they made sure to present Mrs. Mann as the hysterical foreigner. The defense lawyers knew they had to present the proper demeanor, to be respectful, courteous, and dignified when it mattered. The show was the important thing.

Whether they meant to or not, the defense team had created two lines of thought. One looked at the criminal and the other looked at the crime. Of course, the criminal was the enemy of all civilization. Therefore, it was in the best interest of civilization to track down criminals who through the act of murder had disqualified themselves as citizens and taken on the shape of the villain, monster, madman, and lunatic. In a jury trial the ultimate power appeared to be punitive—prescribing tactics of intervention, prevention, and the enacting of penalties. When looking at the criminal, the jury (standing in for the community at large) had to also see a crime. Their punishment had to duplicate the severity of the crime. Fritzie Mann's body was an object that suggested a crime had taken place. What if there had been no crime other than suicide? Then the criminal threatening society was Fritzie Mann, and the punishment had already been enacted.[21]

On the other side of the courtroom was District Attorney Chester Kempley. Though his assistant Guy Selleck had been the one questioning witnesses throughout the trial, Kempley would deliver the closing arguments for the State in the second trial. In so doing, he was writing his own narrative. Had he been a character in *An American Tragedy*, he would have kept parts of the evidence secret and worked to "seal the mouth of everyone who knew." The district attorney would have thought that, since he had personally gathered the evidence and testimony, he deserved a certain amount of recognition in upcoming elections. A murder case could be "opportune" because it took so much time and brought about so much public opinion. A murder case was a "sensation of the first magnitude, with all those intriguingly

colorful, and yet morally and spiritually atrocious elements—
love, romance, wealth, poverty, death. And at once picturesque
accounts of where and how." "How did the killer conceal his
relations with the victim?" the novel asked. The fictional victim's letters, "poetic and gloomy being furnished to the Press for
use," seemed to "paint the picture of a poor, lonely, girl with no
one but him—and he a cruel, faithless—a murderer even. Was
not hanging too good for him?" Dreiser, the novelist, imagined
a moral tragedy so great that it could be a political boon to any
lawyer capable of controlling the narrative in a real courtroom.[22]

To convince the jury, the prosecution, like the defense, had
to decide what type of story to tell. This might seem frivolous,
because the press had already created a story. Mann's friends and
family all had a story to tell as well. In fact, everything about
Fritzie Mann had a kind of fiction to it. With so many timelines
and narrative arcs to pull from, the lawyers had to choose carefully; their narratives, if employed well, could force the jurors to
grasp the meaning of events and objects to which the jury were
not witnesses or participants. The jury would never truly understand the violence of murder, but through the narrative they
could enter the violence, death, and terror as tourists.[23]

The prosecution began their narrative with events the night
Mann died and made her life and murder into a riddle. In their
story, the motif of death underwent a philosophical conversion
that temporally truncated the sequence of her life. The death of
Fritzie Mann took on the meaning of a tragedy with an ultimate
end and a doomed outcome, which oddly is the same conclusion the defense had, though they reached it with a different
narrative.[24]

In the first trial, in April, and again in the second, in July,
the prosecution team of Kempley and Selleck maintained that
the suicide argument ignored the fact that "Frieda Mann never
wanted an illegal operation" and had done everything possible to
avoid having one. Yes, for the prosecution she was Frieda and not
Fritzie. The identity of the body was important because Fritzie
was a stage persona and Frieda was the person, or so the prosecutor wanted the jury to believe. Kempley then personalized
Mann's story for the jury, "Sometimes we think it would hurt
our family for us to marry. Sometimes we think we are better

than the poor little girl." He hinted at Jacobs' motive: "Sometimes we think more of getting ourselves out of trouble, more of maintaining our station in life, than we do of helping someone we may have injured." In both trials, the district attorney contended that pride and Jacobs's love of his "social position" would not permit him to marry one of less social standing.[25]

Though it was not allowed under California law, the prosecution did reference Jacobs's failure to take the stand in his own defense. The district attorney represented the power of the State. His power functioned not only through the State but through his ability to define social norms. In not taking the stand, Jacobs was trying to fight the State's power to define the truth. If he confessed, he would become ensnared in the State's production of truth, and he was more interested in the production of his own power. Nevertheless, the prosecutor saw truth in the details of the crime and in every gesture Jacobs made as a demonstration of guilt.[26] As Nick Caraway explains in *The Great Gatsby*, as if he were describing Jacobs and the wealthy class of citizens shielding him, "I couldn't forgive him or like him but I saw that what he had done was to him, entirely justified. It was all very careless and confused. They were careless people. . . . they smashed up things . . . and then retreated back to their money and their vast carelessness or whatever . . . and let other people clean up the mess they made."[27] The "other people" were the court system. The State's power seeks to permeate the guilty individual's body, which of course it did through executions. Still, it was more than just Jacobs's physical appearance and personality the prosecutor abhorred. He also showed disdain for Jacobs because in not testifying, which was his right, Jacobs refused to allow the State the truth.[28] As the prosecution declared his life forfeit, Jacobs sat smiling as he listened.[29]

The district attorney also voiced his disgust that the defense had introduced a motion that the case be dismissed for lack of evidence of a crime. The medical examiner's office was, according to the defense, unable to show a direct cause of death. Ultimately, the judge dismissed this motion in both trials. Still, the defense maintained in their closing arguments that, if there was a crime, Mann committed it against herself. The district attorney outlined all the physical evidence: "These speak to you the truth. . . . they tell you that certainly Fritzie Mann did not go to the beach of her own volition. If dead or unconscious, she was taken to the beach, it was by no innocent person. Innocent people do not attempt to dispose of the body or a person found by them." Jacobs had killed her, Kempley asserted, and then he attempted to "throw away the undesirable mute evidence of his connection with the little dancer. . . . circumstance after circumstance, each mounting and rising towards the inevitable . . . tells the story of truth."[30]

As a retort to the defense in the first trial's closing arguments and then repeated again in the second, the prosecutors had listed several challenges to the defense's logic: How did Fritzie Mann's body get on the beach with her hands carefully folded if she was not placed there? Who else but the person in attendance at death would cross the hands of the deceased? Why were there no signs of wear or tears on her silk slip or extensive bruises on her body if she had entered the ocean voluntarily to commit suicide, which would have caused her body to be tossed about on that gravel surf? Why should any person contemplating suicide stop to undress down to their slip before their attempt? If she had undressed on the beach, why was so little of her clothing recovered? In both trials, the details of the physical evidence mattered to the prosecution: "If Fritzie Mann had intended to commit suicide, after she left the Blue Sea Cottage with him, there was no reason in God's world why she should have gone more than 100 yards from the cottage." "And that Blue Sea cottage blanket on the beach . . . that is the closest kind of a connecting link between the cottage and the beach. If Fritzie Mann went out to commit suicide, why the blanket?" Indeed, if she had thrown her vanity case, handbag, and clothing on the beach, "how do you account for the fact that, according to several witnesses, there were no tracks around the articles? Except the dog tracks seen by the eminent Mr. Rannels?" The prosecution could have gone even further. If she had walked out into the surf and drowned, how on earth did she manage to keep her shoes on? The prosecutors concluded, "If there exists in your mind any doubt as to how the crime was committed, if you are satisfied that Fritzie came to her death as the result of a criminal agency and that Capt. Jacobs is responsible for her death, it does not make a particle of difference as to how her death occurred."[31]

The only thing the people in court could agree on in either trial was that Fritzie Mann was dead. They did not agree that she had been murdered. They did not agree on the names of the roads or how long it took to travel those roads. Neither could they agree on concepts as fleeting as justice or as complex as anatomy. Expert witnesses testified solely to aid and guide the jury on technical or specialized matters. Yet those experts testifying for the defense had no personal knowledge of the facts. All they could offer were their opinions or speculations. The defense attorneys urged them to hypothesize and expected the jury to know the difference between fact and opinion. The more the various defense attorneys tried to seal off Mann's life from the many contexts she encountered, the more they separated it from the social whole. Meanwhile, the prosecution broke her free from the moorings of performance, which were the ways she defined herself. In the hands of the law, she became a story of the beach, the night, the death, and the grave. They permanently suspended her in a threshold world where she lost her history and physicality. Her body stopped being the corpse and became a text they thought they could read.

Then what was at stake? The defense wanted the trial to be not about Jacobs killing Mann but about her morality and the skills of the investigators. This is not surprising; they were the defense. Running beneath all of their arguments were issues of who led the town and who had the power. Was it the modern city agencies—or was it the old, prominent, wealthy families whose members were among Jacobs's attorneys, his alibis, and his staunch supporters? His attorneys' arguments gave voice to those who wanted to keep power and prevent one of their own from being devoured by the emerging status of women and the working class.

For the prosecution, power had to be in the hands of the police and the coroner's office. There was scientific policing and the rule of law to uphold. They wanted to appear modern, and to exist above the social structure rather than as part of it. To be sure, the police, coroner, and prosecution tolerated the city boosters and the upper crust, but they had no intention of being replaced or voted out of office. In fighting two court cases, they also had no intention of letting a murderer go free or allowing Mann to be forgotten. Yet they could not abandon their expectations of Mann as the girl in trouble and Jacobs as the dishonorable social climber. Mann had flouted all of the socially constructed boundaries and power structures. She had spent the last year of her life creating herself, and in the year after her death everyone in San Diego tried to change her—into the nude body, as the newspapers reported, the victim, as the prosecution argued, the fallen woman, as the defense maintained, and the ghost, for whom her family grieved. Throughout all of these transformations, she was a metaphor that allowed the participants in the discourse to evoke words, ideas, relationships, and above all knowledge, transfiguring her into the imaginary Fritzie Mann.[32]

Where the defense had worked to erase Fritzie Mann's murder, their opposition's narrative tried to link an institution and an individual, a social structure and a subject, events and a biography. They needed the jury to confront the social problem of unwed mothers. Above all, they wanted the jury to be haunted by Frieda, not Fritzie.[33]

Mann understood that what we anticipate helps shape what we see; through "fictions of the self" she created reality.[34] To borrow Nick's description of Gatsby, she possessed "an extraordinary gift for hope" and "a romantic readiness." Like Gatsby, she "literally glowed."[35] Gatsby and Fritzie Mann had much in common. She could not live in a fixed reality any more than Gatsby could live like a gentleman.

The assumption that caused all of the narratives of Fritzie Mann to fail is that her audience believed there was some kind of truth waiting to be uncovered. Their narratives were hollow because they were competing with Mann's own understanding of the power of stories. Her audience would never arrive at the truth. Mann hid it too well. In death, she found fame because she could never fully be known.

12

AFTERWARD

"Not guilty" was the verdict of the second jury in the case of Dr. Louis L. Jacobs, charged with murder. The cloud of suspicion had lifted. The jury, four women and eight men, had deliberated for twenty-four hours. Their first ballot surprised even them. They were in agreement, according to the jury foreman, from the very beginning.

When they read the verdict, Jacobs was sitting forward in his chair. Reporters noticed him swallowing hard as Judge Marsh went through procedures of the court. The bailiff brought the verdict to the judge. The judge read it silently, then handed it back. Then Jacobs heard what he had no doubt hoped to be the outcome. When Dr. Jacobs realized he was free, he sat perfectly still. "I knew it!" were his first words.[1]

"I'll never forget your face—never. Thank you," he said to each juror that filed by him.

Coroner Kelly noted the moment in his scrapbook. Next to a newspaper photo of Jacobs, shot from a low angle to give the innocent man a sinister appearance, Kelly noted that Jacobs was not wearing "spectacles." Kelly clearly believed Jacobs to be guilty and to have faked his way through the trial, in part by wearing his glasses to obscure his appearance.

"I don't know what I'll do now," Jacobs said, when asked about his plans. "I don't know whether I'll go back to Camp Kearny. I didn't expect the jury in until Monday. I was just preparing for a haircut in jail when the bailiff came for me."

Jacobs left the courthouse with his cousin, Louis Shapiro of Detroit, who was also one of his attorneys. Once outside, he turned as if to go to the jail—then checked himself. "I'll be darned if I'll go back to that place," he said. "I have a stack of books and personal effects there but I'll send for them."

The newspaper reporters yelled questions.

"How did I stand it to be accused as I was? An innocent man can stand anything," he said.

"I don't know. I am so upset with this sudden termination of my own trial that I have no definite plans. Why, I had not expected any verdict until next Monday. I was getting ready to have a shave when they called me in the jail and told me the verdict had been obtained. I am too happy for words. Of course, I never did believe they would do anything else but acquit me."

Three days later, Jacobs was still talking to the press. He was sitting on a "luxurious sofa" in the lobby of the Grant Hotel. They wanted to know his plans. Would he leave San Diego? If he left, would he come back?

"I am leaving San Diego but not forever, I will return one day."

Would he marry?

"Going to get married, I should say not. I've got a mountain of debt to dig through."[2]

He did return to work, for the Public Health Service in Chicago and Washington, D.C., where he became a prominent public figure in psychiatry, juvenile delinquency, and addiction treatment.[3]

Rogers Clark, the other suspect in Mann's murder, married his alibi Gladys Flowers, a few minutes after his divorce was finalized.[4]

"One thing more I want to say," Jacobs exclaimed to the press gathered in the hotel lobby. "No one in the world has greater sympathy than I for Mrs. Mann, Fritzie Mann's mother. If I could solve the mystery of Fritzie Mann's death, I should certainly do it. I'd give my right arm . . . to know that secret."

Then he stood and sort of skipped away. At the last moment, he turned and thanked the reporters from the *San Diego Sun*. He felt their coverage had always been fair.

While Jacobs escaped conviction and execution, Clara Phillips, the "Hammer Slayer," faced ten years in prison. She was living in a prison ward meant to house twenty-five but in reality held more than twice as many. When interviewed by the press, she continued to present herself as the victim of fate. She had lost her home and her husband. She had been wrongly accused.[5] The *San Diego Tribune* quipped, "Oh, very well. Now that Clara Phillips is safely locked up, we can resume discussion of the world court."[6]

District Attorney Chester Kempley and his assistant Guy Selleck were indicted in 1926 for accepting a $40,000 bribe and withholding evidence in a murder case. The case hinged on the testimony of a convicted killer and former owner of the Dearborn Hotel, a San Diego brothel. Agnes Keller told a tale of bribery, witness tampering, and connections to the Chicago underworld. Kempley's and Selleck's convictions were overturned in 1928, but their careers were forever tainted.[7]

There was no freedom for the Mann family. Helen, Fritzie's invalid sister, passed away a few months after the second trial. She had succumbed to her grief and to tuberculosis. The people of San Diego noticed her passing only because the newspapers proclaimed her the sister of Fritzie Mann. The tragedy for the Mann family had become total. Amelia, the mother, and William, the brother, buried Helen near Fritzie. Then they left for Colorado. Nearly a decade later, William had his sisters' bodies moved to Colorado too.

Members of the Jacobs jury said they had reached an agreement not to comment on their discussion. Still, one juror said the question of whether the corpus delicti had been proven was given considerable discussion. Their findings left the death of Fritzie Mann as it had always been—a deep mystery. Who was the man who took her to the cottage? Who was the father? Why had she changed her plans at the last minute? The answer to these questions would never be known. *The San Diego Sun* wrote the epitaph, "Fritzie Mann rests in her grave. The world moves on—forgetting."[8]

Appendix

HISTORIOGRAPHY AND METHODOLOGY

By reflecting on historiography and methodology, we can examine how Fritzie Mann's life and death present a framework for understanding the Jazz Age. Her place in the scholarship is significant because she aids the historian in understanding the reasons for and the consequences of the era's fundamental questioning of the meaning of life, self, and freedom. World War I had shaken people's faith in patriotism, loyalty, and honor.[1] As Zelda Fitzgerald explained, the war caused the children of the prewar period to realize "too soon that they had seen the magician's whole repertoire." The war "was the last piece of wizardry" her generation believed.[2] They, both the survivors of the war and those too young to have fought in it, stridently insisted that the meaning of life lay in the act of living and in filling the moment with vitality. As a result, the decade known as the Jazz Age contained more hedonism and narcissism than would seem possible. Freedom was no longer bound to the concept of doing what was morally right and ethically responsible for the whole; rather, people began to define it as doing what was responsible and right for oneself.[3] In *The Great Gatsby*, Nick Caraway, the novel's narrator, summarizes the shift toward the self by pointing out, "Life is much more successfully looked at from a single window, after all."[4] Fritzie Mann's life is the window through which one can see the emergence of the new generation and new age.

Seemingly, everywhere in the Jazz Age there was a call for modernity and social revolution. Women were at the center of this massive postwar social change. Like the war, women's equality had fallen short of its promises of a better world. Though women had fought for the right to vote and all the equalities it implied—such as jury service, the right to work, and the right to divorce—there was emptiness to the demand because the advancements had not made life easier or better. In the early twenties, many women looked back at the gains they had made and felt they were still living in a world dreamed up by men, managed by men, and judged by men. In sum, though they had gained a measure of equality with ratification of the Nineteenth Amendment, they were still only elaborating a society established by men. They were not seeking to live in either a world where men dominated them completely, such as that prior to the war, or a world where men patronizingly permitted them certain freedoms, such as that of working at a department store. Women were looking for a third way.[5] Therefore, Mann's acts of rebellion and quest for liberation, which led to her death and are the focus of this book, were part of a larger moment.[6]

This is a cultural history. In defining my work in this way, I am thinking of Modris Eksteins's argument from *The Rite of Spring* concerning how to do history. He writes that to understand the significance of a moment in history "one must of course deal with the interests and emotions involved in it." This genre of history and writing falls under the "the broad terms of cultural history." Though this type of history might discuss music, fashion, movies, and murder, I have learned from Eksteins that this type of history must "in the end unearth manners and morals, customs and values, either articulated and assumed. As difficult as the task may be, cultural history must at least try to capture the spirit for an age. That spirit is to be located in the society's sense of priorities." Moreover, as Charles Riley argues in *Free as Gods*, cultural history requires some "assembly . . . especially if we want to slip inside the intimate circles" and understand the "public metamorphosis" of figures such as Mann.[7]

Fritzie Mann thrived and died in the Jazz Age city because of its abstractions, improvisations, and hypocrisy. For the most part, the name "Jazz Age" does not conjure images of southern California. Generally, the term raises images of the "lost generation" in Paris, of bootleggers in Chicago, or of musicians in New York City. Recently the literature on the Jazz Age has added a focus on immigrants[8] and drawn on queer theory[9] to expand our understanding of this decade. Lara Putnam's cultural and intellectual history of Harlem, *Radical Moves*, and Andy Fry's *Paris Blues* suggest the connections between emerging music and emerging politics. Delving deeper into the historiography, Lewis A. Erenberg's *Swingin' the Blues* and Michael Alexander's *Jazz Age Jews* also come to mind for their arguments concerning the connection of music, politics, and radicals.[10]

Jazz Age books have certain things in common. They focus on the emergence of urban life and modernity. Their soundtrack-heavy arguments depend on African American music. Immigrants and minorities (be they sexual, political, religious, or racial) play a central role in challenging the status quo, which in turn forces social changes that undermine prewar values. Nevertheless, despite the emphasis on revolutions and upheaval, much of the scholarship focuses on the remaking or transformation of the older established cities: New York, Chicago, and Paris.

Histories of the Jazz Age also frequently claim to be histories of outsiders and rebels. When the focus is exclusively on the long-established urban centers, these histories further a kind of cultural suppression and dominance held by the East and Midwest in American history. By shifting the focus to the borderlands, we can expand our definition of culture to both the beliefs and practices as well as the frontiers and crossroads of these beliefs and practices. In so doing, our scholarship can erode cultural monopolies that present the idea that significant histories focus on the center, either historiographically when examining New York City or geographically when considering Chicago.[11]

Where does Fritzie Mann belong? This is a history of a woman who barely had time to live her life. Her story is a reminder of how much we as students, teachers, and scholars can learn from focusing on a single person in one moment in time. There is a similarity between Mann's life and the histories in Thomas Robisheaux's *The Last Witch of Langenburg*, John Brewer's *A Sentimental Murder*, Carlo Ginzburg's *The Cheese and the Worms*,

Natalie Zemon Davis's *The Return of Martin Guerre,* and Gene Brucker's *Giovannia and Lusanna.* These are all histories pinpointing specific individuals and events rather than groups or structures. They show a predilection for the study of people with obscure lives that act as skeleton keys into the mindset of their respective cultures. "When successful," as Brucker wrote, "this microcosmic focus conveys a sense of immediacy, intimacy, and concreteness that is often absent from analytical histories."[12] Furthermore, these histories rely on court records and police reports to locate individuals who otherwise fall through the cracks, as well as on the skill of the researcher to reconstruct the world as lived. It is my contention that Mann's life and her death offer the opportunity to personalize the conceptual framework of the Jazz Age by making the history as intimate as the crime.

Any history focused on the Jazz Age has to reconcile the importance of primary sources with the reality of the tabloid press. At issue is not so much whether the press fabricated stories, relied on hyperbole, and standardized social fears as whether the focus should be the connection of the press and the readers. In the twenties they were not two entities—one manipulating and the other passively repeating the information. The relationship of the press to the public was one of reciprocation. They consumed each other and in so doing jointly shaped the narrative.[13] In the chapters "News" and "Fantasy," for example, I provide the coverage of the press, a brief history of tabloid journalism, and a discussion of the influence of newspaper serials. With this discussion as a foundation, it becomes clear how the press rather than the police had the power to control the crime narrative. Though the press swung between moralist and sensationalist, the papers are an essential record. I have taken the majority of the San Diego coverage of Mann's death from the scrapbook kept by a coroner central to the case, Schuyler Kelly. The newspapers have even greater significance because a person living through the event used them as a chronicle.

Looking at this history through the lens of Coroner Kelly's scrapbook necessitated connecting the research to the history of violence and crime. As Kristofer Allerfeldt argued in his *Crime and the Rise of Modern America,* the way to present the history of a crime is twofold. First, choose a period in which America experienced significant change. In World War I, the United States found its footing on a world stage and committed itself in the following years to pursuing innovation so as to become an economic, political, and cultural power. Yet this pursuit of perceived destiny brought the mistake of Prohibition, hatred of immigrants, and a sexism that destroyed women while turning them into celebrities. Because of the high degree of immorality and corruption, killers, victims, law enforcement, and those who profited by reporting on crime explain the period well. Second, according to Allerfeldt, choose a structure that reflects the subject. Crime is an obsession for Americans in the Jazz Age, so it presents a way of interpreting that era. This study follows the body from the dumpsite, to the medical examiner, to the media, to the community, and eventually to the trial—thereby involving a degree of social history. Nevertheless, the cultural history approach takes hold because it is the twenties, a time dominated by the purposeful creation of identities—by everyone from the average citizen, to the newspapers, to the city boosters, to Hollywood—rooted in illusion and mythologies. Indeed, the true crime structure provides an ideal conceptual framework for understanding a micro-American cultural history through the life of a woman who was as hyperbolic and invented as the Jazz Age itself.[14]

Throughout, I draw on the archival collections from the San Diego History Center, San Diego State University Special Collections, and the Dittrick Medical History Museum. These archives are at the heart of the project. In "Flapper," I also pull from the collections and expertise of the Western Reserve Historical Society and the Jewish Historical Society of San Diego at San Diego State University.

My research involved not only consulting traditional primary sources found in libraries and archives but also visits to an anatomy lab. In preparation for the chapter "Body," I made extensive visits to the CaseMed anatomy lab, with my students, where I engaged in hands-on, experiential research. To understand the primary sources from the medical examiners' office, it was important for me to view the interiors of the ultimate primary source: the human body. These research trips were the only way to see through the eyes of the medical examiners and to appreciate their written records. Moreover, it was important to this project to understand how and why stories are told about the body. Throughout, the medical examiners' records, testimonies, and methods are juxtaposed with the competing medical theories of the time and scholarly works that consider Mann's performative construction of the body. In other words, the body is an object, a text, contested territory, and the remains of a person.

Selecting an unknown individual and diving headlong into the minutia of her body, death, and life might seem like focusing on the footnotes of history rather than the text. Is this history from below? Is this book an example of how to recover a silent figure from history, as in the New Social History? Indeed, the methodological approaches used throughout the book draw on these schools of thought. Yet *Fritzie: The Invented Life and Violent Murder of a Flapper* goes further toward reducing the scale of history, as Carlo Ginzburg argued, so that the reader can understand how the systems of belief, values, and representations relate to the social affiliations and power relationships that produce the day-to-day culture.[15] Likewise, throughout this book, figures like Zelda Fitzgerald and novels such as *The Great Gatsby* (1925) and *An American Tragedy* (1925) provide access to the minds and motivations of people in this period. Through these writings, we as students of history can locate the voice of the flapper standing in opposition to a socially required—and unjust—life based on conformity.

Moreover, Jazz Age literature, particularly novels, provided a way for readers from the time to recognize themselves and the ambiguous truths at the heart of the era in which they lived. Still, the use of fiction in a history has its limits. Fiction is the work of a single individual with a vibrant imagination and in some cases a need to examine the shortcomings of the world in which they live. Similarly, Zelda Fitzgerald's nonfiction writings about flappers perform the same task. To address these limitations, these works are presented throughout this book, in conjunction with other sources, as part of a cultural whole in which they provide access to the rebellious minds of killers, flappers, and nonconformists.[16]

Like periodicals, I treat novels as primary sources, but there is the argument that they are not primary sources. This argument's subtext wonders if the historian can connect the reader to the period through sources. At stake is the issue of whether these materials are mediated representations of events rather than the events themselves. The same argument could be applied to other sources used throughout this book. Novels, newspaper clippings, and court testimonies are all products of memory and thus could be considered secondary sources.[17] Susan Grigg argues that historians demand primary sources be used but fail to consider how the evidence relates or even why it is important. She calls into question the use of sources in a way that presents them as testimony to an event, because the sources themselves are not in any active or literal way the event. She explains that the classic historical method in the United States had three elements: research, analysis, and interpretation or synthesis.[18] The problems of analysis and synthesis have been interrogated by Giovanni Levi, Sigurour Gylfi Magnússon, and Zoltan Boldizsar Simon.[19] All have questioned the subjectivity of a narrative that seeks to capture the "lived experience," as this book does.[20]

These scholars might ask how and why this book can submerge the reader in the sources and thereby claim the reader will generate a new perspective on history? Indeed, it is my intention that the sources push and define the narrative. My approach is to examine how the competing narratives—those of the police, writers, and media, Mann's persona, and her family's perception of her, for example—work to construct the realities of the case, the era, and Mann. I keep the voices of the time at the forefront of the narrative. As Patricia Cline Cohen wrote in *The Murder of Helen Jewett*, these types of sources are essential to unlocking "an ethic" that acknowledges the "underlying contradiction [that] lay at the heart" of all the stories told about the victim, the killer, and the society. For Cline Cohen, such sources are essential to an understanding of gender and sexuality because they reveal how "seduction narratives bolstered male egos, encouraged men to assert sexual mastery over women, and allowed women the latitude to exhibit sexual energy on their own."[21] Ginzburg might add that, when we use these different types of sources, we see the culture of morality created by the upper classes in tension with the culture created by the other strata of society. Sometimes, according to Ginzburg, to access the lower strata one must use the "intermediaries" of court documents and "popular literature." In the case of Cline Cohen and Ginzburg, the goal is to access the "popular"—meaning the masses—through the use of the "popular"—meaning the mass-produced.[22] Moreover, using these various sources helps to create a history with a respect for the intelligence of those involved while keeping an eye on the nuances the people at the time may not have seen. To fulfill this purpose, the sources present the knowledge of the time and the multiplicity of perspectives.[23]

For these reason, I am not troubled by the extravagances of the media or the novels in the twenties. Rather, these sources intrigue me because I want to understand the culture and how Fritzie Mann fits into it. Here we have a young woman inventing everything about herself to be successful in a culture that is frequently just a fabrication. Her choices illustrate that history has competing narratives that at times overlap or conflict. I maintain that Fritzie Mann's life and death provide an intriguing portal into the Jazz Age as these complex stories yield insight into the nuances of the age. For example, in the chapters "Abortionist," "Death," and "Archetypes," Mann's life and death connect the reader to the various roles women filled at the time, from widows to maids to abortionists.

For the Mann family, I draw on immigration records, census records, and obituaries. They also provided long testimonies in court, which I reproduce in chapters including "News" and "Archetypes," and interviews to the press in which they detailed their lives and views of events. From Fritzie Mann there are surviving letters and photos, which are central to the chapters "Flapper," "Abortionist," and "Death." Because the Mann family first made their home near Denver and then in San Diego, they are strongly part of western history. There were specific reasons for immigrating to California and specific historical experiences that define this community. The pull of Hollywood and the idea that immigrants could be successful was one aspect. The hospitals, sunshine, and still relevant frontier myth of creating a new life were also fundamental to their choices.

By presenting this cultural history as a narrative, this book seeks to appreciate and recognize life in the urban American West in the early Jazz Age in terms of commonly held assumptions about the pathology and normality of violence. Murder investigations were not just vehicles for the production of discourses about deviance: they also inscribed the social and moral geography of the city and its communities.[24] In the chapters "Flapper" and "Abortionist," the book's narrative explores how San Diego grew into prominence by erecting European façades on buildings and by concealing its social problems, including illegal liquor and abortions. In "Archetypes," "Killers," "Rabbit," and "Closings" are examinations of the place of women, law, science, and violence in this Jazz Age city. This is the type of history best pursued by studying crime. I maintain that the most telling crime is not the political fighting or Prohibition violence of the era. As Sace Elder argues in *Murder Scenes*, domestic violence is the key to reading the city, the time, and the people as historic sources.[25] The murder of Fritzie Mann reveals the anxiety of southern California about Jazz Age social leveling and fragmentation, which caused a growing sense of uncertainty regarding class distinctions and the social order.

Mann's relationship to gender and social class exposes evidence of the limits of acceptable female sexual power. Many think of the Jazz Age as a time of female liberation. Indeed, middle-class girls displayed liberal sexual style in their clothing, language, and mannerisms. Popular culture, such as the movies and magazines, encouraged them to date, to dance, and to French kiss. Women in the twenties engaged in premarital sex in greater numbers than in previous decades. Everyone from physicians to educators rejected the Victorian values of the prewar years and seemed to be preaching the importance of heterosexual pleasure.[26] Nevertheless, Fritzie Mann was not middle class. There is a historiography for this type of study focused on the immigrant and working-class woman. Mary Odem in *Delinquent Daughters* and Melissa Klapper in *Ballots, Babies, and Banners of Peace* consider the reforms' attempts to control lower-class women and the legal limits of female sexual expression. Judith Mackrell's *Flappers* considers how socialization and the media arbitrated gender. Angela Latham's *Posing a Threat* and Liz Conor's *The Spectacular Modern Woman* focus on the beauty standard as means of repression and of liberation. Betsy Israel in *Bachelor Girl* considers the social norm of marriage and the women who lived outside that norm. Susan Glenn, in *Daughters of the Shtetl* and *Female Spectacle,* illustrates ethnicity and class holding women in check.[27] Fritzie Mann contributes by presenting the role and culture of violence in gender history.

For the sake of this study, violence is defined as the physical act of infringing on the life or rights of another or oneself. In other words, as the editors of *These Ragged Edges: Histories of Violence along the U.S.-Mexico Border* point out, at its basic level violence is "damage—whether real or threatened—to humans and property."[28] This definition includes murder. It also includes physical abuse, particularly domestic abuse. The focus is Mann's death. Swirling around this story is the larger context of violence in the twenties and its notable rise in homicides, executions, and suicides. What drives this discussion is not the concept of civilization, as in Pieter Spierenburg's *A History of Murder,* a survey of the history of violence over seven centuries, but more as in his *Violence and Punishment,* which discusses the civilizing of the body and how gender became an expression of violence. In San Diego, crime bared the opportunities and boundaries of community, especially for the working-class immigrants compared to the wealthy inhabitants of Coronado.[29] In building my definition of violence, I combine P. D. James and Foucault with an intention of revealing the limits of community, family, and the police.

For these reasons, the structure of this book follows the murder investigation, the media response, and the trials. There are lengthy sections devoted to the newspaper serials, the novels, the films, and the media coverage of murders and the changing social mores. My use of sources enables readers to see and understand how historians explore the reality created by media. My interweaving of sources also insists that the readers understand that these were real people living in a media-driven reality. At times, I present the reader with the raw dialogue from court transcripts and newspaper accounts in order to connect to the voices and the perspectives of the time. My work also values transparency in the presentation of the sources. It is important to understand these sources in their own unique context and in their own voices, because the police investigation involved the process of discovery, and the media transformed the case into a collective community endeavor. By following the footprints left by the sources, it is possible to see the discrepancies, tensions, and the divisions brought on by sexuality and gender. The ways in which I seek to bring readers, especially students and nonacademics, to the sources is one of the chief contributions of this book. The use of sources is also one of the great challenges for the twenty-first-century reader because these materials are striking in how explicitly they discuss the anxieties regarding women and violence. Too often readers come to history hoping to see what the people at the time did not know or to see the roots of our own society. However, the sources throughout this book demand consideration based on their own perspective rather than that of the modern reader.

When readers engage with direct dialogue from court records, they are reading a social script that reflects values and rules. For the women in "Archetypes" who are challenging the social scripts, it is important to let them speak for themselves so that we hear their voices. Likewise, the men who wanted to assert control over Fritzie Mann's body and narrative should also speak for themselves. The intention in the chapters "Rabbit" and Archetypes" is to listen to the history. Hearing the history is important if we are to understand how the social scripts tightened the barriers, as Jennifer Lynn Stover argues regarding race in *The Sonic Color Line,* concerning gender dynamics in the years immediately after World War I and the success of the women's suffrage movement.[30]

Fritzie Mann appeared suddenly, dramatically, and even menacingly on the social scene as a dancer destined for stardom, and fourteen months later she was dead. I argue that her death signaled that a transformation was under way. Women would be the symbol of that transformation because the violence and misogyny of the twenties consumed sexually transgressive women, like Mann, even as it celebrated them. To understand this history one must do more than examine family, class, and consumer habits. Rather, Mann's place in Jazz Age history requires an analysis of the multidimensional complexity of the culture.[31]

NOTES

INTRODUCTION

1. Alice Kessler-Harris, *A Difficult Woman: The Challenging Life and Times of Lillian Hellman* (New York: Bloomsbury Press, 2012), 5.

2. F. Scott Fitzgerald, "Echoes of the Jazz Age," *Scribner's,* November 1931, 459–64.

3. Paula S. Fass, *The Damned and the Beautiful: American Youth in the 1920s* (New York: Oxford University Press, 1977), 3; Charles A. Riley II, *Free as Gods: How the Jazz Age Reinvented Modernism* (Lebanon, NH: University Press of New England, 2017), 8, 235–36.

4. Larry Wolfe, *The Idea of Galicia: History and Fantasy in Habsburg Political Culture* (Stanford, CA: Stanford University Press, 2010), 13–14.

5. Wolfe, *Idea of Galicia,* 1, 305, 403, 404.

6. Zelda Fitzgerald, "Eulogy for the Flapper," in *Zelda Fitzgerald: The Collected Writings,* ed. Matthew J. Bruccoli (New York: Collier Books, 1992), 391; Sarah Churchwell, *Careless People: Murder, Mayhem, and the Invention of The Great Gatsby* (London: Virago, 2015), 11.

7. Frederick Lewis Allen, *Only Yesterday: An Informed History of the 1920s* (New York: Harper and Brothers, 1931; reprint, New York: Harper and Row, 1964), 97 (page references are to the 1964 edition); Maureen A. Molly, *On Creating a Usable Culture: Margaret Mead and the Emergence of American Cosmopolitanism* (Honolulu: University of Hawai'i Press, 2008), 43–44; F. Scott Fitzgerald, *The Great Gatsby* (original publication

1925, New York: Simon and Schuster, 1995), 26, 98, 189 (page references are to the 1995 edition).

8. Kessler-Harris, *Difficult Woman*, 4–5, 15.

CHAPTER 1. BEACH

1. Opening statement by District Attorney Chester C. Kempley, *The People of the State of California v. Louis L. Jacobs*, case 38832, Superior Court of the State of California, San Diego County, San Diego and San Diego Court Appellate Briefs Collection, boxes 5–19, San Diego State University Special Collections and University Archive, Library and Information Access (hereafter *People v. Louis L. Jacobs*). All testimony and other documents from the Jacobs case cited in this book are from this collection unless otherwise noted.

2. "Torrey Pines Park Graced by Beautiful Adobe Lodge," *San Diego Union*, January 1, 1923.

3. Opening statement by District Attorney Chester C. Kempley.

4. Testimony of Clarence Matthews, *People v. Louis L. Jacobs*.

5. Testimony of John R. Chase, *People v. Louis L. Jacobs*.

6. Testimony of Harley Sachs, *People v. Louis L. Jacobs*.

7. Testimony of Clarence Matthews.

8. Testimony of Clarence Matthews; Testimony of Robert Bowman, *People v. Louis L. Jacobs*.

9. Testimony of Harley Sachs.

CHAPTER 2. BODY

1. Testimony of Dr. John Shea, *People v. Louis L. Jacobs*. The following discussion of the first Mann autopsy is drawn from this testimony, supported by the other sources noted.

2. William Scott Wadsworth, *Post-mortem Examinations* (Philadelphia: W. B. Saunders Company, 1915), 518. I am indebted to the archivists and curators at the Dittrick Medical History Center, Cleveland, Ohio, for this source.

3. Wadsworth, *Post-mortem Examinations*, 25–26.

4. Wadsworth, *Post-mortem Examinations*, 18; Bill Brown, *A Sense of Things* (Chicago: University of Chicago Press, 2003), 4, 11.

5. Wadsworth, *Post-mortem Examinations*, 169.

6. Wadsworth, *Post-mortem Examinations*, 140–41.

7. Wadsworth, *Post-mortem Examinations*, 142–48; Christine Montross, *Body of Work: Meditations on Mortality from the Human Anatomy Lab* (New York: Penguin Press, 2007), 66.

8. Wadsworth, *Post-mortem Examinations*, 32.

9. Wadsworth, *Post-mortem Examinations*, 33–35, 46, 149, 155, 487. I am grateful to Victor Guinto at Case Western Reserve University School of

Medicine for inviting me to the school's anatomy lab, where I experienced and came to understand these issues firsthand.

10. Wadsworth, *Post-mortem Examinations,* 154–55.

11. Wadsworth, *Post-mortem Examinations,* 150–51, 155, 327.

12. Wadsworth, *Post-mortem Examinations,* 40–41, 44.

13. "Girl Murdered, Police Say, Solution Is Near," *San Diego Union,* January 18, 1923; "Two Held in Mann Case," *San Diego Tribune,* January 19, 1923.

14. Testimonies of Richard Chadwick and George Sears, *People v. Louis L. Jacobs.*

15. La Verne T. Ryder, "Photographs as Evidence," *Photo-Era,* May 1919, 248–50.

16. "Owner of 'Love Cottage' Sees Photo of Clark; Says He Resembles Fritzie Mann's Companion," *San Diego Union,* January 19, 1923. Camp Kearny (now on the grounds of Miramar Naval Air Station) was several miles inland from Torrey Pines.

17. "Jacobs Listens Smiling while State Declares His Life Forfeit," *San Diego Union,* April 13, 1923.

18. "Owner of 'Love Cottage.'"

19. Testimonies of Drs. Shea and H. A. Thompson, *People v. Louis L. Jacobs;* Wadsworth, *Post-mortem Examinations,* 47, 480–84, 498.

20. Testimonies of Drs. Shea and Thompson; Wadsworth, *Post-mortem Examinations,* 518.

21. "Death of Dancer Followed Auto Trip, Charge; Companions Sought," date and publication unknown, articles saved in Kelly's scrapbook.

22. Discussion of the second autopsy is drawn the testimonies of Drs. Shea, Kelly, and Thompson and the other sources specified below; Wadsworth, *Post-mortem Examinations,* 514–15, 519. "Moral imperatives shift accordingly, to combat first the temptations of the imagination and then subjectivity. Quests for truth and quests for objectivity do not produce the same kind of sciences or the same kind of scientist. It is the integral involvement of the scientific self in the process of knowing that accounts for the interweaving of ethos and epistemology in all these historical episodes." Lorraine Daston and Peter Galison, *Objectivity* (New York: Zone Books, 2007), 232–33.

23. Eugene A. Arnold, "Autopsy: The Final Diagnosis," in *Images of the Corpse: From the Renaissance to Cyberspace,* ed. Elizabeth Klaver (Madison: University of Wisconsin Press, 2004), 3–5; P. D. James, *The Murder Room* (New York: Random House, 2003), 7. I am grateful to Theresa Mudrock for introducing me to P. D. James.

24. Wadsworth, *Post-mortem Examinations,* 498–99.

25. Wadsworth, *Post-mortem Examinations,* 511–12.

26. "Think Girl Died from Illegal Anesthetic," *San Diego Tribune,* January 19, 1920.

27. "Bones Unearthed at Doctor's Home," *San Diego Union,* September 2, 1920; "Kelly Answers Criticism of Verdict," *San Diego Evening Tribune,* September 21, 1920.

28. Dr. John George Spenzer Collection, "Corrosive Poisons," plate 45, Dittrick Museum of Medical History, Cleveland, OH (hereafter Spenzer Collection); Wadsworth, *Post-mortem Examinations,* 479.

29. "Charge Former San Diego Man with Murder," *San Diego Tribune,* April 28, 1921; Wadsworth, *Post-mortem Examinations,* 479.

30. E. E. Free, "The Detective's Laboratory," *San Diego Tribune,* November 11, 1922.

31. "Slayer Strangled Girl, Says Doctor," *San Diego Union,* July 29, 1920.

32. Wadsworth, *Post-mortem Examinations,* 513.

33. Spenzer Collection, "Corrosive Poisons," plates 34, 36, 37.

34. "D— Fool Altruism Blamed by Jacobs; Whiskey Clue Fails," *San Diego Tribune,* January 19, 1923.

35. "Death, Only Way Out," *San Diego Union,* July 29, 1920.

36. "Wife of Slain Man Testifies," *San Diego Union,* February 21, 1923; "Tells Jury How He Killed with Pickaxe Handle," *San Diego Union,* February 22, 1923; "Murder Case Nearing End," *San Diego Sun,* February 28, 1923.

37. "Rendering the city legible proved to be increasingly difficult over the Weimar years. There developed in the 1920s a palpable anxiety about the uncertainty of class distinctions and the social order." Sace Elder, *Murder Scenes: Normality, Deviance, and Criminal Violence in Weimar Berlin* (Ann Arbor: University of Michigan Press, 2010), 3.

38. "Most of the homicidal violence committed in Berlin (as indeed elsewhere) was not stranger violence but rather 'everyday' homicides, by which is meant those acts of violence that arose out of normal, everyday life that could potentially affect anyone." Elder, *Murder Scenes,* 7; "Kelly Answers Criticism of Verdict."

CHAPTER 3. NEWS

1. "S.D. Coroner Called to Torrey Pines," *San Diego Tribune,* January 15, 1923.

2. "Woman's Body on Beach," *San Diego Sun,* January 16, 1923.

3. Sace Elder continues this discussion throughout her book. Through the press, society began to see murder as a way of evaluating the effectiveness of the police and civil reformers. The apparent increase in violent acts, particularly homicide, appeared to be evidence of the impact of war, inflation, and revolution. The idea of a "moral panic" started to take hold of the public imagination. Looking at Jazz Age America, a similar argument could be made. Elder, *Murder Scenes,* 6, 43.

4. "Fritzie's Letters Stolen," *San Diego Sun,* January 20, 1923; "Woman's Body on Beach."

5. "Fritzie's Letters Stolen."

6. Patricia Cline Cohen, *The Murder of Helen Jewett* (New York: Vintage Books, 1998), 26–29, 43–45; Neal Gabler, *Life: The Movie—How Entertainment Conquered Reality* (New York: Knopf, 1998), 61–63.

7. Gabler, *Life*, 53, 54, 62, 66, 67, 74; Charles Taylor, *Sources of the Self: The Making of Modern Identity* (Cambridge, MA: Harvard University Press, 1989), 458. Elder terms this phenomenon "the visual and spectacular nature of the criminal investigation" and then draws on Janet Ward's term "surface culture." "Sites of surface culture included advertising, the film industry, and shop windows." The press could be considered an important part of this type of culture in that newspapers made the city "observable" and people could "imagine themselves as part of a wider community." Elder, *Murder Scenes*, 66–67.

8. "Trial by Headline" *Saturday Evening Post*, August 16, 1924, 22.

9. "Getting Away with Murder," *Saturday Evening Post*, March 22, 1924, 21, 101, 102, 105.

10. Gabler, *Life*, 72–77.

11. "Poison Gas and Probation," *The Independent*, February 5, 1921, 137–38.

12. "District Attorney's Theory of the Elwell Murder; Someone He Well Knew and Not Feared, Killed Elwell," *New York Times*, June 17, 1920.

13. "Roscoe Arbuckle Faces an Inquiry on Woman's Death," *New York Times*, September 11, 1921; "Arbuckle Accused of Manslaughter by Coroner's Jury," *New York Times*, September 15, 1921; "Hays Sanctions Arbuckle Return; Causes Protests," *New York Times*, December 21, 1922; "Will Hays Defends Arbuckle Decision," *New York Times*, December 24, 1922.

14. "Question Movie Stars in Director's Murder," *San Diego Union*, February 3, 1922.

15. Allen, *Only Yesterday*, 67; "Youth Shot Pastor and Choir Singer by Mistake Says Pal Who Was with Him," *The World*, October 22, 1922.

16. "Ideal Crime Tours for Motorists," *New York Tribune*, November 19, 1922.

17. Boyden Spanks, "When Murder Lifts a Small Town's Lid," *New York Tribune*, October 22, 1922.

18. Churchwell, *Careless People*, 291–92.

19. Gabler, *Life*, 60, 72, 96.

20. Churchwell, *Careless People*, 261–62.

21. "Girl Murdered Police Say," *San Diego Union*, January 18, 1923.

22. "Arrest Expected after Probe of Dancing Girl's Mysterious Death Here," *San Diego Union*, January 18, 1923; "Indictment May Result from Grand Jury Probe into Death of Dancer," *San Diego Sun*, January 26, 1923.

23. "Dancing Feet of Fritzie Are Stilled," *San Diego Sun*, January 16, 1923.

24. "Dress Lying Near above Tide-Line," *San Diego Union*, January 16, 1923.

25. "Two Are Arrested for Dancer's Death," *New York Times*, January 19, 1923; "Her Mother Breaks Down," *San Diego Sun*, January 19, 1923.

26. Allen, *Only Yesterday*, 83–84.

27. "Fritzie's Letters Stolen."

28. "Wife of Oil Man Taken from the Train," *San Diego Union*, July 14, 1922.

29. "Eye-Witness Sickened by Blood as Mrs. Phillips Beat Her Victim to Death, Testimony at Inquest," *San Diego Tribune*, July 17, 1922.

30. "Mrs. Phillips Not Present at Inquest," *San Diego Tribune*, July 17, 1922; "Accuser Repeats Charge against Mrs. Phillips as Woman Is Jailed," *San Diego Union*, July 17, 1922.

31. "Accuser Repeats Charge against Mrs. Phillips."

32. "Mrs. Phillips Not Present at Inquest."

33. "Forced to Flee Jail, Clara Declares," *San Diego Tribune*, May 31, 1923.

34. "Long Search for Slayer Is Finished," *San Diego Union*, April 16,1923.

35. "Accuser Repeats Charge against Mrs. Phillips."

36. Robert Hughes, *The Shock of the New* (New York: Knopf Doubleday, 2013), 17.

37. "Owner of 'Love Cottage' Sees Photo of Clark; Says He Resembles Fritzie Mann's Companion," *San Diego Union*, January 19, 1923.

38. "Girl Murdered Police Say."

39. "Owner of 'Love Cottage.'" The following extended discussion of William Mann's testimony, including quotations, is drawn from this source.

40. Otis M. Wiles, "Secret Carried to Grave," *Los Angeles Times*, January 23, 1923.

41. Wiles, "Secret Carried to Grave."

42. "Motion Picture Director Arrested in Connection with Dancer's Death," *San Diego Union*, January 19, 1923.

43. "Owner of 'Love Cottage.'"

44. "Owner of 'Love Cottage.'"

45. "Dr. Jacobs Held without Bail for Murder of S.D. Girl," *San Diego Union*, February 18, 1923; " 'D— Fool Altruism' Blamed by Jacobs, Whisky Clue Fails," *San Diego Tribune*, January 19, 1923; "Motion Picture Director Held in Connection with Dancer's Death."

46. "Dancer Seen in Struggle with Man at Night," *San Diego Tribune*, January 20, 1923.

47. "Dr. Louis L. Jacobs Granted Release on Habeas Corpus Writ," *San Diego Tribune*, January 22, 1923.

48. "Girl Hurled into Surf while Alive," *Oregon Daily Journal*, January 20, 1923.

49. Testimony of Rogers V. Clark, *People v. Louis L. Jacobs*.

50. Sandra E. Bonura, *Empire Builder: John D. Spreckles and the Making of San Diego* (Lincoln: University of Nebraska, 2020), 138–40.

51. "Owner of 'Love Cottage.'" This *San Diego Union* report is the source for the following discussion.

52. "Friends of Dancing Girl Involved Doctor Deeper in Case; He Plans Fight," *San Diego Sun*, January 19, 1923.

53. Bonura, *Empire Builder*, 140.

54. "Friends of Dancing Girl."

55. Bonura, *Empire Builder*, 140.

56. "Dancer Seen in Struggle with Man at Night."

57. "Dr. Louis L. Jacobs Granted Release on Habeas Corpus Writ."

58. "Dancer Seen in Struggle with Man at Night."

59. "Landlord Not Certain Kearny Physician Is Man Last Seen with Dancer," *San Diego Union*, January 21, 1923.

60. Charles L. Briggs, "Mediating Infanticide: Theorizing Relations between Narrative and Violence," *Cultural Anthropology* 22 (Fall 2007): 330–31.

61. "Camp Kearny Doctor Faces Indictment Charging Him with Fritzi Mann Murder," *San Diego Sun*, March 26, 1923.

62. "Conspiracy Is Hunted, "*San Diego Sun*, January 23, 1923.

63. "S.D. Grand Jury Sifts Mystery of Girl's Death," *San Diego Union*, January 25, 1923; "Grand Jury Probes Case," *San Diego Sun*, January 25, 1923; "Indictment May Result from Grand Jury Probe into Death of Dancer," *San Diego Sun*, January 26, 1923; "Dr. Jacobs Held without Bail for Death of S.D. Girl."

64. Wiles, "Secret Carried to Grave."

65. "And the Dance Is on Again," *San Diego Sun*, January 18, 1923; Molly, *On Creating a Usable Culture*, 43.

CHAPTER 4. FANTASY

1. "Panorama View of the City: One of Real Beauty," *San Diego Union*, January 1, 1921. Sace Elder explains that the construction of the deviant personality by the press also allowed the press to describe areas of the city or nation that could then be defined as part of the crime. Elder, *Murder Scenes*, 67–68. To see the implications of this kind of reporting in US history, it is important to look to Mary Ting Yi Lui's *The Chinatown Trunk Mystery: Murder, Miscegenation, and Other Dangerous Encounters in Turn-of-the-Century New York City* (Princeton, NJ: Princeton University Press, 2007).

2. "San Diego Home Life Is Ideal," *San Diego Union*, January 1, 1923; "Blessed with Unsurpassed Year," *San Diego Union*, January 1, 1923.

3. Ida McGlone Gibson, "Starlight," *San Diego Union*, February 13, 1922.

4. "Starlight," February 20, 1922.

5. "Starlight," February 21, 1922.

6. Kevin F. White, *The First Sexual Revolution: The Emergence of Male Heterosexuality in Modern American* (New York: New York University Press, 1993), 58–59.

7. Steven J. Ross, *Working-Class Hollywood: Silent Film and the Shaping of Class in America* (Princeton, NJ: Princeton University Press, 1998), 11–12, 28: Allen, *Only Yesterday,* 83–85.

8. Anthony Slater, "June Mathis's Valentino Scripts," *Cinema Scripts* 50 (Fall 2010), 99–101.

9. Gavin Lambert, *Nazimova: A Biography* (New York: Random House, 1998), 223.

10. "Last Day 'Ladies Must Live' with Betty Compson," movie advertisement, *San Diego Union,* December 3, 1921.

11. Movie advertisements, *San Diego Union,* July 30, 1922; Douglas Fairbanks, "From Left to Right in the Movies," in *Bohemians, Bootleggers, Flappers, and Swells: The Best of Early Vanity Fair,* ed. Graydon Carter and David Friend (New York: Penguin Press, 2014), 86–87.

12. Lambert, *Nazimova,* 246, 249, 223, 205; "No Sympathy with Tears Now: Alice Terry Forgoes Emoting and Aids Ingram in Costuming," *Los Angeles Times,* April 2, 1922.

13. David S. Shields, *Still: American Silent Motion Picture Photography* (Chicago: University of Chicago Press, 2013), 194.

14. "New Years' Edition," *San Diego Union,* January 1, 1921; Bahr Ehrhard, *Weimar along the Pacific: German Exile Culture in Los Angeles and the Curse of Modernism* (Berkeley: University of California Press, 2008), 71. Also see Roger W. Lotchin, *Fortress California: 1910–1961* (Champaign: University of Illinois Press, 2002), 1–6.

15. "New Years' Edition"; Ehrhard. *Weimar,* 71; Lotchin, *Fortress California,* 7–8, 11, 13, 16.

16. "Colonial's New Bill Draws Large Crowd," *San Diego Union,* January 8, 1922.

17. Shields, *Still,* 10, 60, 63.

18. "A Wrap and Gown Made to Spend Their Evenings Together," *Harper's Bazaar,* March 1922, 51.

19. "Florence O'Denishawn," photo, *Cosmopolitan,* January 1922, 52; "Marguerite Marsh," photo, "Shirley Vernon," and "Lillian Russell," *Cosmopolitan,* May 1922, 50, 52, 69–70.

20. Gabler, *Life,* 53–55, 86.

21. Susan A. Glenn, *Female Spectacle: The Theatrical Roots of Modern Feminism* (Cambridge, MA: Harvard University Press, 2002), 36; Vicki Callahan, ed., *Reclaiming the Archive: Feminism and Film History* (Detroit: Wayne State University Press, 2010), 231, 260. For an in-depth explanation of the shifting terms of gender and sexuality as they pertain to the postwar woman, see Anna Carden-Coyne and Laura Doan, "Gender in Sexuality,"

in *Gender and the Great War*, ed. Susan R. Grayzel and Tammy M. Proctor (New York: Oxford University Press, 2017).

22. Shields, *Still*, 86–88.

23. Shields, *Still*, 88.

24. Shields, *Still*, 10, 63.

25. Shields, *Still*, 98. *American Magazine*, May 1922, back cover Kodak advertisement, "There's always another story waiting for your Kodak."

26. Riv-Ellen Prell, *Fighting to Become American: Assimilation and the Trouble between Jewish Women and Jewish Men* (Boston: Beacon Press, 1999), 44, 41.

27. John D'Emilio and Estelle B. Freedman, *Intimate Matters: A History of Sexuality in America* (Chicago: University of Chicago, 2012), 256, 231, 240.

28. Peter Metcalf, *They Lie, We Lie: Getting On with Anthropology* (New York: Routledge, 2003), 1.

29. Testimony of Amelia Mann, *People v. Louis L. Jacobs*. As a comparison, in 1920 Jews living in the old and congested downtown Governeur District of New York City had a tuberculosis mortality rate of 83 percent, whereas it was only 52 percent in the newer and more open Bronx-Tremont District. In a period when germ theory was known but antibiotics were not, living conditions were a controllable factor. If they could, they would opt to change their situation because people believed it was the difference between life and death. Emily K. Abel, *Tuberculosis and the Politics of Exclusion* (New Brunswick, NJ: Rutgers University Press, 2007), 30–35; Rene Jules Dubos, *White Plague: Tuberculosis, Man, and Society* (New Brunswick, NJ: Rutgers University Press, 1952), 193.

30. Diane Price Herndl, *Invalid Women: Figuring Feminine Illness in American Fiction and Culture, 1890–1940* (North Carolina Press, 1993), 213–14.

31. "Tijuana Bar and Café," advertisement, *San Diego Tribune*, January 7, 1922.

32. "And the Dance Is on Again," *San Diego Sun*, January 18, 1923.

33. Fred Rosenbaum, *Cosmopolitans: A Social and Cultural History of the Jews of the San Francisco Bay Area* (Berkeley: University of California Press, 2009), 234.

34. Margaret Pinckney Allen, "Women on the Witness Stand," *North American Review* 213 (April 1921): 489–93.

35. Zelda Fitzgerald, "Looking Back Eight Years," in Bruccoli, *Zelda Fitzgerald*, 408–9.

36. Max Hastings, *Catastrophe 1914: Europe Goes to War* (New York: Alfred A. Knopf, 2013), 2.

37. See Marc Ferro, *The Great War, 1914–1918* (London: Routledge and Kegan Paul, 1973), 3; Paul Fussel, *The Great War and Modern Memory* (New York: Oxford University Press, 1975), 74, 21; Modris Eksteins, *The*

Rite of Spring: The Great War and the Birth of the Modern Age (Boston: Houghton Mifflin, 1989), 211; Hughes, *Shock of the New,* 56–57.

38. William E. Leuchtenburg, *The Perils of Prosperity: 1914–1932* (Chicago: University of Chicago Press, 1958), 29. As Camus wrote, "The absurd does not liberate; it binds." Albert Camus, "The Absurd Mann," in *The Myths of Sisyphus and Other Essays,* trans. Justin O'Brien (New York: Alfred A. Knopf, 1955), 50.

39. Fitzgerald, "Looking Back Eight Years," 410. Also see E. E. Cummings to his father, August 19, 1919, *Selected Letters of E. E Cummings,* ed. F. W. Dupree and George Stade (New York: Harcourt, Brace and World, 1969), 50–51.

40. Leuchtenburg, *Perils of Prosperity,* 152.

41. *San Diego Union,* February 8, 1922.

42. *San Diego Union,* February 22, 1922

43. Riley, *Free as Gods,* 9, 29. Here I am applying Riley's definitions of Jazz Age aesthetics to Mann's style and performances.

44. "Scarcity of Dancing Girls Worrying Ballet Producers; Turn to Other Occupations," *San Diego Tribune,* August 21, 1922.

45. "Starlight," February 21, 1922.

46. "Attends Valentine Party," *San Diego Union,* February 16, 1922.

47. "Point Loma Home Scene of Party," *San Diego Union,* March 20, 1922.

48. "Starlight," February 16, 1922.

49. Brett Gray, *Dirty Works: Obscenity on Trial in America's First Sexual Revolution* (Stanford, CA: Stanford University Press, 2021), 2.

50. "Dangerous Odds in Hollywood," *Literary Digest,* August 23, 1924; "When Women Sit in Judgment," *Good Housekeeping,* April 1920, 46–47; "Hollywood and American States of Mind," *Harper's Monthly Magazine,* May 1923, 689–96. For more on the treatment of young women and girls in Los Angeles in this period, read Joan Jacobs Brumberg, "Something Happens to Girls: Menarche and the Emergence of the Modern American Hygienic Imperative," Kathy Peiss, "Putting on Style," and Vicki L. Ruiz, "'Star Struck': Acculturation, Adolescence, and Mexican American Women, 1920–1950," in *The Girls History and Culture Reader: Twentieth Century,* ed. Miriam Forman-Brunell and Leslie Paris (Champaign: University of Illinois Press, 2011).

51. "Spanish Dinner-Dance Declared Big Success," *San Diego Union,* February 9, 1922.

52. "Terpsichorean Artist, Protégé of Pavlowa, to Entertain at 13th Annual Charity Ball," *San Diego Union,* February 6, 1922.

53. "Starlight," May 26, 1922.

54. "Greatest Carnival Crowd Ever Assembled Here Gathers at Shrine Mardi Gras in Balboa Park," *San Diego Union,* May 16, 1922; "Shriners

Start on Last Week of Pre-circus Work Vigorously," *San Diego Union,* May 9, 1922.

55. "Entries for Great Fashion Parade at Coronado: Tent City Sunday Is Showing Rapid Increase," *San Diego Union,* June 23, 1922; Baron De Meyer, "Paris Gossip by a Mere Man," *Harper's Bazaar,* September 1922, 39.

56. Shields, *Still,* 66.

57. "The Barn," advertisement, *San Diego Tribune,* July 18, 1922.

58. "By transforming the natural body into a cultural body the individual subordinates himself to the common social values of his group. The body may even become a kind of model of society, which aesthetically communicates customs and the role of relationships from individual to individual." Robert Brain, *The Decorated Body* (New York: Harper and Row, 1979), 14–15.

59. "In reality, anatomy by itself is silent. The physical differences that we use to distinguish between sexual categories of human beings and other animals exist outside of language, yet we depend on language to conceptualize and understand those differences. What becomes apparent in the space between the silence of anatomy and the articulation of culture are variations in the ways people construct the concept of sex and consequently of gender." William Johnston, *Geisha, Harlot, Strangler, Star: A Woman, Sex, and Morality in Modern Japan* (New York: Columbia University Press, 2005), 6.

60. Brain, *Decorated Body,* 124, 188, 107; Callahan, *Reclaiming the Archive,* 260.

61. According to Marchetti, the tension between the performer and the performance is that "erotic fantasies can be indulged, sexual taboos broken. However, any radical deviation from the mainstream . . . tends to be a flirtation with the exotic rather than an attempt at any genuine intercultural understanding." Here Marchetti is leaning on Edward Said's *Orientalism.* Marchetti continues to argue that there exists a "metaphoric justification for this domination. Any act of domination brings with it opposition, guilt, repression, and resistance, which also must be incorporated into these myths and silenced, rationalized, domesticated, or otherwise eliminated," which applies well to Mann as she moved from performer to murder victim. Gina Marchetti, *Romance and the Yellow Peril: Race, Sex, and Discursive Strategies in Hollywood Fiction* (Los Angeles: University of California Press, 1994), 1, 6. Boone recommends rethinking the binaries of the dominant and dominated, as well as East and West. Instead, he suggests looking for the "slipages" that "simultaneously betray and disguise" the "interpretive possibilities" that "exist between the lines." Doing so may help erode the reliance on binary thinking about sexual identities as being normative and non-normative, and all other sexual oppositional thinking. This argument applies well to Mann because of her shape-shifting identity.

Joseph A. Boone, *The Homoerotics of Orientalism: Mappings of Male Desire in Narratives of the Near and Middle East* (New York: Columbia University Press, 2014), xxiii–xxiv.

62. I am drawing on Robert G. Lee here. Lee argues that "the mobilization of national identity under the sign 'America' has never been a simple matter of imposing elite interests and values on the social formation, but is always a matter of negotiation between the dominant and the dominated." His argument accesses the Global Social Theory of Antonio Gramsci when he writes, "Subordinated groups offer resistance to the hegemony of the elite culture; they create subaltern popular cultures and contest for a voice in the dominant public sphere." His argument assists us in understanding Mann's Orientalist performance as being in conflict with the gendered class system she inhabited while seeking to distort that same system's desires." Robert G. Lee, *Orientals: Asian Americans in Popular Culture* (Philadelphia: Temple University Press, 1989), 6. Kang adds to the argument concerning Mann as an Orientalist by arguing, "All of these surface modifications and affections were marshaled to enable the credible illusion of Asianness as performed by a non-Asian body . . . to encode a body cinematically . . . and to 'mark' that a white actor was performing." Laura Hyun Yi Kang, *Compositional Subjects: Enfiguring Asian/American Women* (Durham, NC: Duke University Press, 2002), 105.

63. F. Scott Fitzgerald, *The Great Gatsby* (original publication 1925, New York: Simon and Schuster, 1995), 6 (page references are to the 1995 edition).

64. Kang argues that blackface and yellowface performances were "linked but also differentially premised on a racist fortification of the unique plasticity and malleability of the white body"—so much so that, "I would say that such practices also were necessary reassurances that only a white body can be remade, can remake itself to 'look like' its racial others." Kang, *Compositional Subjects*, 106. Here I draw on Kang because Mann's performances raise questions about her perceptions of her own body. Because of her Jewish background, many around her would not have considered her to be white, and we have no direct evidence of her verbally explaining or writing about her own identity definition. What is clear from the available information from her performances and advertisements is that she saw herself as remakeable. She did not invest in a static identity. For scholars of whiteness, this would define her as white because only the white body has this performable characteristic. Nevertheless, here Mann might be illustrating the gap between the lived experience as an ethnic other "doing" Orientalism and the scholarship on whiteness.

65. "Love's Masquerade," advertisement, *San Diego Union*, May 23, 1922.

66. Ben Hecht, "The Adventures of the Broken Mirror," *Harper's Bazaar*, September 1922, 64.

67. "Reputation," advertisement, *Harper's Bazaar*, December 1922, 99.

68. "Woodbury Facial Soap," advertisement, *Harper's Bazaar*, December 1922, 99.

69. According to the Margaret Herrick Library, Academy of Motion Picture Arts and Sciences, Clark never worked, in any capacity, in the film industry. However, James Stewart, in his book *Mystery at the Blue Sea Cottage: A Story of Murder in Jazz Age San Diego* (Denver: WildBlue Press, 2021), indicates that Clark may have worked as an actor at the Fellow Motion Pictures Corporation. Stewart was unable to locate more information on this possible connection or on the studio itself.

70. "Artists Differ over Female Beauty," *San Diego Tribune*, March 13, 1922.

71. "Holiday Dance Is Delightful Social Event," *San Diego Union*, 1 January 1, 1922.

72. "Honor Visitor with Enjoyable Bridge Party," *San Diego Union*, March 19, 1922.

73. "Dancing Party Is Enjoyed by Club," *San Diego Tribune*, January 30, 1922.

74. "Permit Issued for New School Building," *San Diego Union*, January 30, 1922.

75. "Bishop's School Girl Going to France," *San Diego Union*, October 25, 1920.

76. "CPO Stag Party Features Fine Music, Dancing," *San Diego Union*, November 11, 1922.

CHAPTER 5. FLAPPER

1. The following discussion of Chief Patrick's interviews with Jacobs is drawn from Patrick's testimony, *People v. Louis L. Jacobs*, along with other cited sources.

2. "C.L.U Delegates," *Cleveland Plain Dealer*, August 15, 1900; "Peddler Makes Trouble for Police," *San Diego Tribune*, January 12, 1914; "The Profiteer Goes Free," *Literary Digest*, March 19, 1921, 17; "Profiteer Jailed," *Literary Digest*, May 1920. I am grateful to the Greenbaum family and the Jewish Historical Society of San Diego at San Diego State University, San Diego History Center for their assistance with this research.

3. Lewis Mumford, *The City in History: Its Origins, Its Transformations, and Its Prospects* (New York: Harcourt, Brace and World, 1961), 546.

4. Robert M. Fogelson, *Fragmented Metropolis: Los Angeles, 1850–1930* (Berkeley: University of California Press, 1993), 43–62. Also see Dennis Drabelle, *The Great American Railroad War: How Ambrose Bierce and Frank Norris Took On the Notorious Central Pacific Railroad* (New York: St. Martin's Press, 2012).

5. Mumford, *Interzones*, 154–155, 157. Many of the transformations to the American city had happened before. In the 1870s and 1880s, young women

had flocked to the cities, where they lived in boarding houses, enjoyed their anonymity, used contraceptives, and worked in shops. After the American Civil War, there was an intense surge among women to separate reproduction from sexuality. Critics worried about the traditional female gender roles eroding and society slipping into anarchy. Also see Rickie Solinger, *Pregnancy and Power: A Short History of Reproductive Politics and America* (New York: New York University Press, 2005), 64–65. The twenties was not just a decade about urbanization and vice; it was also about image, both reproducible images and recordable images, which is something Fritzie Mann understood well.

6. "The US Grant Hotel: A Palace of Concrete and Marble in the Far-Famed Resort by the Sea, San Diego, California" (Chula Vista, CA: Denrich Press, 1910); Mumford, *City in History*, 547.

7. "Old Style Parents and New Style Songs," *New York Tribune*, August 13, 1922; Beth L. Bailey, *From the Front Porch to Back Seat: Courtship in Twentieth-Century America* (Baltimore: Johns Hopkins University Press, 1989), 3. For more on the diversity of the flappers, read Vicki L. Ruiz, *From out of the Shadows: Mexican Women in Twentieth-Century America* (New York: Oxford University Press, 1998).

8. Zelda Fitzgerald, "Save Me the Waltz," in Bruccoli, *Zelda Fitzgerald*, 9.

9. "Old Style Parents and New Style Songs."

10. "Old Style Parents and New Style Songs."

11. "Why They Won't Marry the Modern Girl," *Delineator*, December 1921, 2, 76.

12. "Why They Won't Marry the Modern Girl," 2, 80, 82. This bachelor was complaining about the shift in power women possessed in the relationship, but he was also noting an economic shift. The men observing the flappers often thought they had to spend money on the young women, which felt like buying a date. The use of the word "date" came from the realm of prostitution and gained legitimate acceptance in this period. Bailey, *From the Front Porch*, 22–23.

13. White, *First Sexual Revolution*, 3.

14. Dorothy Rothschild (Parker), "Men: A Hate Song," in Carter and Friend, *Bohemians, Bootleggers*, 65–67; "Contradicts Testimony Given by Witness against Jacobs," *San Diego Tribune*, April 10, 1923.

15. Ellen Welles Page, "A Flapper's Appeal to Parents," *Outlook*, December 6, 1922.

16. Fitzgerald, "Eulogy on the Flapper," in Brucolli, *Zelda Fitzgerald*, 392–93. Notably, young women had begun, in large numbers, to work in department stores. By 1927 the average department store buyer had started work as a salesgirl at about sixteen years of age. Within two years she enjoyed promotion. By the end of the decade, many were working in management positions. Furthermore, the department store invested in its employees because it was eager to reduce the rate of turnover and accompanying

expense of training new hires. Those in sales positions could quickly compile a group of clientele who would follow them to a new store. During the thirties, managers at New York's and Chicago's Filene's, Weibolt's, and Jordan Marsh, for example, hit on the idea of paying for part of employees' college tuition, for training courses, and other benefits that would keep an employee loyal. In this way, the young women had remade the retail industry, which in turn had remade them into employees. Their gains had been materialistic rather than atavistic. Susan Porter Benson, *Counter Cultures: Saleswomen, Managers, and Customers in American Department Stores, 1890–1940* (Champagne: University of Illinois Press, 1988), 164–65.

17. Mary Alden Hopkins, "Women's Rebellion against Fashion" *New Republic* 16 (August 1922), 331–32; Joan Jacobs Brumberg, "Fasting Girls: The Emerging Ideal of Slenderness in American Culture," in *Women's America: Refocusing the Past,* ed. Linda K. Kerber, Jane Sherron de Hart, Cornelia Hughes, and Judy Tzu-Chun Wu (New York: Oxford University Press, 2016), 421.

18. Einav Rabinovitch-Fox, *Dressed for Freedom: The Fashionable Politics of American Feminism* (Champaign: University of Illinois Press, 2021), 79.

19. "The Debutant versus the Married Woman" and "The Debutant versus her Mater's Ideal" appeared side by side in *Vogue,* September 15, 1921, 52, 53, 98, 100.

20. Gabler, *Life,* 192–95.

21. "Do You Decorate Walls at Balls?" *Seattle Star,* July 18, 1922.

22. Rabinovitch-Fox, *Dressed for Freedom,* 78.

23. Allen, *Only Yesterday,* 97.

24. "Debutante versus the Married Woman" and "Debutant versus Her Mother's Ideal."

25. Brian Donovan, *American Gold Digger: Marriage, Money, and the Law from the Ziegfeld Follies to Anna Nicole Smith* (Chapel Hill: University of Carolina Press, 2020), 10–11.

26. Fitzgerald, "Eulogy on the Flapper," 392. In the nineteenth century, upper-class women attended colleges and seminaries to find social and intellectual freedom from their families. Similarly, the daughters of working-class families went to work in the textile mills rather than stay on the farm. For all of these women there was an emphasis on "purity." As World War I remade the world, the war also created an opportunity for women to shift their dependence away from their family to a boyfriend. The rise of dating culture was essential to this social transformation. The emphasis placed on popularity and dating continued into the 1930s and 1940s. The *Woman's Home Companion* explained to its readers that having "dates aplenty" was the "hallmark of personality and popularity." Where in previous decades this type of perception fell to women in the college or the upper classes, in the thirties there was less of a class distinction between the expectations

for women. Ruth M. Alexander, *The "Girl Problem": Female Sexual Delinquency in New York, 1900–1930* (Ithaca: Cornell University Press, 1995), 19–21; Bailey, *From the Front Porch*, 29.

27. "Hard Dies Demon Rum, and the Bootlegger Makes It Harder," *Literary Digest*, April 26, 1919, 106–7. When the Eighteenth Amendment became law, Congress charged the Coast Guard with the task of enforcing Prohibition along the nation's coasts but did not assign them greater funding to help until 1925. Stephen T. Moore, *Bootleggers and Borders: The Paradox of Prohibition on Canada-US Borderlands* (Lincoln: University of Nebraska Press, 2014), 78.

28. Clifford Walker, *One Eye Closed, the Other Red: The California Bootlegging Years* (Barstow, CA: Back Door, 1999), 52–53, 65, 160. "Prohibition Has More Than Doubled the Vineyardists Income," *Literary Digest*, December 18, 1920, 47.

29. Walker, *One Eye Closed*, 62–63.

30. Guy Debord, *The Society of the Spectacle and Other Films* (New York: Zone Books, 1994), n57.

31. "City of San Diego Has Efficient Police Force," *San Diego Union*, January 1, 1923; "Women Charged with Conducting Disorderly House," *San Diego Tribune*, October 31, 1910; Roger M. Showley and Richard Crawford, *San Diego: Perfecting Paradise* (San Diego: Heritage Media, 2000), 103.

32. The city did not report arrest rates for 1921. Ernest Hurst Cherrington, ed., *The Anti-Saloon League Year Book 1921: An Encyclopedia of Facts and Figures Dealing with the Liquor Traffic and the Temperance Reform* (Westerville, OH: Anti-Saloon League of America, 1920), 68–69; Walker, *One Eye Closed*, 62–63.

33. Mumford, *City in History*, 546.

34. Elizabeth Alice Clement, *Love for Sale: Courting, Treating, and Prostitution in New York City, 1900–1945* (Chapel Hill: University of North Carolina Press, 2006), 172, 224.

35. Mary E. Odem, *Delinquent Daughters: Protecting and Policing Adolescent Female Sexuality in the United States, 1885–1920* (Chapel Hill: University of North Carolina Press, 1995), 24–24. Odem explains that African American women in Black progressive clubs defined sexual danger differently than their white and Jewish counterparts. For Anna Julia Cooper, famous Black leader of the turn of the century, the greatest danger to young Black women was lower-class white men who seduced the girls. In this way, Black women considered the racist society a threat to the purity of the young.

36. Mabel Dodge Luhan, *The Suppressed Memoirs of Mabel Dodge Luhan: Sex, Syphilis, and Psychoanalysis in the Making of Modern American Culture*, ed. Lois Palken Rudnick (Albuquerque: University of New Mexico Press, 2012), 64.

37. Testimony of Ben Shelley, *People v. Louis L. Jacobs*.

38. Fitzgerald, *Great Gatsby*, 118.

39. According to the news coverage after her death and the available sources at the Margaret Herrick Library, Academy of Motion Pictures Arts and Sciences. Also, when the *San Diego Tribune* checked with night club owners in Culver City where Mann claimed employment, they had never heard of her. "Kearny Doctor Held," *San Diego Tribune*, January 18, 1923.

40. "Dancer's Love Revealed: Chum Declares 'Certain Man' Could Shed Light," *Los Angeles Times*, January 18, 1923; Letter from Fritzie Mann to Bernice Edwards, January 12, 1923, *People v. Louis L. Jacobs*.

41. Testimony of Chief Patrick.

42. "Dancer's Love Revealed."

43. Letter from Fritzie Mann to Louis Jacobs, January 6, 1923, *People v. Louis L. Jacobs*.

44. "Dancer's Love Revealed."

45. Letter from Fritzie Mann to Louis Jacobs, January 2, 1923.

46. I am grateful to Matt Brown for this insight.

CHAPTER 6. DEATH

1. Testimony of Mrs. Spencer, *People v. Louis L. Jacobs*.

2. Testimony of Dr. Wagner, *People v. Louis L. Jacobs*.

3. Theodore Dreiser, *An American Tragedy* (originally published in 1925, New York: Signet, 1964), 492 (page references are to the 1964 edition).

4. Dreiser, *American Tragedy*, 492.

5. Dreiser, *American Tragedy*, 492–93.

6. Testimony of Amelia Man, *People v. Louis L. Jacobs*.

7. Telegrams and letters from January 1923, read into the court transcript during Chief Patrick's testimony.

8. Testimony of Bernice Edwards, *People v. Louis L. Jacobs*.

9. Letter from Fritzie Mann to Bernice Edwards, January 12, 1923, *People v. Louis L. Jacobs*.

CHAPTER 7. KILLERS

1. "Jacobs Facing Second Trial," *Casper Daily Tribune*, April 18, 1923.

2. "Statements of Suspect Are Checked," *San Diego Sun*, April 20, 1923.

3. Testimony of Chief Patrick, *People v. Louis L. Jacobs*.

4. Testimony of Frank Wisler, *People v. Louis L. Jacobs*.

5. "Murder as Diversion," *The Living Age*, November 1, 1924.

6. John Brazil, "Murder Trials, Murder, and Twenties America," *American Quarterly* 33 (1981): 181–82; "Murders and Suicides Increase," *World's Work*, August 1924, 362–63; "America's Murder Record," *Outlook*, July 11, 1923; "The Death Penalty No Cure for Murder," *Literary Digest*, June 28, 1924; "Murder by Wholesale," *Literary Digest*, July 22, 1922.

7. "Crime Increase," *Chariton Courier*, August 13, 1920. Though still a story in San Diego, Mann's murder was by this time receiving less regional and national coverage. Her name reigned in headlines for only a few days before other events began to supersede, though it returned from time to time. The second week in January 1923, just a few days after the discovery of Fritzie Mann's body, movie star Wally Reid passed away from complications of drug addiction, which caused a shift in newspaper coverage in California. "Thirty Thousand Honor Wallace Reid's Memory," *Los Angeles Times*, January 21, 1923; "The Sins of Hollywood" (1922), in *Movies in Our Midst: Documents in the Cultural History of Film in America*, ed. Gerald Mast (Chicago: University of Chicago Press, 1982), 176–79.

8. Brazil, "Murder Trials, Murder," 181–82.

9. "The Rising Tide of Murder," *Literary Digest*, December 23, 1922.

10. Brazil, "Murder Trials, Murder." I am grateful to Elanda Goduni for our discussions of this topic.

11. Milton Frederic Thrasher, *The Gang: A Study of 1,313 Gangs in Chicago* (Chicago: University of Chicago Press, 1963), 293; Lloyd Vernon Briggs, *Capital Punishment Not a Deterrent: It Should Be Abolished* (Berkeley: University of California Press, 1940), 74–84.

12. "Jazz Girl Trial Will Open Today," *Los Angeles Times*, March 23, 1925, 9; "Jazz Girl Sobs in Courtroom," *Los Angeles Times*, March 23, 1925, 7. I am grateful to Elizabeth Doolittle and Kevin Smith for our discussions of this murder.

13. "Olivia Stone Murder Case Goes to Jurors," *Philadelphia Public Ledger*, April 6, 1922; "Jury Acquits Olivia Stone," *New York Tribune*, April 7, 1922.

14. "Olivia Stone, Who Shot Kinkead and Went Free, a Suicide, Telling Real Reason for Killing Him," *New York Times*, December 2, 1922.

15. "Intellectual Murder in Chicago," *Literary Digest*, July 5, 1924, 41–46.

16. As cited in Harrison Kinney, *James Thurber: His Life and Times* (New York: Henry Holt, 1995), 285.

17. "Death Penalty No Cure for Murder."

18. "Murder Most Foul," *Outlook*, September 24, 1924, 115–16.

19. "Murder Most Foul."

20. Harry L. Davis, "Death by Law," *Outlook*, July 26, 1922, 525–28.

21. "Trial by Headline," *Saturday Evening Post*, August 16, 1924, 22.

22. "Arrest Expected after Probe of Dancing Girl's Mysterious Death Here," *San Diego Union*, January 18, 1923; "Indictment May Result from Grand Jury Probe into Death of Dancer," *San Diego Sun*, January 26, 1923.

23. "Dr. Jacobs Formally Charged with Murder of Dancer Fritzie Mann," *Anchorage Daily Times*, February 20, 1923, 1; "Dashing Doctor Is Indicted by San Diego Jury in Mann Killing," *Denver Post*, February 17, 1923, 1; "Doctor Again Arrested," *Cordova Daily Times*, February 17, 1923, 9;

"Camp Kearny Doctor Faces Indictment Charging Him with Fritzi Mann Murder," *San Diego Sun*, March 26, 1923.

24. "Great Interest Shown in Trial of Army Doctor Defendant Calm," *San Diego Union*, March 23, 1923; "Five Witness Testify to Finding Dancer's Body," *San Diego Union*, March 29, 1923; "Witnesses for State Declare All Exhibits Written by Jacobs," *San Diego Tribune*, July 7, 1923. His coworkers at the hospital and waitresses at his favorite spots testified that they had not seen him wearing glasses until around the time of Mann's murder.

25. "Camp Kearny Doctor Faces Indictment."

26. "Great Interest Shown in Trial of Army Doctor"; "Camp Kearny Doctor Faces Indictment."

27. "Camp Kearny Doctor Faces Indictment"; "Great Interest Shown in Trial of Army Doctor."

28. Michel Foucault, *Discipline and Punish: The Birth of the Prison* (New York: Random House, 1995), 44–45.

29. "Two Will Be Hanged Friday Unless Governor Cuts In," *The Searchlight* (Redding, California), January 24, 1923; Sheila O'Hare, Irene Berry, Silva Jesse, *Legal Executions in California: A Comprehensive Registry, 1851–2005* (Jefferson, NC: McFarland: 2006), 270.

30. "Is Coolest on State Gallows," *San Diego Tribune*, June 29, 1923.

31. "Coolest Man Pays for Fresno Murder," *San Diego Tribune*, June 29, 1923; O'Hare et al., *Legal Executions in California*, 273–74.

32. "Execution by Gas, " *Literary Digest*, March 1, 1924, 17.

33. "Execution by Gas"; Laurentine Figuroa, "Making Death Easy," *Overland Monthly and Out West Magazine*, April 1921, 30–34. I am grateful to Ryan Brubaker for our discussions of Parisi.

34. Figuroa, "Making Death Easy"; "Executions by Gas."

35. "Death Penalty No Cure for Murder."

36. "Fritzie's Letters Stolen," *San Diego Sun*, January 20, 1923.

37. Testimony of Ben Shelley, *People v. Louis L. Jacobs*.

38. "Especially for Women," *Washington Times*, January 20, 1919.

39. "Owner of 'Love Cottage' Sees Photo of Clark; Says He Resembles Fritzie Mann's Companion," *San Diego Union*, January 19, 1923.

40. "Lies and the Fearful Price of Feminine Falsehood," *Oregonian*, July 16, 1922.

41. Erving Goffman, *The Presentation of Self in Everyday Life* (New York: Doubleday, 1959), 141–42.

42. Kathy J. Ogren, *The Jazz Revolution: Twenties America and the Meaning of Jazz* (New York: Oxford University Press, 1989), 4.

43. Phil Pastras, *Dead Man Blues: Jelly Roll Morton Way Out West* (Berkeley: University of California Press, 2002), 109–10, 115. Morton's presence in San Diego predated the explosion of jazz in Los Angeles, where Kid Orey recorded in 1921. There were also several Black-owned recording

companies in Los Angeles, which provided the region with access to the music. Bete Yarbrough Cox, "The Evolution of Black Music in Los Angeles," in Autry Museum of Western Heritage, *Seeking El Dorado: African Americans in California* (Seattle: University of Washington Press, 2001), 257.

44. Catherine Christensen, "Mujeres Publicas: American Prostitutes in Baja California, 1910–1930," *Pacific Historical Review* 82 (May 2013): 222, 224.

45. Erika Lee, *At America's Gates: Chinese Immigration during the Exclusion Era, 1882–1943* (Chapel Hill: University of North Carolina Press, 2003).

46. Christensen, "Mujeres Publicas," 222, 224

47. Clement, *Love for Sale*, 191.

48. Rachel St. John, *Line in the Sand: A History of the Western U.S.-Mexico Border* (Princeton, NJ: Princeton University Press, 2011), 1–2, 151–53.

49. Christensen, "Mujeres Publicas," 219, 221, 222.

50. "Famous Tent City Is Summer Home of Thousands: Hotel Del Coronado Entertains Notable Guests," *San Diego Union*, January 2, 1922, 3; "Coronado without Equal as Place of Residence," *San Diego Union*, January 2, 1922; "Nature Made San Diego," *San Diego Union*, January 2, 1922, 7; Bonura, *Empire Builder*, 203, 207–8.

51. Dreiser, *American Tragedy*, 254–55.

52. "Mencken to Dreiser," March 4, 1921, in *Dreiser-Mencken Letters: The Correspondence of Theodore Dreiser and H. L. Mencken 1907–1945*, Vol. 2, ed. Thomas P. Riggio (editors notes) (Philadelphia: University of Pennsylvania Press, 1986), 429, 508.

53. "Book-Censorship Condemned as Un-American and Undesirable," *Current Opinion*, October, 1922, 517–18.

54. "Why They Won't Marry the Modern Girl," *Delineator*, December 1921, 2.

55. "What a Woman of Forty Thinks about Men," *Harper's* 143 (October 1921), 610–13.

56. "Getting Away with Murder," *Saturday Evening Post*, March 22, 1924.

57. "Long Search for Slayer Is Finished," *San Diego Union*, April 16, 1923.

58. "Will Reveal True L. A. Slayer Threat," *San Diego Tribune*, May 29, 1923.

59. "When Law Clashes with Feminine Charmers Dainty Defendants Usually Win Verdicts," *San Diego Tribune*, November 3, 1922.

60. Gordon Morris Bakken and Brenda Farrington, *Women Who Kill Men: California Courts, Gender, and the Press* (Lincoln: University of Nebraska Press, 2009), 13, 191–92, 197–98.

61. For example, "Why They Won't Marry the Modern Girl," 2, 76.

62. "Why Do Juries So Often Acquit Women in Murder Cases? Three Reply," *Ogden Standard-Examiner,* November 27, 1922.

63. "Forced to Flee Jail, Clara Declares," *San Diego Union,* May 31, 1923.

64. "Why They Can't Convict a Woman," *Day Book,* December 27, 1916.

65. "Getting Away with Murder."

CHAPTER 8. ABORTIONIST

1. "Prosecution in Dr. Jacobs Trial Seeks to Prove Motive Existed," *San Diego Union,* April 4, 1923; "Nurse Takes Stand against Dr. Jacobs in Abortion Case," *Searchlight,* April 4, 1923, 1; "Blood Stains Found in Cottage Where Fritzi Mann Visited," *Denver Post,* April 4, 1923, 15; testimony of Wilma Miner, *People v. Louis L. Jacobs.*

2. Robert M. Fehrenbacher, *Lincoln in Text and Context: Collected Essays* (Stanford, CA: Stanford University Press, 1987), n15, 338.

3. Fehrenbacher, *Lincoln in Text and Context,* 250, 257. For the court, she gave her name as Miner, which is what she is called throughout this book because it was how she identified herself in an official document. The newspapers reported her name as "Miss Minor." Jacobs also wrote his checks to "Minor." It appears that she may have been unhappily married and hiding out under an assumed name, which is possibly the name she gave to the court. In the 1910 census, there was a Wilma F. Minor, married to Frank N. Minor, born in Ohio, living in Missouri for three years. She reported her age as twenty-one, birthplace as California, and occupation as actress. The 1920 census does list a Wilma F. Minor in Long Beach, California, where she was living in a rooming house with her Ohio-born husband Frank N. Minor, age thirty-nine, a caulker who worked in the shipyards. This Wilma F. Minor's birthplace was Kansas. She named no occupation. If this is the same Wilma, then somehow in two years she had radically changed her life to the point that she was living part of the year in an apartment on Coronado among the wealthy and famous. Robert Fehrenbacher, in his research, gives her name as Wilma Francis Minor, but he was unaware of her activities in San Diego in the early twenties and her role in this trial.

4. Marie Lyons, "Beauty Must Be Framed as Well as Dressed," *Harper's Bazaar,* January 1922, 43.

5. Fehrenbacher, *Lincoln in Text and Context,* 250.

6. Fehrenbacher, *Lincoln in Text and Context,* 250.

7. Fehrenbacher, *Lincoln in Text and Context,* 262, 252.

8. Testimony of Wilma Miner.

9. Letter from Louis Jacobs to Fritzie Mann, December 6, 1922. All letters and telegrams between Jacobs and Mann were read during the testimony of Chief Patrick. *People v. Louis L. Jacobs.*

10. Letter From Louis Jacobs to Fritzie Mann, December 18, 1922. At the time, Mann was staying at the Hotel Rosslyn. Letter from Louis Jacobs to Fritzie Mann, December 20, 1922.

11. Letter from Louis Jacobs to Fritzie Mann, December 5, 1922, *People v. Louis L. Jacobs.* Mann was still staying at the Hotel Rosslyn.

12. Gray, *Dirty Works*, 5, 9, 105.

13. Miner testimony; "Great Interest Shown In Trial of Army Doctor Defendant Calm," *San Diego Union,* March 23, 1923, 1, 3.

14. Letter from Louis Jacobs to Fritzie Mann, undated.

15. "Will Wage War on Evil Which Cuts 30,000 births," *Day Book,* June 1, 1915.

16. "Nurses Open Fight to Close Private Maternity Homes," *Tacoma Times,* November 2, 1915. Rickie Solinger suggests that the focused construction of the image of poor women as immoral directed attention away from the deplorable living and working conditions of the poor as well as the high infant mortality rate. Solinger, *Pregnancy and Power*, 68.

17. "Salvation Army's Rescue and Maternity Homes," *San Jose Mercury News,* May 7, 1921.

18. "Curran Body Starts Out on Maternity Homes," *Day Book,* April 27, 1914.

19. "Babies Sold Like Dogs in Los Angeles," *San Diego Union,* November 6, 1912.

20. "Kelly Answers Criticism of Verdict," *San Diego Evening Tribune,* September 21, 1920.

21. "Midwives Perform Abortions Is Charge, Poor Girls and Rich Patients," *Day Book,* June 5, 1915.

22. Solinger, *Pregnancy and Power,* 71–72.

23. Solinger, *Pregnancy and Power,* 95, 102, 73.

24. Leslie J. Reagan, *When Abortion Was a Crime: Women, Medicine, and Law in the United States, 1867–1973* (Berkeley: University of California Press, 1997), 14–15, 70-71.

25. Gray, *Dirty Works,* 220.

26. Solinger's *The Abortionist: A Woman against the Law* focuses on the role and perception of the abortionist after the 1920s. Though most of the book does not pertain to this time, the argument that abortion laws "created opportunities for individuals—sleazy entrepreneurs and ambitions politicians—who did not perform abortions, but positioned themselves to benefit from women's desperation, at women's expense" does apply to the Mann case. Solinger goes on to write, "The story of the illegal era provides a glaring example of how, when an activity is simultaneously illegal, culturally taboo, and perceived as one of life's necessities by women, the opportunities abound for exploiting women while enhancing the power of men." Solinger, *Abortionist,* xi.

27. Odem, *Delinquent Daughters,* 16–17, 19. 39, 58.

28. Solinger, *Pregnancy and Power*, 71–75.

29. Odem, *Delinquent Daughters*, 100–101.

30. "Charge Doctor with Illegal Operation" *Evening Tribune*, June 24, 1921; "Think Girl Died from Illegal Anesthetic," *Evening Tribune*, January 29, 1920; "Six Members of Jury Refuse to Sign Verdict," *San Diego Union*, April 12, 1921; "Murder," *Evening Tribune*, April 12, 1921; "Criminal Calendar to Begin on May 24," *San Diego Union*, May 11, 1921; "Charges Illegal Operation Made," *Evening Tribune*, October 27, 1920; "Nab Doctor in Death of Girl," *Evening Tribune*, May 12, 1921.

31. "Will Wage War on Evil.

32. Morris Kahn, "A Municipal Birth Control Clinic," *New York Medical Journal* 54 (April 28, 1917), 166–67.

33. Clement, *Love for Sale*, 225–26. Klapper points out that at the time those against any form of birth control were quick to associate prevention of pregnancies with abortion. Moreover, Klapper cites numerous Yiddish plays on the topics of birth control and abortion and the large Jewish presence in activist groups. Melissa R. Klapper, *Ballots, Babies, and Banners of Peace: American Jewish Women's Activism, 1890–1940* (New York: New York University Press, 2013), 96–99.

34. "To Fight Abortionists with State Institutions" *Day Book*, June 7, 1915.

35. "To Fight Abortionists with State Institutions."

36. "Tells of the Workings of the 'Abortion Ring,'" *Day Book*, June 11, 1915.

37. "Puzzled over Illegal Acts Midwives Must Register," *Day Book*, June 17, 1915.

38. "Lucy Hagenow Bares Cause of Abortion Wave: Legitimatize Child, Her Remedy for Evil," *Chicago Tribune*, January 15, 1922. The interview with Hagenow quoted in the remainder of the chapter is from this source.

39. J. Dixon Mann, *Forensic Medicine and Toxicology* (London: Charles Griffin, 1893), 122–25.

40. I am grateful to Sam Esterman for sharing his research on Hagenow.

41. Mann, *Forensic Medicine and Toxicology*, 104–5.

42. Dreiser, *American Tragedy*, 400.

43. Dreiser, *American Tragedy*, 398, 401, 402,

44. Testimony of Wilma Miner.

45. Dreiser, *American Tragedy*, 384–85.

46. Dreiser, *American Tragedy*, 385, 388.

47. Letter Louis Jacobs to Fritzie Mann, December 5, 1922, special delivery Hotel Rosslyn, Los Angeles, California.

48. Letter from Louis Jacobs to Fritzie Mann, December 5, 1922.

49. Letter from Louis Jacobs to Fritzie Mann, January 5, 1923. By this time, Mann had left the hotel and moved in with Bernice.

50. Letter from Jacobs to Fritzie Mann, January 6, 1923.

51. "Find Letters of Man Held," *San Diego Sun*, January 19, 1923.

52. Testimony of Wilma Miner.

53. Letter from Louis Jacobs to Fritzie Mann, undated "Saturday"; testimony of Wilma Miner. Miner's transcript confirms her nickname.

54. Testimony of Wilma Miner.

55. Letter from Louis Jacobs to Fritzie Mann, undated "Wednesday." Addressed to Miss F. Mann, 505 Loma Avenue, Long Beach, California. She was still staying at Bernice's house.

56. Testimony of Wilma Miner.

CHAPTER 9. RABBIT

1. Testimony of A. F. Wagner, *People v. Louis L. Jacobs*. All quoted material in this chapter is from the Wagner testimony except where otherwise noted.

2. Mann, *Forensic Medicine and Toxicology*, 216.

3. Mann, *Forensic Medicine and Toxicology*, 216.

4. Mann, *Forensic Medicine and Toxicology*, 215, 217–18.

5. Mann, *Forensic Medicine and Toxicology*, 230–31.

6. Mann, *Forensic Medicine and Toxicology*, 229.

7. Mann, *Forensic Medicine and Toxicology*, 229.

8. On July 11, 1923, the afternoon session took place in the vicinity where the body of Fritzie Mann "is said to have been found." The source is the transcript of that afternoon.

9. "Extraordinary Situation Looms: Expected Conflict of Analysts," *Los Angeles Times*, December 27, 1918; "Mrs. Gibbons Free Today," *Los Angeles Times*, January 17, 1919.

10. "Man in Billiard Hall Killing Is Held to Answer," *Los Angeles Times*, March 24, 1922.

11. "Suicide Hint in Mystery: Autopsy Gives Officers Clew in Gray Death," *Los Angeles Times*, January 30, 1922.

12. "Thacker Autopsy Ordered: Evidence Bearing on Foul Play in Rumors Causes Acton," *Los Angeles Times*, November 23, 1920.

13. "What Kern Said," *San Diego Sun*, June 30, 1923,

14. Spenzer Collection, "Corrosive Poisons," plate 45.

15. Spenzer Collection, "Corrosive Poisons," plate 45.

16. "Jacobs Listens Smiling while State Declares His Life Forfeit," *San Diego Union*, April 13, 1923; "Both Sides Make Pleas," *San Diego Sun*, April 13, 1923; "To Jacobs' Defense, Prosecution on Alibi—Physician Won't Testify," *San Diego Sun*, April 12, 1923; Florence Holbrook, *The Book of Nature Myths for Children* (Boston: Houghton, Mifflin, 1902), 70.

17. Donald Elms Core, *Functional Nervous Disorders: Their Classification and Treatment* (Bristol, UK: Wright and Songs, 1922), 210.

18. "Murders and Suicides Increase," *World's Work*, August 1924, 362–63. The Save-A-Life League indicated that the rate of suicide among women had increased from the previous year but offered no statistics to prove this point. They reported that there had been no increase in the rates among men.

19. Crystal Eastman, "Now We Can Begin" (1919), in *Crystal Eastman: On Women and Revolution*, ed. Blanche Wiesen Cook (New York: Oxford University Press, 1978).

20. Churchwell, *Careless People*, 338.

CHAPTER 10. ARCHETYPES

1. Hyman Strunsky, "Are Odd Women Really Odd?" in Carter and Friend, *Bohemians, Bootleggers*, 24–26. To compare the social understanding of women in journalism and in court, basically the most public positions possible because in both women could shape perceptions of gender and the law, to women's roles prior to the Nineteenth Amendment, consider the argument that women displaced the idea of public and private gender roles through their role as journalists in the late nineteenth century, which is central to Karen Roggenkamp, *Sympathy, Madness, and Crime: How Four Nineteenth-Century Journalists Made the Newspaper Women's Business* (Kent: Ohio: Kent State University Press, 2016).

2. Irvin S. Cobb, "Oh Well You Know How Women Are," *American Magazine*, October 1919, 10–11.

3. Gilbert Frankau, "The Psychology of the Woman Criminal," *Forum* 69, April 1923, 1399, 1402.

4. Frankau, "Psychology of the Woman Criminal," 1401–2.

5. G. J. Barker-Benfield, *The Horrors of the Half-Known Life: Male Attitudes toward Women and Sexuality in Nineteenth-Century America* (New York: Harper-Row, 1976), xiii.

6. "The Kind of Evidence That Most Impresses a Jury," *Current Opinion* 71, September 1921, 351–52.

7. "Plea to Women," *The Freeman* 6, February 21, 1923.

8. Frankau, "Psychology of the Woman Criminal."

9. "Jurywoman and Modesty: Should Women Serve as Jurors in Divorce Cases?" *Current Opinion*, April 1921, 511–12.

10. "Twelve Good Women," *Saturday Evening Post*, January 22, 1921.

11. "Jurywoman and Modesty," 511.

12. The Woman, "Eleven Men and One Woman: An Account of an Experience on a Jury," *Outlook*, March 30, 1921, 508–9.

13. Testimony of Blanche Jones, *People v. Louis L. Jacobs*. The Kearny gatekeeper had testified that he saw Jacobs's car return to the camp at 9:00, but District Attorney Kempley discredited the witness when the gatekeeper suddenly remembered that three other cars had returned at the same time.

14. Mary Sargent Potter, "A Plea for First-Class Women," *North American Review* 211, March 1920, 366–37.

15. Pinckney Allen, "Woman on the Witness Stand."

16. "Human Interest Document Introduced as Evidence," *San Diego Union*, July 11, 1923.

17. Goffman, *Presentation of Self*, 9, 102.

18. "Nurse's Testimony in Jacobs Case May Cost Her Own Happiness," *San Diego Sun*, July 9, 1923; "Nurse Tells of Dash by Night," *San Diego Sun*, July 9, 1923.

19. Goffman, *Presentation of Self*, 141–42. Goffman outlines several types of secrets, the first being "dark secrets." These are "double secrets" because they conceal vital information and are never freely admitted. A second type of secret that applies to Mrs. Jones is "strategic," in which information is withheld because it might become useful or more significant as time passes.

20. Foucault, *Discipline and Punish*, 37; Riley, *Free as Gods*, 170–71.

21. "Nurse's Testimony in Jacobs Case"; "Nurse Tells of Dash by Night"; "Mann Case Alibi Is Hit," *Los Angeles Times*, July 10, 1923. Richard McCauley, her patient and companion that night, did testify and support her claims of seeing Jacobs. During the cross-examination, the defense mostly focused on whether he could tell the difference between types of automobiles rather than his morality.

22. "Burch's Counsel Asks Dismissal of Entire Panel," *Bakersfield Morning Echo*, March 31, 1922; "Rabbit Death Test Is Hit in Jacobs' case," *San Diego Sun*, July 17, 1923.

23. Goffman, *Presentation of Self*, 7, 9.

24. "Mann Case Alibi Is Hit."

25. Testimony of Ella Worthington, *People v. Louis L. Jacobs*. Mrs. Worthington's testimony was also used against several waitresses who testified that they did not see Jacobs on January 14.

26. "What a Woman of Forty Thinks about Men," *Harper's*, October 1921, 610–13.

27. Goffman, *Presentation of Self*, 103.

28. "What a Woman of Forty Thinks about Men."

29. "What a Woman of Forty Thinks about Men."

30. Cora Harris, "Concerning Widows: How to Be a Widow," *Ladies' Home Journal* 37, September 1920, 13.

31. Ellen N. La Motte, "Widows and Orphans," *Century Magazine* 100, September 1920, 586–94.

32. Testimony of Amelia Mann, *People v. Louis L. Jacobs*.

33. "Concerning Widows," 13, 64.

34. "Widows Know the World, Girl," *The Delineator*, July 1920, 46, 92.

35. "Concerning Widows," 64.

36. "Concerning Widows," 13, 64.

37. Irene McMullin, *Time and the Shared World: Heidegger on Social Relations* (Evanston, IL: Northwestern University Press, 2013), 16.

38. Richard Harker, Cheleen Mahar, and Chris Wilkes, "The Basic Theoretical Position," in *An Introduction to the Work of Pierre Bourdieu: The Practice of Theory*, ed. Harker, Mahar, and Wilkes (New York: St Martin's Press, 1990), 2, 10.

39. "European Women Seeking Husbands, Homes, and Happiness in America," *Literary Digest*, March 19, 1921; Elizabeth Reinbold MacPhail, *The Influence of German Immigrants on the Growth of San Diego* (San Diego: San Diego Historical Society, 1986), 71.

40. Testimony of Alyce Wolfensparger, *People v. Louis L. Jacobs*.

41. Testimony of William Mann, *People v. Louis L. Jacobs*.

42. Testimony of Rogers V. Clark, *People v. Louis L. Jacobs*.

CHAPTER 11. CLOSINGS

1. "Kempley Opens Final Plea to Jury," *San Diego Tribune*, July 19, 1923.

2. M. H. Abrams, *The Mirror and the Lamp: Romantic Theory and the Critical Tradition* (Oxford: Oxford University Press, 1953), 4–5.

3. Abrams, *Mirror and the Lamp*, 4–5. What if race had played a role in this case and trial? For an analysis of this topic, read Kali Nicole Gross, *Hannah Mary Tabbs: A Tale of Race, Sex, and Violence in America* (New York: Oxford University Press, 2016). Gross explains that violence was part of everyday life for Black women in the late 1800s. More often than not, violence highlighted the beginning and the end of Black women's lives. It also taught them about the power of violence. Hannah Mary Tabbs, who murdered and dismembered her lover, found that violence gave her agency.

4. "Prosecutor Will Close for State," *San Diego Union*, July 19, 1923.

5. Briggs, "Mediating Infanticide," 316.

6. "Prosecutor Will Close for State."

7. Foucault, *Discipline and Punish*, 101.

8. "Prosecutor Will Close for State."

9. Testimonies of Harley Sachs, Clarence Matthews, and John R. Chase, *People v. Louis L. Jacobs*; "Fritzie's Letters Stolen," *San Diego Sun*, January 20, 1923.

10. "Rabbit Death Test Is Hit in Jacobs' Case," *San Diego Sun*, July 17, 1923.

11. "Rabbit Death Test Is Hit in Jacobs' Case"; testimonies of Chief Patrick and Wilma Miner, *People v. Louis L. Jacobs*.

12. According to Elder, "Transgressions of those limits were generally either attributed to individual pathology or a broader social problem having little to do with gender." Elder, *Murder Scenes*, 188.

13. "Prosecutor Will Close for State."

14. Briggs, "Mediating Infanticide," 328–29.

15. "Prosecutor Will Close for State."

16. "Prosecutor Will Close for State."

17. Frank Kermode, *The Genesis of Secrecy: On the Interpretation of Narrative* (Cambridge, MA: Harvard University Press, 1979), 122–23.

18. "Prosecutor Will Close for State."

19. Abrams, *Mirror and the Lamp*, 104–5, 265.

20. "The Kind of Evidence That Most Impresses a Jury," *Current Opinion*, September 1921, 351–52.

21. Foucault, *Discipline and Punish*, 101.

22. Dreiser, *American Tragedy*, 576–77.

23. Briggs, "Mediating Infanticide," 331.

24. M. M. Bakhtin, *The Dialogic Imagination: Four Essays* (Austin: University of Texas Press, 2010), 47, 216.

25. "Jacobs Listens Smiling while State Declares His Life Forfeit," *San Diego Union*, April 13, 1923; "Both Sides Make Pleas," *San Diego Sun*, April 13, 1923; "To Jacobs' Defense Prosecution on Alibi—Physician Won't Testify," *San Diego Sun*, April 12, 1923; "Kempley Opens Final Plea to Jury," *San Diego Tribune*, July 19, 1923.

26. Margaret A. McLauren, *Feminism, Foucault, and Embodied Subjectivity* (Albany: State University of New York Press, 2002), 58.

27. Fitzgerald, *Great Gatsby*, 187.

28. McLauren, *Feminism*, 58.

29. "Jacobs Listens Smiling."

30. "Kempley Opens Final Plea."

31. Otis M. Wiles, "Jacobs Seeks to Prove Alibi," *Los Angeles Times*, April 10, 1923; "Jacobs Listens Smiling"; "Both Sides Make Pleas"; "To Jacobs' Defense."

32. Bakhtin, *Dialogic Imagination*, 169.

33. Kessler-Harris, *Difficult Woman*, 14; Kermode, *Genesis of Secrecy*, 123; Foucault, *Discipline and Punish*, 301.

34. Churchwell, *Careless People*, 74.

35. Fitzgerald, *Great Gatsby*, 6, 94.

CHAPTER 12. AFTERWARD

1. "Agreement Reached in Less than 24 hours," *San Diego Tribune*, July 21, 1923.

2. "Defendant in Fritzie Case Goes," *San Diego Sun*, July 23, 1923.

3. "PTA to Hear Hegstrom on Child Delinquency," *Washington Evening Star*, January 5, 1944; "Dr. Louis Jacobs to Speak Tomorrow," *Illinois State Journal*, January 11, 1952.

4. "Rogers V. Clark Is Wedded Here," *San Diego Tribune*, July 6, 1923.

5. "Clara Misses Xmas Cosmetics in Prison Cell but Finds Love Only Thing in World," *San Diego Tribune*, December 25, 1923.

6. "Quillen's Quips," *San Diego Tribune*, June 20, 1923.

7. People v. Kempley, 271 P. 478 (Cal. 1928).

8. "The Long Case Ends in an Acquittal," *San Diego Sun*, July 21, 1923.

APPENDIX. HISTORIOGRAPHY AND METHODOLOGY

1. S. Macauley "Patriotism, Old and New," *The Toiler*, November 13, 1920, 10.

2. Fitzgerald, "Looking Back Eight Years," in Bruccoli, *Zelda Fitzgerald*, 408–9.

3. Eksteins, *Rite of Spring*, 256–57.

4. Fitzgerald, *Great Gatsby*, 9.

5. Clemence Dane, "Have Women Got What They Want," *World's Work*, April 24, 1924, 626–30. Here I am using a woman from the era to sum up what women were looking for. This topic is one many scholars have considered. One of the best is Billie Melman, who argues that there were six popular images of women in the Jazz Age: the disenfranchised, the superfluous, the oversexed, the precocious, the immigrant, and the manual laborer. All six are present in the life of Fritzie Mann. All were looking for something more than the Nineteenth Amendment. Billie Melman, *Women and the Popular Imagination in the Twenties* (New York: St. Martin's Press, 1988).

6. Eksteins, *Rite of Spring*, xv–xvi.

7. Eksteins, *Rite of Spring*, xv–xvi; Riley, *Free as Gods*, 3.

8. Maria Montserrat Feu Lopez, "The U.S. Hispanic Flapper: Pelonas and Flapperismo in U.S. Spanish-Language Newspapers, 1920–1929," *Studies in American Humor* 1 (2015): 192–217.

9. Victor Bascara, "'A Spot of Pleasure and Importance': Jazz as Contact Zone," *GLC: A Journal of Lesbian and Gay Studies* 21 (2014): 667–69.

10. Lara Putnam, *Radical Moves: Caribbean Migrants and the Politics of Race in the Jazz Age* (Chapel Hill: University of North Carolina Press, 2013); Andy Fry, *Paris Blues: African American Music and French Popular Culture, 1920–1960* (Chicago: University of Chicago Press, 2014); Lewis A. Erenberg, *Swingin' the Blues: Big Band Jazz and the Rebirth of American Culture* (Chicago: University of Chicago Press, 1998); Michael Alexander, *Jazz Age Jews* (Princeton, NJ: Princeton University Press, 2001).

11. Alejandro Lugo, "Reflections of Border Theory, Culture, and the Nation," in *Border Theory: The Limits of Cultural Politics*, ed. Scott Michaelsen and David E. Johnson (Minneapolis: University of Minnesota Press, 1997).

12. Gene Brucker, *Giovanni and Lusanna: Love and Marriage in Renaissance Florence* (Berkeley: University of California Press, 1986), ix; Thomas

Robisheaux, *The Last Witch of Langenburg* (New York: W. W. Norton, 2009); John Brewer, *A Sentimental Murder: Love and Madness in the Eighteenth Century* (New York: Farrar, Straus and Giroux, 2005); Carlo Ginzburg, *The Cheese and the Worms: The Cosmos of a Sixteenth-Century Miller* (Baltimore: Johns Hopkins University Press, 1980); Natalie Zemon Davis, *The Return of Martin Guerre* (Cambridge, MA: Harvard University Press: 1984).

13. Melman, *Women and the Popular Imagination*, 15.

14. Kristofer Allerfeldt, *Crime and the Rise of Modern America: A History from 1865–1941* (New York: Routledge, 2011), 2–3.

15. Ginzburg, *Cheese and the Worms*, xx–xxi; J. Munday, "Using Primary Sources to Produce a Microhistory of Translation and Translators: Theoretical and Methodological Concerns," *Translator: Studies in Intercultural Communication* 20, no. 1 (2014): 4–5.

16. Mario Vargas Llosa, "Why Literature? The Premature Obituary of the Book," *New Republic*, May 13, 2001.

17. Munday, "Using Primary Sources," 5.

18. Susan Grigg, "Archival Practice and the Foundations of Historical Method," *Journal of American History* 78 (June 1991): 228–39.

19. Giovanni Levi, "On Microhistory," in *New Perspectives on Historical Writing*, ed. Peter Burke, 93–113 (Cambridge, UK: Polity Press, 2001); Sigurour Gylfi Magnússon, "The Singularization of History: Social History and Microhistory within the Postmodern State of Knowledge," *Journal of Social History* 36 (Spring 2003): 701–35; Zoltan Boldizsár Simon, "Microhistory: In General," *Journal of Social History* 49 (September 2015): 237–48; Zoltan Boldizsár Simon, "Historicism and Constructionism: Rival Ideas of Historical Change," *History of European Ideas* 45 (November 2019): 1171–90.

20. Munday, "Using Primary Sources," 5.

21. Cline Cohen, *Murder of Helen Jewett*, 404–5.

22. Ginzburg, *Cheese and the Worms*, xvi–xvii.

23. Randolph D. Pope, "The Importance of Literary History in a Cultural Context," *Hispania* 95 (September 2012): xvi–xvii.

24. Here I am thinking about Sace Elder's *Murder Scenes*. I am also influenced by Mary Ting Yi Lui's *The Chinatown Trunk Mystery: Murder, Miscegenation, and Other Dangerous Encounters in Turn-of-the Century New York City* (Princeton, NJ: Princeton University Press, 2007); Paul Collin's *The Murder of the Century: The Gilded Age Crime That Scandalized a City and Sparked the Tabloid Wars* (New York: Crown, 2011); and T. J. English, *The Savage City* (New York: Deckle Edge, 2011).

25. Elder, *Murder Scenes*, 3, 7.

26. Odem, *Delinquent Daughters*, 188–89; Susan A. Glenn, *Daughters of the Shtetl: Life and Labor in the Immigration Generation* (Ithaca: Cornell University Press, 1991), 4–5; Gray, *Dirty Works*; Rabinovitch-Fox, *Dressed for Freedom*; Donovan, *American Gold Digger*.

27. Odem, *Delinquent Daughters*; Klapper, *Ballots, Babies*; Judith Mackrell, *Flappers: Six Women of a Dangerous Generation* (New York: Pan Macmillan, 2013); Angela Latham, *Posing a Threat: Flappers, Chorus Girls, and Other Brazen Performers of the American 1920s* (Middletown, CT: Wesleyan University Press, 2000); Liz Conor, *The Spectacular Modern Woman: Feminine Visibility in the 1920s* (Bloomington: Indiana University Press, 2004); Betsy Israel, *Bachelor Girl: The Secret History of Single Women in the Twentieth Century* (New York: HarperCollins, 2002); Glenn, *Daughters of the Shtetl*; Glenn, *Female Spectacle*.

28. Andrew J. Torget and Gerardo Gurza-Lavalle, eds., *These Ragged Edges: Histories of Violence along the U.S.-Mexico Border* (Chapel Hill: University of North Carolina Press, 2022), 7.

29. Elder, *Murder Scenes*, 5; Pieter Spierenburg, *A History of Murder* (Malden, MA: Polity Press, 2008).

30. Jennifer Lynn Stover, *The Sonic Color Line: Race and the Cultural Politics of Listening* (New York: New York University Press, 2016).

31. Fass, *Damned and Beautiful*, 3, 6–8.

BIBLIOGRAPHY

PRIMARY SOURCES

ARCHIVES AND RESEARCH INSTITUTIONS

Case Western Reserve University School of Medicine, Anatomy Lab, Cleveland, OH

Dittrick Medical History Museum, Cleveland, OH
   Dr. John George Spenzer Collection

Jewish Historical Society of San Diego, San Diego State University, San Diego, CA

Margaret Herrick Library, Academy of Motion Pictures Arts and Sciences, Beverly Hills, CA

San Diego History Center, San Diego, CA

Special Collections and Archives, San Diego State University, San Diego, CA

The People of the State of California v. Louis L. Jacobs, case 38832. Superior Court of the State of California, San Diego County, San Diego, and San Diego Court Appellate Briefs Collection. Boxes 5–19.

Western Reserve Historical Society, Cleveland, OH

NEWSPAPERS

Anchorage Daily Times
Casper Daily Tribune
Chicago Daily Tribune
Colorado Springs Gazette

Cordova Daily
Day Book
Denver Post
Evening Tribune
Illinois State Journal
Los Angeles Examiner
Los Angeles Times
New York Times
New York Tribune
Ogden Standard-Examiner
Oregon Daily Journal
Oregonian
Philadelphia Public Ledger
Public Ledger
Richmond-Times Dispatch
San Diego Sun
San Diego Union
San Diego Tribune
San Jose Mercury News
Searchlight
Seattle Star
Tulsa Daily World
Washington Evening Star
Washington Herald
Washington Times
World (New York)

MAGAZINES

American Magazine
Atlantic Monthly
Century Magazine
Chariton Courier
Cosmopolitan
Current Opinion
Delineator
Forum
Freeman
Harper's Bazaar
Independent
Ladies' Home Journal
Literary Digest
Living Age
Nation

New Republic
Outlook
Overland Monthly and Out West Magazine
Photo-Era
Saturday Evening Post
Scribner's
Vogue
World's Work

PUBLISHED PRIMARY SOURCES

Allen, Frederick Lewis. *Only Yesterday: An Informed History of the 1920s.*
New York: Harper and Brothers, 1931. Reprint. New York: Harper and
Row, 1964. Page references are to the 1964 edition.

Briggs, Lloyd Vernon. *Capital Punishment Not a Deterrent: It Should Be
Abolished.* Berkeley: University of California Press, 1940.

Camus, Albert. "The Absurd Mann." In *The Myths of Sisyphus and Other
Essays.* Translated by Justin O'Brien. New York: Alfred A. Knopf, 1955.

Carter, Graydon, and David Friend, eds. *Bohemians, Bootleggers, Flappers,
and Swells: The Best of Early Vanity Fair.* New York: Penguin Press,
2014.

Cherrington, Ernest Hurst, ed. *The Anti-Saloon League Year Book 1921:
An Encyclopedia of Facts and Figures Dealing with the Liquor Traffic
and the Temperance Reform.* Westerville, OH: Anti-Saloon League of
America, 1920.

Core, Donald Elms. *Functional Nervous Disorders: Their Classification
and Treatment.* Bristol, UK: Wright and Songs, 1922.

Cummings. E. E. *Selected Letters of E. E Cummings.* Edited by F. W. Dupree
and George Stade. New York: Harcourt, Brace and World, 1969.

Dreiser, Theodore. *An American Tragedy.* New York: Boni and Liveright,
1925. Reprint with an afterword by Irving Howe. New York: Signet
Classics, 1964. Page references are to the 1964 edition.

Dreiser, Theodore, and H. L. Mencken. *Dreiser-Mencken Letters: The Correspondence of Theodore Dreiser and H. L. Mencken 1907–1945,*
Vol. 2. Edited by Thomas P. Riggio. Philadelphia, University of Pennsylvania Press, 1986.

Eastman, Crystal. "Now We Can Begin" (1919). In *Crystal Eastman: On
Women and Revolution.* Edited by Blanche Wiesen Cook. New York:
Oxford University Press, 1978.

Finney, Patrick A. *The Moral Problems in Hospital Practice, a Practical
Handbook.* St. Louis, MO: Herder, 1922.

Fitzgerald, F. Scott. *The Great Gatsby.* New York: Charles Scribner's Sons,
1925. Reprint with preface and notes by Matthew J. Bruccoli. New
York: Collier Books, 1995. Page references are to the 1995 edition.

Fitzgerald, Zelda. *Zelda Fitzgerald: The Collected Writings*. Edited by Matthew J Bruccoli. New York: Collier Books, 1992.

Godkin, Edwin Lawrence. *Reflections and Comments 1865–1895*. New York: Charles Scribner's Sons, 1895.

Holbrook, Florence. *The Book of Nature Myths for Children*. Boston: Houghton Mifflin, 1902.

Jacob, Abraham. "Birth Control." *Free Synagogue Pulpit* 3 (December 1915): 181–209.

Kahn, Morris. "A Municipal Birth Control Clinic." *New York Medical Journal* 54 (April 28, 1917).

Larson, John A. "Psychology in Criminal Investigation." *Annals of the American Academy of Political and Social Science* 146 (1929): 258.

Mann, Jacob Dixon. *Forensic Medicine and Toxicology*. London: Charles Griffin, 1893.

Munsterberg, Hugo. *The Photoplay: A Psychological Study*. New York: D. Appleton, 1916.

O'Malley, Austin. *The Ethics of Medical Homicide and Mutilation*. New York: Devin-Adair, 1922.

Pinckney Allen, Margaret. "Women on the Witness Stand." *North American Review* 213 (April 1921): 489–93.

Rygier-Nalkowska, Sofya. *Kobiety: A Novel of Polish Life*. New York: G. P. Putnam's Sons, 1920.

San Diego in the 1930s: The WPA Guide to America's Finest City. Berkeley: University of California Press, 2013.

Sanger, Margaret. *The Case for Birth Control: A Supplementary Brief and Statement of Facts*. New York: Modern Art Printing, 1917.

Sargent Potter, Mary. "A Plea for First-Class Women." *North American Review* 211 (March 1920): 366–70.

Schroeder, Theodore. *The List of References on Birth Control*. New York: H. W. Company, 1918.

Thrasher, Milton Frederic. *The Gang: A Study of 1,313 Gangs in Chicago*. Chicago: University of Chicago Press, 1963.

Torget, Andrew J., and Gerardo Gurza-Lavalle, eds. *These Raged Edges: Histories of Violence along the U.S. Mexico Border*. Chapel Hill: University of North Carolina Press, 2022.

The US Grant Hotel: A Palace of Concrete and Marble in That Far-Famed Resort by the Sea, San Diego, California. Chula Vista, CA: Denrich Press, 1910.

Wadsworth, William Scott. *Post-mortem Examinations*. Philadelphia: W. B. Saunders, 1915.

Watzek, Ferdinand. "Searching for and Recording Circumstantial Evidence." *American Journal of Police Science* 1 (May-June 1930): 272–75.

Wilkinson, Lupton A. "The Divine Right of Newspapers." *North American Review* 230 (November 1930): 610–16.

SECONDARY SOURCES

Abel, Emily K. *Tuberculosis and the Politics of Exclusion.* New Brunswick, NJ: Rutgers University Press, 2007.

Abrams, M. H. *The Mirror and the Lamp: Romantic Theory and the Critical Tradition.* Oxford: Oxford University Press, 1953.

Alexander, Michael. *Jazz Age Jews.* Princeton, NJ: Princeton University Press, 2001.

Alexander, Ruth M. *The "Girl Problem": Female Sexual Delinquency, 1900–1930.* Ithaca, NY: Cornell University Press, 1995.

Allerfeldt, Kristofer. *Crime and the Rise of Modern America: A History from 1865–1941.* New York: Routledge, 2011.

Autry Museum of Western Heritage. *Seeking El Dorado: African Americans in California.* Seattle: University of Washington Press, 2001.

Axelrod, Jeremiah B. C. "Keeping the 'L' Out of Los Angeles": Race, Discourse, and Urban Modernity in 1920s Southern California." *Journal of Urban History* 34 (November 2007): 3–37.

Bailey, Beth L. *From the Front Porch to Back Seat: Courtship in Twentieth-Century America.* Baltimore: Johns Hopkins University Press, 1989.

Bakhtin, M. M. *The Dialogic Imagination: Four Essays.* Austin: University of Texas Press, 2010.

Bakken, Gordon Morris, and Brenda Farrington. *Women Who Kill Men: California Courts, Gender, and the Press.* Lincoln: University of Nebraska Press, 2009.

Barker-Benfield, G. J. *The Horrors of the Half-Known Life: Male Attitudes toward Women and Sexuality in Nineteenth-Century America.* New York: Harper-Row, 1976.

Bascara, Victor. "'A Spot of Pleasure and Importance': Jazz as Contact Zone." *GLC: A Journal of Lesbian and Gay Studies* 21 (2014): 667–69.

Baud, Michiel, and Willen Van Schendel. "Towards a Comparative History of Borderlands." *Journal of World History* 8 (Fall 1997): 211–42.

Benson, Susan Porter. *Counter Cultures: Saleswomen, Managers, and Customers in American Department Stores, 1890–1940.* Champaign: University of Illinois Press, 1988.

Berman, Marshall. *All That Is Solid Melts into Air.* New York: Simon and Schuster, 1982.

Blum, Deborah. *The Poisoner's Handbook: Murder and the Birth of Forensic Medicine in Jazz Age New York.* New York: Penguin Books, 2010.

Boldizsár Simon, Zoltan. "Historicism and Constructionism: Rival Ideas of Historical Change," *History of European Ideas* 45 (November 2019): 1171–90.

———. "Microhistory: In General." *Journal of Social History* 49 (September 2015): 237–48.

Bonura, Sandra E. *Empire Builder: John D. Spreckles and the Making of San Diego.* Lincoln: University of Nebraska Press, 2020.

Boone, Joseph A. *The Homoerotics of Orientalism: Mappings of Male Desire in Narratives of the Near and Middle East.* New York: Columbia University Press, 2014.

Brain, Robert. *The Decorated Body.* New York: Harper and Row, 1979.

Brazil, John. "Murder Trials, Murder, and Twenties America." *American Quarterly* 33 (1981): 181–82.

Brewer, John. *A Sentimental Murder: Love and Madness in the Eighteenth Century.* New York: Farrar, Straus and Giroux, 2005.

Briggs, Charles L. "Mediating Infanticide: Theorizing Relations between Narrative and Violence." *Cultural Anthropology* 22 (Fall 2007): 315–56.

Brown, Bill. *A Sense of Things.* Chicago: University of Chicago Press, 2003.

Brucker, Gene. *Giovanni and Lusanna: Love and Marriage in Renaissance Florence.* Berkeley: University of California Press, 1986.

Buffington, Robert. "Prohibition in the Borderlands: National Government-Border Community Relations." *Pacific Historical Review* 63 (February 1994): 19–38.

Butler, Judith. *Gender Troubles: Feminism and Subversion of Identity.* New York: Routledge, 2011.

Callahan, Vicki, ed. *Reclaiming the Archive: Feminism and Film History.* Detroit: Wayne State University Press, 2010.

Christensen, Catherine. "Mujeres Publicas: American Prostitutes in Baja California, 1910–1930." *Pacific Historical Review* 82 (May 2013): 215–47.

Churchwell, Sarah. *Careless People: Murder, Mayhem, and the Invention of The Great Gatsby.* London: Virago, 2015.

Clement, Elizabeth Alice. *Love for Sale: Courting, Treating, and Prostitution in New York City, 1900–1945.* Chapel Hill: University of North Carolina Press, 2006.

Cline Cohen, Patricia. *The Murder of Helen Jewett.* New York: Vintage Books, 1998.

Collin, Paul. *The Murder of the Century: The Gilded Age Crime That Scandalized a City and Sparked the Tabloid Wars.* New York: Crown, 2011.

Conor, Liz *The Spectacular Modern Woman: Feminine Visibility in the 1920s.* Bloomington: Indiana University Press, 2004.

Cruz, Teddy. "Two-Way Journeys: Border Walls, Border Cities, and the Two-Headed Trojan Horse of Tijuana." *Thresholds* 20 (2000): 72–77.

Daston, Lorraine, and Peter Galison. *Objectivity.* New York: Zone Books, 2007.

Davis, Marni. *Jews and Booze: Becoming American in the Age of Prohibition.* New York: New York University Press, 2012.

Davis, Natalie Zemon. *The Return of Martin Guerre.* Cambridge, MA: Harvard University Press, 1984.

Debord, Guy. *The Society of the Spectacle and Other Films.* New York: Zone Books, 1994.

D'Emilio, John, and Estelle B. Freedman. *Intimate Matters: A History of Sexuality in America.* Chicago: University of Chicago Press, 2012.

Donovan, Brian. *American Gold Digger: Marriage, Money, and the Law from the Ziegfeld Follies to Anna Nicole Smith.* Chapel Hill: University of North Carolina Press, 2020.

Dubos, Rene Jules. *White Plague: Tuberculosis, Man, and Society.* New Brunswick, NJ: Rutgers University Press, 1952.

Duncan, Robert H. "The Chinese and the Economic Development of Northern Baja California, 1889–1929." *Hispanic American Historical Review* 74 (November 1994): 615–47.

Ehrhard, Bahr. *Weimar along the Pacific: German Exile Culture in Los Angeles and the Curse of Modernism.* Berkeley: University of California Press, 2008.

Eksteins, Modris. *The Rite of Spring: The Great War and the Birth of the Modern Age.* Boston: Houghton Mifflin, 1989.

Elder, Sace. *Murder Scenes: Normality, Deviance, and Criminal Violence in Weimar Berlin.* Ann Arbor: University of Michigan Press, 2010.

Emerson, Charles. *1913: In Search of the World before the Great War.* New York: PublicAffairs, 2013.

English, T. J. *The Savage City.* New York: Decle Edge, 2011.

Erenberg, Lewis A. *Swingin' the Blues: Big Band Jazz and the Rebirth of American Culture.* Chicago: University of Chicago Press, 1998.

Fass, Paula S. *The Damned and the Beautiful: American Youth in the 1920s.* New York: Oxford University Press, 1977.

Fehrenbacher, Don E. *Lincoln in Text and Context: Collected Essays.* Stanford, CA: Stanford University Press, 1987.

Ferro, Marc. *The Great War, 1914–1918.* Translated by Nicole Stone. London: Routledge and Kegan Paul, 1973.

Fogelson, Robert M. *Fragmented Metropolis: Los Angeles, 1850–1930.* Berkeley: University of California Press, 1993.

Foltyn, Jacque Lynn. "Dead Famous and Dead Sexy: Popular Culture, Forensics, and the Rise of the Corpse." *Mortality* 13 (May 2008): 153–73.

Forman-Brunell, Miriam, and Leslie Paris eds. *The Girls' History and Culture Reader: The Twentieth Century.* Champaign: University of Illinois Press, 2011.

Foucault, Michel. *Discipline and Punish: The Birth of the Prison.* New York: Random House, 1995.

Fry, Andy. *Paris Blues: African American Music and French Popular Culture, 1920–1960.* Chicago: University of Chicago Press, 2014.

Fussell, Paul. *The Great War and Modern Memory.* New York: Oxford University Press, 1975.

Gabler, Neal. *Life: The Movie: How Entertainment Conquered Reality.* New York: Knopf, 1998.

Ginzburg, Carlo. *The Cheese and the Worms: The Cosmos of a Sixteenth-Century Miller.* Baltimore: Johns Hopkins University Press, 1980.

Glenn, Susan A. *Daughters of the Shtetl: Life and Labor in the Immigration Generation.* Ithaca: Cornell University Press, 1991.

———. *Female Spectacle: The Theatrical Roots of Modern Feminism.* Cambridge, MA: Harvard University Press, 2002.

Goffman, Erving. *The Presentation of Self in Everyday Life.* New York: Doubleday, 1959.

Gray, Brett. *Dirty Works: Obscenity on Trial in America's First Sexual Revolution.* Stanford, CA: Stanford University Press, 2021.

Grayzel, Susan R., and Tammy M. Proctor, eds. *Gender and the Great War.* New York: Oxford University Press, 2017.

Grigg, Susan. "Archival Practice and the Foundations of Historical Method." *Journal of American History* 78 (June 1991): 228–39.

Gross, Kali Nicole. *Hannah Mary Tabbs: A Tale of Race, Sex, and Violence in America.* New York: Oxford University Press, 2016.

Hansen, Arlen. *Gentlemen Volunteers: The Story of the American Ambulance Drivers in the First World War.* New York: Arcade, 2011.

Harker, Richard, Cheleen Mahar, and Chris Wilkes, eds. *An Introduction to the Work of Pierre Bourdieu: The Practice of Theory.* New York: St. Martin's Press, 1990.

Hastings, Max. *Catastrophe 1914: Europe Goes to War.* New York: Alfred A. Knopf, 2013.

Hughes, Robert. *The Shock of the New.* New York: Knopf Doubleday, 2013.

Israel, Betsy. *Bachelor Girl: The Secret History of Single Women in the Twentieth Century.* New York: William Morrow, 2002.

James, P. D. *The Murder Room.* New York: Random House, 2003.

Johnston, William. *Geisha, Harlot, Strangler, Star: A Woman, Sex, and Morality in Modern Japan.* New York: Columbia University Press, 2005.

Kerber, Linda K., et al., eds. *Women's America: Refocusing the Past.* New York: Oxford University Press, 2016.

Kermode, Frank. *The Genesis of Secrecy: On the Interpretation of Narrative.* Cambridge: Harvard University Press, 1979.

Kessler-Harris, Alice. *A Difficult Woman: The Challenging Life and Times of Lillian Hellman.* New York: Bloomsbury Press, 2012.

Kinney, Harrison. *James Thurber: His Life and Times*. New York: Henry Holt, 1995.

Klapper, Melissa R. *Ballots, Babies, and Banners of Peace: American Jewish Women's Activism, 1890–1940*. New York: New York University Press, 2014.

Klaver, Elizabeth, ed. *Images of the Corpse: From the Renaissance to Cyberspace*. Madison: University of Wisconsin Press, 2004.

Lambert, Gavin. *Nazimova: A Biography*. New York: Random House, 1998.

Latham, Angela. *Posing a Threat: Flappers, Chorus Girls, and Other Brazen Performers of the American 1920s*. Middletown, CT: Wesleyan University Press, 2000.

Lee, Erika. *At America's Gates: Chinese Immigration during the Exclusion Era, 1882–1943*. Chapel Hill: University of North Carolina Press, 2003.

Lee, Robert G. *Orientals: Asian Americans in Popular Culture*. Philadelphia: Temple University Press, 1989.

Lehan, Richard. *Theodore Dreiser: His World and His Novels*. Carbondale: Southern Illinois University Press, 1969.

Leuchtenburg, William E. *The Perils of Prosperity: 1914–1932*. Chicago: University of Chicago Press, 1958.

Levi, Giovanni. "On Microhistory." In *New Perspectives on Historical Writing*. Edited by Peter Burke, 93–113. Cambridge, UK: Polity Press, 2001.

Lewis, Tiffany. "Winning Woman Suffrage in the Masculine West: Abigail Scott Duniway's Frontier Myth." *Western Journal of Communication* 75 (March 2011): 127–47.

Luhan, Mabel Dodge. *The Suppressed Memoirs of Mabel Dodge Luhan: Sex, Syphilis, and Psychoanalysis in the Making of Modern American Culture*. Edited by Lois Palken Rudnick. Albuquerque: University of New Mexico Press, 2012.

Lui, Mary Ting Li. *The Chinatown Trunk Mystery: Murder, Miscegenation, and Other Dangerous Encounters in Turn-of-the-Century New York City*. Princeton, NJ: Princeton University Press, 2007.

Mackrell, Judith, *Flappers: Six Women of a Dangerous Generation*. New York: Farrar, Straus and Giroux, 2013.

Magnússon, Sigurour Gylfi. "The Singularization of History: Social History and Microhistory within the Postmodern State of Knowledge." *Journal of Social History* 36 (Spring 2003): 701–35.

Marchetti, Gina. *Romance and the Yellow Peril: Race, Sex, and Discursive Strategies in Hollywood Fiction*. Los Angeles: University of California Press, 1994.

Martin, Eliza L. "Growth by the Gallon: Water, Development and Power in San Diego, California 1890–1947." PhD diss., University of California Santa Cruz, 2010.

Mast, Gerald. *Movies in Our Midst: Documents in the Cultural History of Film in America.* Chicago: University of Chicago Press, 1982.

McDowell Alternus, Althea. *Big Bosses: A Working Girls' Memoir of Jazz Age America.* Chicago: University of Chicago Press, 2016.

McLauren, Margaret A. *Feminism, Foucault, and Embodied Subjectivity.* Albany: State University of New York Press, 2002.

Melman, Billie. *Women and the Popular Imagination in the Twenties.* New York: St. Martin's Press, 1988.

Metcalf, Peter. *They Lie, We Lie: Getting On with Anthropology.* New York: Routledge, 2003.

Miller, Nathan. *New World Coming: The 1920s and the Making of Modern America.* New York: Da Capo Press, 2004.

Molly, Maureen A. *On Creating a Usable Culture: Margaret Mead and the Emergence of American Cosmopolitanism.* Honolulu: University of Hawai'i Press, 2008.

Montross, Christine. *Body of Work: Meditations on Mortality from the Human Anatomy Lab.* New York: Penguin Press, 2007.

Montserrat Feu Lopez, Maria. "The U.S. Hispanic Flapper: Pelonas and Flapperismo in U.S. Spanish-Language Newspapers, 1920–1929." *Studies in American Humor* (2015): 192–217.

Moore, Stephen T. *Bootleggers and Borders: The Paradox of Prohibition on Canada-US Borderlands.* Lincoln: University of Nebraska Press, 2014.

Mumford, Kevin J. *Interzones: Black/White Sex District in Chicago and New York in the Early Twentieth Century.* New York: Columbia University Press, 1997.

Mumford, Lewis. *The City in History: Its Origins, Its Transformations, and Its Prospects.* New York: Harcourt, Brace and World, 1961.

Munday, J. "Using Primary Sources to Produce a Microhistory of Translation and Translators: Theoretical and Methodological Concerns." *Translator: Studies in Intercultural Communication* 20, no. 1 (2014): 4–5.

Odem, Mary E. *Delinquent Daughters: Protecting and Policing Adolescent Female Sexuality in the United States, 1885–1920.* Chapel Hill: University of North Carolina Press, 1995.

Ogren, Kathy J. *The Jazz Revolution: Twenties America and the Meaning of Jazz.* New York: Oxford University Press, 1989.

O'Hare Sheila Ann, Irene Berry, and Jesse Silva. *Legal Executions in California: A Comprehensive Registry, 1851–2005.* Jefferson, NC: McFarland, 2006.

Okrent, Daniel. *Last Call: The Rise and Fall of Prohibition.* New York: Simon and Shuster, 2010.

Pastras, Phil. *Dead Man Blues: Jelly Roll Morton Way Out West.* Berkeley: University of California Press, 2002.

Perretti, Burton W. *Nightclub City: Politics and Amusement in Manhattan.* Philadelphia: University of Pennsylvania Press, 2013.

Pope, Randolph D. "The Importance of Literary History in a Cultural Context." *Hispania*, 95 (September 2012): xvi–xvii.

Price Herndl, Diane. *Invalid Women: Figuring Feminine Illness in American Fiction and Culture, 1890–1940.* Chapel Hill: University of North Carolina Press, 1993.

Putnam, Lara. *Radical Moves: Caribbean Migrants and the Politics of Race in the Jazz Age.* Chapel Hill: University of North Carolina Press, 2013.

Rabinovitch-Fox, Einav. *Dressed for Freedom: The Fashionable Politics of American Feminism.* Champaign: University of Illinois Press, 2021.

Ramey, Jessie. "The Bloody Blonde and the Marble Woman: Gender and Power in the Case of Ruth Snyder." *Journal of Social History* 37 (Spring 2004): 625–50.

Reagan, Leslie, J. *When Abortion Was a Crime: Women, Medicine, and Law in the United States, 1867–1973.* Berkeley: University of California Press, 1997.

Recio, Gabriela. "Drugs and Alcohol: US Prohibition and the Origins of the Drug Trade in Mexico, 1910–1930." *Journal of Latin American Studies* 34 (February 2002): 21–42.

Reinbold MacPhail, Elizabeth. *The Influence of German Immigrants on the Growth of San Diego.* San Diego: San Diego Historical Society, 1986.

Riley, Charles A. *Free as Gods: How the Jazz Age Reinvented Modernism.* Lebanon, NH: University of New England Press, 2017.

Robisheaux, Thomas. *The Last Witch of Langenburg.* New York: W. W. Norton, 2009.

Roggenkamp, Karen. *Sympathy, Madness, and Crime: How Four Nineteenth-Century Journalists Made the Newspaper Women's Business.* Kent: OH: Kent State University Press, 2016.

Rose, Peter I. "Tempest-Tost: Exile, Ethnicity, and the Politics of Rescue." *Sociological Forum* 8 (March 1993): 5–24.

Rosenbaum, Fred. *Cosmopolitans: A Social and Cultural History of the Jews of the San Francisco Bay Area.* Berkeley: University of California Press, 2009.

Ross, Steven J. *Working-Class Hollywood: Silent Film and the Shaping of Class in America.* New Haven, NJ: Princeton University Press, 1998.

Ruiz, Vicki L. *From out of the Shadows: Mexican Women in Twentieth-Century America.* New York: Oxford University Press, 1998.

Schantz, Eric Michael. "All Night at the Owl: The Social and Political Relations of Mexicali's Red-Light District, 1913–1925." *Journal of Southwest* 43 (Winter 2001): 549–602.

Shields David S. *Still: American Silent Motion Picture Photography.* Chicago: University of Chicago Press, 2013.

Showley, Roger M., and Richard Crawford. *San Diego: Perfecting Paradise.* San Diego: Heritage Media, 2000.

Slater, Anthony. "June Mathis's Valentino Scripts." *Cinema Scripts* 50 (Fall 2010): 99–120.

Slide, Anthony. *Hollywood Unknowns: A History of Extras, Bit Players, and Stand-Ins.* Jackson: University of Mississippi Press, 2012.

Solinger, Rickie. *The Abortionist: A Woman against the Law.* New York: Free Press, 1994.

———. *Abortion Wars: A Half Century of Struggle, 1950–2000.* Berkeley: University of California Press, 1998.

———. *Pregnancy and Power: A Short History of Reproductive Politics in America.* New York: New York University Press, 2005.

Spierenburg, Pieter. *A History of Murder: Personal Violence in Europe from the Middle Ages to the Present.* Oxford: Polity, 2008.

———. *Violence and Punishment: Civilizing the Body through Time.* New York: John Wiley and Sons, 2013.

Stewart, James. *Mystery at the Blue Sea Cottage: A True Story of Murder in San Diego's Jazz Age.* Denver: WildBlue Press, 2021.

St. John, Rachel C. "Line in the Sand: The Desert Border between the United States and Mexico, 1848–1934." PhD. diss, Stanford University, 2005.

———. *Line in the Sand: A History of the Western U.S.-Mexico Border.* Princeton, NJ: Princeton University Press, 2011.

Stover, Jennifer Lynn. *The Sonic Color Line: Race and the Cultural Politics of Listening.* New York: New York University Press, 2016.

Sui, Daniel, and Dydia DeLyser. "Crossing the Qualitative-Quantitative Chasm: Hybrid Geographies, the Spatial Turn, and Volunteered Geographic Information (VGI)." *Progress in Human Geography* 36 (Winter, 2012): 111–24.

Susman, Warren. *Culture as History: The Transformation of American Society in the Twentieth Century.* New York: Pantheon Books, 1984.

Taylor, Charles. *Sources of the Self: The Making of Modern Identity.* Cambridge, MA: Harvard University Press, 1989.

Thomas, Carol. *Finding People in Early Greece.* Columbia: University of Missouri Press, 2005.

Vargas Llosa, Mario. "Why Literature? The Premature Obituary of the Book." *New Republic,* May 13, 2001.

Walker, Clifford. *One Eye Closed, the Other Red: The California Bootlegging Years.* Barstow, CA: Back Door, 1999.

Weinbaum, Alys Eve, ed. *The Modern Girl around the World: Consumption, Modernity, and Globalization.* Durham, NC: Duke University Press, 2005.

White, Kevin F. *The First Sexual Revolution: The Emergence of Male Heterosexuality in Modern America.* New York: New York University Press, 1992.

Wolfe, Larry. *The Idea of Galicia: History and Fantasy in Hapsburg Political Culture.* Stanford, CA: Stanford University Press, 2010.

Yeh, Rihan. "Passing: An Ethnography of Status, Self and the Public in a Mexican Border City." PhD. diss., University of Chicago, 2009.

Zeitz, Joshua. *Flapper: A Madcap Story of Sex, Style, Celebrity, and the Women Who Made America Modern.* New York: Three Rivers Press, 2006.

INDEX

Printed in the USA
CPSIA information can be obtained
at www.ICGtesting.com
CBHW030618130224
4305CB00002B/87

9 780806 192895